A THEOLOGY TO LIVE BY

HERMAN A. PREUS

A THEOLOGY
to Live By

The Practical Luther
for the Practicing Christian

CONCORDIA PUBLISHING HOUSE · SAINT LOUIS

To Florence Catherine

This edition published in 2005 by Concordia Publishing House

Copyright © 1977 Concordia Publishing House
3558 S. Jefferson Ave., St. Louis, MO 63118-3968
1-800-325-3040 • www.cph.org

Scripture quotations are from The Holy Bible, English Standard Version, copyright © 2001 by Crossway Bibles, a division of Good News Publishers. Used by permission. All rights reserved.

Quotations from vols. 1, 3, 6, 12, 13, 14, 21, 22, 24, 26, 27, 29, 30, and *Companion Volume* of *Luther's Works*, American Edition, copyright © 1958, 1961, 1970, 1955, 1956, 1958, 1956, 1957, 1961, 1963, 1964, 1968, 1967, 1959, respectively, by Concordia Publishing House, all rights reserved.

Quotations from vols. 31, 32, 34, 35, 36, 37, 40, 41, 44, 48, 51, 53, 54 of *Luther's Works*, American Edition, edited by Harold J. Grimm, George W. Forell, Lewis Spitz, E. Theodore Bachmann, Abdel Ross Wentz, Robert H. Fischer, Conrad Bergendoff, Eric W. Gritsch, James Atkinson, Gottfried G. Krodel, John W. Doberstein, Ulrich S. Leupold, Theodore G. Tappert, respectively, copyright © 1957, 1958, 1960, 1960, 1959, 1961, 1958, 1966, 1966, 1963, 1959, 1965, 1967, respectively, used by permission of Augsburg Publishing House.

Manufactured in the United States of America

Library of Congress Cataloging in Publication Data

Preus, Herman Amberg, 1896-
A theology to live by.
Includes bibliographical references.
Luther, Martin, 1483–1546—Theology. I. Title.
BR333.2.P73   230'.4'1   76-42203
ISBN 0-570-03739-5

1 2 3 4 5 6 7 8 9 10   14 13 12 11 10 09 08 07 06 05

CONTENTS

Preface   7

Abbreviations   9

Part I: Theologia Crucis   11

    Chapter One: Theology and Life   13

    Chapter Two: From Luther to Paul—
       The Making of the Reformer   27

    Chapter Three: The Theology of the Cross   51

Part II: What Is Man?   67

    Introductory Comments   69

    Chapter Four: Man in the Image of God   75

       1. Man Was Created by God   75

       2. Man Was Created in the Image of God   82

    Chapter Five: Man in Sin   87

       1. The Cause of the Fall   87

       2. The Nature of the Fall   88

       3. The Consequences of the Fall   89

       4. Law and Gospel   98

5. Free Will   102

6. Man Is Guilty and Under the Wrath and
Judgment of God   111

7. God Saves Man by a Miracle of Grace   115

Chapter Six: Man in Grace   123

Chapter Seven: Righteous but Still a Sinner   135

Part III: The Christian Life—Its Dynamic and Destiny   147

Chapter Eight: The Life We Live—Under the Cross   149

Chapter Nine: The Life We Receive—
The Means of Grace   167

1. The Word of God   169

2. The Sacraments   183

a. The Necessity of the Sacraments   183

b. The Sacrament of Baptism   189

c. The Sacrament of the Altar   195

Unio sacramentalis   198

Manducatio oralis   202

Communio indignorum   204

Communion   207

Chapter Ten: Immortality and Resurrection   217

Notes   227

PREFACE

D o we really need another book about Martin Luther? Is there any side of Luther—his person, his life, his theology—that has not been explored by theologians, philosophers, psychiatrists, historians, and sociologists? Even if the answer were no, does that mean that nothing more need be written about him? Or is there good reason why books should continue to be written about Luther and Calvin, St. Augustine and St. Francis, Rembrandt and Leonardo? Are there not a few in history who have contributed so much to culture, religion, and civilization that their voices deserve to be heard in every generation? If so, then books will continue to be written about them, lest we slide into a mediocrity of contemporary thought with blinders on, an existentialism that ignores history. It was Cicero who said that the nation that does not learn from history is doomed to repeat its mistakes. And what is true of a nation is true of the Church.

But one more book about Martin Luther? The author is driven by a dual purpose. In the first place, we are faced with a multitude of Luther scholars—many good ones—each giving his or her own picture of Luther, each his or her own interpretation of Luther's theology. Which one shall we accept as the true one? Will the real Luther please stand up? Luther's theology of justification has been picked apart, piece by piece, and has frequently shared the fate of Humpty Dumpty. They could not put Humpty—or Luther—together again. Even galaxies of theologians assembled to probe the depths of Luther's thinking have a hard time coming up with a clear definition of his theology. This is the situation that gives birth to this book. The aim is to let Luther speak, and to speak louder than all his interpreters, thus possibly giving us answers to questions that continue to plague Luther scholars. Hence no apology is offered for the mass of quotations, some of inordinate length.

The second aim of this book is to expose students, pastors, and laypeople to a Christ-centered theology that can serve as a dynamic for Christian living and thinking. This is what Luther's theology has done for the author through decades of study, lectures, seminars, and international conferences. It may do the same for others.

In conclusion, I should like to express my appreciation to my friend and colleague Dr. Charles S. Anderson, who was kind enough to read the manuscript and give valuable help toward its completion.

H. A. P.

ABBREVIATIONS

Erl.   Luther, Martin. *Dr. Martin Luther's sämmtliche Werke.* 67 vols. Erlangen: C. Heyder, 1826–1857.

Lenker   Lenker, John Nicholas, ed. *The Precious and Sacred Writings of Martin Luther.* 31 vols. Minneapolis: Lutherans in All Lands Co., 1903–.

LW   Luther, Martin. *Luther's Works.* American Edition. General editors Jaroslav Pelikan and Helmut T. Lehmann. 56 vols. St. Louis: Concordia, and Philadelphia: Muhlenberg and Fortress, 1955–86.

Pauck   Pauck, Wilhelm, ed. *Luther: Lectures on Romans.* Vol. 15, *Library of Christian Classics.* Philadelphia: Westminster Press, 1951.

Phila.   Luther, Martin. *Works of Martin Luther.* Philadelphia Edition. 6 vols. Philadelphia: Muhlenberg Press, 1915–43.

Tappert   Tappert, Theodore G. ed. *The Book of Concord.* Philadelphia: Fortress, 1959.

Triglotta Concordia Triglotta: The Symbolical Books of the Evangelical Lutheran Church. St. Louis: Concordia, 1921.

WA Luther, Martin. *D. Martin Luthers Werke. Kritische Gesamtausgabe. Schriften.* 68 vols. Weimar: Hermann Böhlaur Nachfolger, 1883–1999.

WABr *D. Martin Luthers Werke. Kritische Gesamtausgabe. Briefwechsel.* 18 vols. Weimar: Hermann Böhlaus Nachfolger, 1930–85.

Walch Joh. Georg Walch, ed. *Dr. Martin Luthers sämmtliche Schriften.* St. Louis: Concordia, 1881–1910.

WATr Luther, Martin. *D. Martin Luthers Werke. Kritische Gesamtausgabe. Tischreden.* 6 vols. Weimar: Hermann Böhlaus Nachfolger, 1912–21.

PART I

THEOLOGIA CRUCIS

CHAPTER
ONE

THEOLOGY AND LIFE

Jesus said it in His Sermon on the Mount: "Not everyone who says to Me, 'Lord, Lord,' will enter the kingdom of heaven, but the one who does the will of My Father who is in heaven" (Matthew 7:21). St. Francis said it to his mendicant followers: "Even Religious are killed by the letter if they are not prepared to follow the spirit of the Word of God, but are content merely to know it and explain it to others." Christians in every century have said it, and Dorothy Sayers, theologian and mystery writer, says it well for the twentieth century: "It is worse than useless for Christians to talk about the importance of Christian morality, unless they are prepared to take their stand upon the fundamentals of Christian theology. It is a lie to say that dogma does not matter; it matters enormously. . . . It is absolutely impossible to teach Christianity without teaching Christian dogma."[1] And she drives it home to our generation with a scathing indictment that applies to our country and our churches as well as to her own.

Theologically, this country is at present in a state of utter
chaos, established in the name of religious toleration,
and rapidly degenerating into the flight from reason and
the death of hope. We are not happy in this condition
and there are signs of a very great eagerness, especially
among the younger people, to find a creed to which they
can give wholehearted adherence. . . . the reason why the
Churches are discredited today is not that they are too
bigoted about theology, but that they have run away
from theology.[2]

Martin Luther chided his Wittenberg parishioners for praising God on Sundays for the recovery of the Gospel of grace and
the theology of the cross and then living all week as though they
had never heard of either. It was this divorce of theology and life
that as much as anything caused Luther to burst out of the Wartburg at the risk of his life to thunder from his Wittenberg pulpit:

I notice that you have a great deal to say of the doctrine
of faith and love which is preached to you, and this is no
wonder; an ass can almost intone the lessons, and why
should you not be able to repeat the doctrines and for-
mulas? Dear friends, the kingdom of God,—and we are
that kingdom—does not consist in talk or words [I Cor.
4:20], but in activity, in deeds, in works and exercises.
God does not want hearers and repeaters of words [Jas.
1:22], but followers and doers, and this occurs in faith
through love. For a faith without love is not enough—
rather it is not faith at all, but a counterfeit of faith. . . .[3]

Luther's first task in the Reformation was undoubtedly to
straighten out the theology of the Church. But he never ceased
preaching that theology—doctrine, faith—must show itself in a
Christian life. This is the side of Luther that is coming to life, as we
would expect in a day when the password is "social action." Now
we suddenly wake up to the fact that the cry for social action in the
Church is threatening to deaden the Church's concern for theol-

ogy. That is why voices like Dorothy Sayers's and Martin Luther's become so terribly important just at this moment.

As Christians we believe that our life is determined by our theology—not by anthropology, though we must learn to live with people; not by cosmology, though we must know the world and the universe we live in; not by the immediate situation, though some theologians are tantalized by "situation ethics." As for life in the world with people in the contemporary situation, the key to all this is living with God, knowing God, knowing His will, and committing oneself in faith and obedience to His will as revealed to us in Scripture, particularly in the person of Jesus Christ. Right living with those around us is determined by our relation to God, recognizing that He created us and redeemed us. "For we are His workmanship, created in Christ Jesus for good works, which God prepared beforehand, that we should walk in them" (Ephesians 2:10).

God has "designed us" for "good deeds" for Christian living. To make this possible, as Luther saw it, He has given us a "theology," a *Theou Logos*, a Word of God, a Word from God, a Word about God, His person, His will for the life and salvation of the world, and His mighty acts in accomplishing His purpose. He created us to be His sons. We rebelled and became His enemies. He redeemed us through the sacrifice of His Son, and through faith in Him, created in Holy Baptism, the Holy Spirit has made us again the children of God. As such He has given us a life to live and a "theology" to live by. It is a theology of revelation and a theology of faith and love. No one since the apostles has expressed this theology more beautifully than Luther did when he said in his great treatise *The Freedom of a Christian*:

> We conclude, therefore, that a Christian lives not in himself, but in Christ and in his neighbor. Otherwise he is not a Christian. He lives in Christ through faith, in his neighbor through love. By faith he is caught up beyond himself into God. By love he descends beneath himself

into his neighbor. Yet he always remains in God and in
his love. . . .[4]

Add to this formula of the life in faith and love the life in
hope, and you have the heart of the theology of Martin Luther,
which he drew from the life and teachings of Jesus and of St. Paul
and of the entire Scripture. And no one realized more keenly and
preached more powerfully than Luther that this theology was not
a mere playground for theologians, but a platform, an inspiration,
and a dynamic for Christian living.

Luther not only taught the theology of the Word when he
preached and lectured and wrote, but he also lived it. And in his
preaching and teaching he persistently called his hearers and readers to live it in a life of faith and love and hope.[5] How closely life
is connected with theology is clearly illustrated in Luther. His
momentous rediscovery of the theology of justification by grace
alone through faith alone is the watershed. The picture of "the
Christian man" we see in Luther before this "discovery" is quite
different from the one we see after this so-called "tower experience."

The young Luther was brought up and educated in the
medieval Roman Catholic theology of scholasticism and mysticism. It drove him into a monastery, where he sought to please
God by self-denial, prayer, good works, and strict obedience to
the law of God and the authority of the Church. God is just, who
rewards the good and punishes the evil.

Then came the "tower experience" and the great discovery.
God is love. Forgiveness is free. Salvation is not a reward for our
good works but a gift of God through faith in the atoning work of
Christ. The Gospel was discovered. The Christian life was no
longer seen as a slavery to the Law and a struggle to pacify a just
God with self-mortification and good works. It was rather a free
expression of a faith that thankfully accepts the sacrifice of the
cross as the atonement for sin and the perfect proof of God's love.
Look at Luther's life before and after the "discovery" and you see

two versions of the Christian life, each determined by the theology behind it.

This did not mean to Luther that the one was all good, the other all bad. Luther was no iconoclast. He was no schismatic. He was a child of the Church, believing in the unity and the continuity of the one holy, catholic, and apostolic Church. His call was to preserve this unity and continuity by reforming the organized Church in theology and life. This meant to eliminate error, to correct aberrations, to preserve the good, and to restore what was lost of the faith and life of the apostolic Church. To this he was called. To this he bore witness both in his theology and in his life.

Theology and life—these have always been joined together in holy wedlock, whether in the twentieth century or in the first. But why go back to Luther? Why go back at all? Does not the Christian life look different in the twentieth century than in the sixteenth? Indeed it looks different. But its basic character is the same, whether in the twentieth or in the sixteenth or in the first century. The principles, ideals, and motives for Christian living are the same. They do not change. Like the Word of God, like Christ Himself, they are "the same yesterday, today, and forever." For God has established them and set them before us in the Holy Scriptures and in the life and teaching of Jesus Christ.

Why turn to Luther and the dim past? Because without the light that comes out of the past, we shall be groping in darkness in the present. We shall be wasting time trying solutions and remedies that have already been tried and have failed. We shall be dissipating an inheritance of wisdom and experience that has enriched life in every generation. To interpret life in the present without a historical perspective is like sailing a ship while despising the use of a compass because it was invented 4,000 years ago. The cult of "contemporary theology" has reached such proportions in some theological seminaries that we need to remind each other and our students of what Wilhelm Loehe said about a century ago: "Great thoughts are not born in the latter days, but were given by the Lord to His Church from the beginning. Novelty and falsehood are synonymous, if said of things we cannot look into. Every novelty in matters of religion ought to be doubted."[6] Edmund Smits of Luther Theological Seminary said recently:

> There is a theology in Scripture which is implicit, and it is our business to make it explicit. As such it is a given thing like a *regula fidei*, a rule of faith which emanates from Scripture and runs up through the fathers and through the church. Surely it is attacked, it is perverted, it is mixed with error from time to time. But the *regula fidei* is there, rising like a tree out of Scripture and reaching for the stars, yes, for the Star that leads wise men to the truth.

A historical perspective is particularly important when dealing with things spiritual and eternal, things pertaining to God and our relation to God. The Ten Commandments are as relevant to life today as they were the day they were given on Mount Sinai. So is the Gospel of God's love in Christ. So are the Beatitudes in the Sermon on the Mount. So is the theology of the Bible. If I want to extract the true theology of the Bible, I need the help of the saints and scholars who through the ages have struggled with the same problems.

Martin Luther is himself a fine example of this kind of scholarship. He spent a lifetime extracting the theology of the Bible. His basic principle of interpretation was to let Scripture interpret Scripture. But before he gave his theology to the Church, he checked his interpretation with the fathers and teachers and saints of the Church. He was early led into the theological tradition of the Church fathers through his studies of the *Sentences* of Peter Lombard. He made constant use of the fathers, ancient and medieval. For example, in his lectures on Hebrews he made abundant use of Chrysostom's *Homilies on Hebrews*, and in his *Romans Lectures* he frequently consulted medieval theologians like William of Occam and Gabriel Biel. Augustine, of course, was to

Luther the greatest of all the fathers and is therefore the one most quoted by Luther.

In other words, Luther was a man of the Church. Luther knew that Christ came not to pick out a lot of individuals and start them off one by one on their lonely way to eternal life. Christ came to build the Church and asked no disciple to walk the way alone. He asked him to live his Christian life in the fellowship of believers as a member of His body, the Church. Luther never forgot this, whether he was formulating his theology or his pattern for Christian living.

So as we search for a theology to live by, one path at least leads us back to Luther, just as Luther looked back to St. Augustine, St. Chrysostom, St. Ambrose, and other great fathers of the Church. Sitting at the feet of Luther, we are in a sense sitting at the feet of Mother Church, as he loved to call her. For all the experience and scholarship and theology of the Church were weighed and strained through the mind and faith of Luther, so that when he speaks, one hears the voice and the wisdom and the faith of Mother Church speaking.

Some will call this hero worship. If it is, no apology is offered. How the world could use a few hero worshipers! Our country would be in better state if our youth were brought up to venerate the names of Lincoln and Washington and St. Augustine and St. Francis and Savonarola and Luther. People must pick their own heroes. The hero of this book is Martin Luther. For his theology was a theology to live by. And, to put it in reverse, his life was both a reflection and a proof of his theology. If I were trying to persuade someone that Luther's theology was worth serious study, I could do worse than point him to Luther's life. A life with the heroic dimensions of Luther's must have a great theology behind it.

Let no one suggest that Luther was a saint without spot or blemish. He was, in the truest sense of the phrase, both saint and sinner. Volumes have been written about Luther the sinner. Start-

ing with Johannes Cochlaeus (1479–1552), Martin Luther was for
four centuries the object of a smear campaign unparalleled in the
history of the Church. As Adolf Herte, a Roman Catholic Luther
scholar, points out,[7] the opponents of Luther and the Reformation, following the cue of Cochlaeus, have drawn a picture of
Luther that reeks with immorality and lust, selfishness and greed,
dishonesty and hypocrisy. These writers make Luther a proud,
deceitful, lying egomaniac in league with Satan, a heretic and a
false prophet. Herte decries this libelous treatment that his fellow
Catholics have given Luther right up to the twentieth century. It
has robbed the Roman Church of many good things that she
should have embraced from the Reformation.

So the sins and weaknesses, foibles and failures of Luther
have never been hidden from public view. But now the tide has
turned. With scholars like Herte and Joseph Lortz[8] there has arisen
a whole new school of Roman Catholic Luther scholars, sympathetic to Luther and seeking to correct the false image created by
centuries of unprincipled polemics.

This spirit of reconciliation that marks the new Catholic
approach to Luther deserves a response from Lutheran scholars in
their Reformation research. No one is asked to abandon hero worship of the great Reformer. But let it be tempered by a spirit of reconciliation and by the same desire to heal the breach that Luther
nursed so passionately. He despised schism. His Reformation was
no call to the "faithful" to leave the Roman Catholic Church. It
was a call to reform and purify the Church in head and members
in order that the unity of the Church might be preserved. Luther
refused all his life to take the blame for the breach that occurred.
Rome tried in every way to label Luther not only a heretic but also
a schismatic. As such they excommunicated him. But when he
burned the papal bull *Exsurge Domine*, he was saying to the world
that he was neither heretic nor schismatic. He was a man of the
Church. As he said to Rome years later, "With this we have now
proven that we are the true ancient church, one body with the

entire holy Christian Church and a communion of saints. . . . I will prove that you are the new false church which is ever apostate from the ancient true church. . . . "[9] Here Luther is saying to Rome, "We have not broken the unity of the church—you have."

Here we see again Luther as the man of the Church. He loved his Holy Mother and would have no dealings with the sectarian individualism that some enthusiasts have attributed to him in an effort to make him a "Protestant." He was a catholic Christian to the end of his life. One of the first doctrines to mature in the mind of the emerging Reformer was the doctrine of the Church. As early as 1520 he could write,

> I believe that there is on earth, through the whole wide world, no more than one holy, common, Christian Church, which is nothing else than the congregation, or assembly of the saints, i.e., the pious, believing men on earth, which is gathered, preserved, and ruled by the Holy Ghost, and daily increased by means of the sacraments and the Word of God.[10]

Behind this clear definition of the Church lay the long and tortuous theological pilgrimage from Rome to Wittenberg. Years of controversy and debate forced him to face the problem of the nature of the Church. The pope's excommunication of Luther brought it to a head. When the bull of excommunication struck, Luther was unafraid, for now he knew that though the pope might exclude him from the man-made organization with headquarters in Rome, he could not exclude him from the one, holy, catholic, and apostolic Church, which was the communion of saints, the fellowship of all believers in Christ.

At this point we cannot fail to see the existential nature of Luther's theology. Doctrine and life, theology and life, go hand in hand. While he is proclaiming his theology of the Church, we find him living his Christian life as a member of the Church, not as a lone-wolf sectarian. He shares the joys and sorrows, the fears and hopes of the fellowship of believers.

Thus I have the same faith, doctrine, and sacrament with you, likewise also the same weakness, lack of wisdom, the same want and poverty as you. Are you naked? So am I. That is, I cannot rest until you are clothed. Are you hungry, thirsty? Then we come together to share in one pot; my food is yours and your hunger and thirst are mine. Likewise, are you a sinner? I am too. Am I happy and strong? Then I approach your sorrow and weakness and do not rest until you are like me. Thus my joy is your joy and vice versa. Your sorrow is mine. That is the meaning of one spirit and one body. Thus Christians shall be one united people, who have everything in common, as we pray in our Confession of Faith: "I believe One Catholic Church, the Communion of Saints."[11]

This is the Christian life born out of the Reformation theology of faith and love. Luther's followers in the twentieth century have, at least to some extent, kept the theology but have failed to live the life it was meant to produce. The "Luther Renaissance" has inspired a formidable resurgence of Luther research. The greater part of the mass of literature that has emanated from it has been concerned with his theology. Now with the awakening of social consciousness in Church and society comes the necessity of applying this theology to life in the twentieth century. Luther scholars are turning to the task. And we are discovering that Luther has much to say toward the solving of our social problems today. Suffering, poverty, authority, civil disobedience, war, peace—how can Christians live their theology in the face of all this? Luther faced the same problems, and he developed a theology adequate to deal with them all. This had to be a theology of faith and love, a theology to be lived not for myself but for my neighbor; a theology that embraces the crucified and risen Christ in faith, knows the love of Christ, and turns it loose to the good of the neighbor. This is Luther's *theologia crucis*, the theology of the cross.

A theology to live by must have the inner strength to stand the test of life. It must have the power of truth to answer the ques-

tions of the skeptics and to unmask the errors of false teachers. It
must have the vigor to remain unshaken and to guide Christians
through periods of temptation. It must sustain in the hour of
Anfechtung and hold fast in the conviction that in every life situation God's grace is sufficient. For there will be times of suffering,
of doubt, of temptation, yes, of despair. There will be for every
Christian and for the Church the "little whiles" of which Jesus
warned the disciples. To Luther this meant the "little while" of
despair between the cross and the resurrection, between defeat
and victory, between earthly sorrow and heavenly bliss. "We will
experience the same as the disciples . . . " says Luther, "although we
know and hear that trials, misfortune and sorrow endure but a little while, yet we see that it constantly appears different than we
believe. Then we despair and waver, and cannot be reconciled to
it."[12] As Gerhard Ebeling points out:

> Luther once said at table that if he lived longer he would
> like to write a book about temptations, for without them
> man could understand neither the holy scripture, nor
> faith, nor fear and love of God. For the only real under-
> standing is that which endures when it is put to the test,
> as Luther emphasized in similar terms on numerous
> occasions: "From the literal and historical point of view
> these words are . . . easy to understand . . . but the confu-
> sion comes when one has to test them and take them
> and bring them into life or experience; this is a real trial
> of understanding and can be very difficult. . . . "[13]

To meet these "little whiles" in life the Church must have
what Luther calls a theology of certainty. Erasmus, the skeptic,
cannot abide the "dogmatic assertions" of Luther and the certainty
with which he speaks in matters of doctrine. Luther responds: "To
take no pleasure in assertions is not the mark of a Christian heart;
indeed, one must delight in assertions to be a Christian at all. . . .
Take away assertions, and you take away Christianity."[14] Luther
finds himself here in the company of the saints and apostles.

> Away, now, with Sceptics and Academics from the com-
> pany of us Christians; let us have men who will assert,
> men twice as inflexible as very Stoics! Take the Apostle
> Paul—how often does he call for that "full assurance"
> which is, simply, an assertion of conscience, of the high-
> est degree of certainty and conviction. . . . Woe to the
> Christian who doubts the truth of what is commanded
> him and does not follow it!—for how can he believe
> what he does not follow? . . . The Holy Spirit is no Scep-
> tic, and the things He has written in our hearts are not
> doubts or opinions, but assertions—surer and more cer-
> tain than sense and life itself.[15]

A theology to live by can only be that when it is a theology
of certainty. And it can be a theology of certainty only when it is a
theology of the Word. For Luther found his certainty not in theological speculation, not in the voice of tradition, not in pro-
nouncements of the pope, but in the Word of God. When he
struggles to understand the purpose of God's "little whiles," he
declares that they come "[i]n order that we should not despair but
hold fast to the Word."[16] So faith to Luther means assurance and
conviction, the very words used to define faith in Hebrews: "Now
faith is the assurance of things hoped for, the conviction of things
not seen" (11:1). There is always this triumphant note when
Luther talks about faith.

> Faith is and, indeed, must be a steadfastness of the heart,
> which does not waver, wobble, shake, tremble, or doubt,
> but stands firm and is sure of its case. . . . When this
> Word enters the heart by true faith, it makes the heart as
> firm, sure and certain as it is itself, so that heart is
> unmoved, stubborn, and hard in the face of every temp-
> tation, the devil, death, and anything whatever, boldly
> and proudly despising and mocking everything that
> spells doubt, fear, evil, and wrath. For it knows that
> God's Word cannot lie. [17]

In the last analysis Luther's theology of certainty is rooted in the cross. There is no contradiction between a theology of the Word and a theology of the cross. Luther cannot conceive of the one without the other. Our faith must be a blind faith, like that of the Jews before the brazen serpent. "So we, too, must close our eyes, take captive our reason, look at Christ on the Cross, and believe the Word. . . . We should cling to the Word which Christ speaks: He who believes in the Son of Man, raised on the Cross, shall be saved."[18]

CHAPTER TWO

FROM LUTHER TO PAUL—
THE MAKING OF THE REFORMER

H ow did Luther arrive at his theology of the cross, the theology of faith and love? Some people like to say that his theology grew out of his experience. When he attacked Rome, the counterattack was so violent that he was driven into a corner, put on the defensive, and forced to formulate his "Protestant" theology. Or, they say, he found the Roman theological system so enslaving that when he was set free by the Gospel of grace alone, he had only to describe his own experience, and out of that his theology grew.

This has a kernel of truth in it, but it is of course an oversimplification. It fails to take account of the prime element in Luther's experience and in the formulation of his theology. Both his experience and his theology were the creation of God through His Word. It was God who by His Word took Luther through the refiner's fire, made him restless under slavery to the Law and led him into the freedom of the Gospel. It was God who by His Word took Luther through years of *Anfechtung* under the legalism of the Catholic system. It was God who through the Gospel opened Luther's eyes to see that one is justified not by good works *and* faith, but by grace through faith in the crucified and risen Christ. This theology of the cross is a theology not arrived at by rational speculation. It is a theology of revelation.

If we ask where Luther got his theology, how he became the Reformer, or how the Reformation came about, we can start with Luther and work back through the history of dogma until we come to St. Paul. Or we can start with the theology of St. Paul and work forward and see what happens to it through the centuries until it gets its full expression in the theology of Luther. The first method seems to serve our purpose best.

When we look at Luther and ask where his theology came from, we can most certainly trace a line back to the apostle Paul. But as we study the history of dogma, we see very clearly that this is no straight line. For we have to pick our way back through movements and trends, heresies and aberrations, which sometimes make it hard to discern the line that has its source in the theology of St. Paul.[1]

Luther was a child of the Medieval Church. He grew up and was educated in medieval thought. He was an heir of the theology that contained within it the theology of all the four great movements: scholasticism, nominalism, humanism, and mysticism. When he started teaching theology at the universities of Erfurt and Wittenberg, every one of these movements contributed to his theology and showed itself in his lectures. Using the standard textbook of medieval theology, he first lectured on the *Sentences* of Peter Lombard. Little by little he began to strain this theology through the tightly knit sieve of Holy Scripture. All the theologies of the four schools that were his inheritance were put through the strainer. As he probed deeper and deeper into the Scriptures, the mesh of his sieve became finer and finer. By the time he began lec-

turing on Romans, the theological aberrations in these movements began to stick in the sieve and wouldn't go through. And
what came out was a new theology, new to the Medieval Church,
but not at all new in the true sense as Luther saw it. For he had
found his way slowly and tortuously through the medieval theology back to the theology of Augustine and the Church fathers, to
the Early Church, and to the great apostle himself.

If you ask who led Luther into the "holy of holies" of discipleship with Christ, the answer would have to be Paul. It was the
apostle who pulled aside from Luther's eyes the rheum of theological error so he could see clearly the doctrine of grace. It was
Paul who taught Luther the way of salvation, the way of justification by grace through faith. It was Paul who led him back into the
clear light of "the faith that was once for all delivered to the saints"
(Jude 1:3). And when Luther's Reformation theology finally
emerges, one does not have to look twice to see where he got it to
see who his teacher was. His language, his concepts, and his theological thought patterns all reveal a disciple of the apostle. When
Luther characterizes his theology in summary as a theology of the
cross, anyone can hear that it is a disciple of Paul who is speaking.

Certainly we cannot forget that, like his great teacher, Luther
was an Old Testament scholar, and his theology of the cross had its
roots way back there. Thus when he is speaking about "the books
and office of Moses" in the Prefaces to the Old Testament, he
writes:

> Make the high priest Aaron, then, to be nobody but
> Christ alone, as does the Epistle to the Hebrews.... Like-
> wise, as the same epistle announces . . . it is certain that
> Christ himself is the sacrifice—indeed even the altar
> [Heb. 13:10]—who sacrificed himself with his own
> blood. Now whereas the sacrifice performed by the
> Levitical high priest took away only the artificial sins,
> which in their nature were not sins, so our high priest,
> Christ, by his own sacrifice and blood, has taken away
> the true sin, that which in its very nature is sin. He has

gone in once for all through the curtain to God to make
atonement for us [Heb. 9:12]. Thus you should apply to
Christ personally, and to no one else, all that is written
about the High Priest.[2]

Luther says that nowhere in the Bible is the story of the Passion of
our Lord told more beautifully than in Isaiah 53.

It is evident that Luther found his theology of the cross in
the four Gospels, as he did in the Old Testament and in the whole
of Scripture. But it is particularly from Paul's Epistles that he
draws this theology. The apostle extracts the divine message from
the Gospel story, interprets it for us, and presents us with his
unique theology of the cross. The cross is the lodestar of his faith
and life: "But far be it from me to boast except in the cross of our
Lord Jesus Christ, by which the world has been crucified to me,
and I to the world" (Galatians 6:14). The guide for his preaching
is Paul's great word: "[W]e preach Christ crucified" (1 Corinthians
1:23). And, as if to burn this theology into the conscience of the
Church, he says, "For I decided to know nothing among you
except Jesus Christ and Him crucified" (1 Corinthians 2:2).

Studying, explaining, and teaching Paul's Epistles through
the years, Luther could not resist the passion of the apostle, driving him to his theology of the cross. Captivated by this theology,
Luther could not escape proclaiming the "theology of the Reformation," so frequently characterized as "grace alone," "faith alone,"
and "Word alone." When we stand by the cross and realize how far
God's love had to go to save us, it is hardly less than blasphemy to
say that we must contribute some of our own meritorious works
toward our salvation. "For by grace you have been saved through
faith. And this is not your own doing; it is the gift of God" (Ephesians 2:8). This told Luther that he was saved by grace alone,
through faith alone, and that this was not his own doing; it was the
gift of God. Faith, too, is a part of this gift of grace. "That is why it
depends on faith, in order that the promise may rest on grace"
(Romans 4:16).

The Word alone, or Scripture alone, was a necessary part of the theology of the cross. To Luther the whole of Scripture revolved around the crucified and risen Christ. From Paul he learned that "[a]ll Scripture is breathed out by God" (2 Timothy 3:16), and from the apostle's frequent use of *gegraptai* ("it is written") Luther was confirmed in his faith in Holy Scripture as the Word of God. In the well-known language of Luther, it is the *verbum Dei infallibile*, the infallible Word of God.[3] It is "His own witness concerning Himself."[4] Hence Luther says, "You should so deal with Scripture that you believe God Himself is speaking."[5]

Take all these together and put them through the meat grinder of Luther's teaching and preaching and there emerges the basic theology of the Reformation: justification by grace through faith. This is Luther's theology of the cross that he learned above all from St. Paul.

But as already mentioned, there is no straight line that Luther could trace back to the apostle. Like a drowning man, he saw the line thrown to him when he read Paul's Epistle to the Romans. He grabbed it, and it was the lifeline that saved him. But as he then struggled to work his way along that line to its moorings in the Epistles of Paul, he found the line, like the hawser of an anchored ship, made slippery with the accumulated accretions of centuries of theological barnacles. Luther had to wade through the shoals of humanism and through the rarified air of a spiritualistic mysticism. He had to fight his way past "the bargaining God" of Occamism and the *theologia gloriae* of the scholastics. He had to throw off the synergistic shackles of Peter Lombard, whose *Sentences* were the textbook of every theological student right into the sixteenth century.

Every one of these movements bent the line that should have led from Paul straight to Luther and the Reformation. And every irritating bend in the line was a thorn in the flesh of Luther in his search for truth. The Reformation itself could only be accomplished if God would straighten out that line. He used

Luther to do it, but it meant that Luther had to treat every one of these schools of thought with the scalpel of Scripture, until there emerged again the original theology of the cross of the great apostle.

Who would be sufficient for such an assignment? Had Luther stopped to count the cost or to consider the magnitude of the job, he would surely have thrown up his hands and said like Moses, "Who am I that I should . . . bring the children of Israel out of Egypt?" (Exodus 3:11). But instead of counting the cost, Luther went to work, feeling that he was chosen by God for the task. Who would suggest that the Reformation would ever have been accomplished without the assurance of such a divine appointment?

Under the guidance of Holy Scripture, Luther proceeded to put his late medieval theology through his sieve, straining it through the Word of God. This meant that every one of the prevailing theological movements had to go through this strainer.

Lecturing on the *Sentences* of Peter Lombard from 1509 through 1511, Martin Luther met scholastic theology head on. He had already been soaked in it as a student. He had a good philosophical background for understanding it, having lectured on Aristotle at the University of Wittenberg in 1508. And now, as he studied the "father of schoolmen," Luther found himself wading up to his neck in the well-springs of scholastic theology. Augustine heavily influenced Luther's doctrine of sin and justification. More than most of the scholastics, he emphasized faith above reason. There was much in Lombard that pleased Luther to begin with. But he soon began to see that Lombard's doctrine of original sin and free will was not in accord with Paul's theology of grace alone.

The great scholastic theologians picked up where Lombard left off, and it must be said to their credit that they did face the big problems of life, death, and eternity, starting with God. But Luther found that in answering these great questions, they were appealing to both theology and philosophy, which frequently meant appealing to philosophy instead of theology, to reason instead of faith, and to science instead of revelation. Being men of profound scholarship, they examined the sources of knowledge. In doing so they could go back to Aristotle just as easily as to Augustine. Sometimes they seemed to give philosophy the same authority as theology. Aristotle, Plato, and Socrates became almost as important to their answers as the Church fathers themselves. Luther objected to the exaltation of reason to the point where it tried to search out the mysteries of God. He attacked this as the *theologia gloriae* that presumed to probe the mysteries of the *Deus nudus* (the naked God), peering into the very majesty of God Himself. Luther rejected their effort to prove biblical doctrine by reason and dialectic.

Luther saw God as both hidden and revealed. God has revealed Himself through Jesus Christ, and in Holy Scripture He has revealed as much as you need to know about God to be saved and to fulfill your destiny in your life on earth. But there are many things God has not revealed about Himself. And neither reason nor any natural theology is capable of discovering this God. It is sin to even dare to try to find God by this means. The god humans find is only a half-god, who rules the world with power. But the God of love who reaches out to save lost sinners is not found by this way. Here you see God only on His left hand, as Luther describes it, and not on His right hand. You see the God of righteousness, but not the God of love; the God of wrath, but not the God of grace; the God of Law, but not the God of Gospel. You are seeing only a half-God, for you are peering into the mysteries of the hidden God (*Deus absconditus*) instead of keeping to the revealed God (*Deus revelatus*). You have not come to the true knowledge of God because you have sought Him in your own human, natural, rational way. You have not sought God where He may be found and where alone He may be grasped. You have sought Him apart from Christ. And God reveals Himself in His full saving relation to humankind only in Christ. Jesus Christ is on the right hand of the Father. It is no use therefore to seek Him on the left hand.

Reason can arrive at a "legal knowledge" of God. It is conversant with God's Commandments and can distinguish between right and wrong. The philosophers, too, had this knowledge of God. But the knowledge of God derived from the Law is not the true knowledge of Him, whether it be the Law of Moses or the Law instilled into our hearts.[6]

But Luther sees another knowledge of God that emerges from the Gospel.

There we learn that all the world is by nature an abomination before God, subject to God's wrath and the devil's power, and is eternally damned. From this the world could not extricate itself except through God's Son, who lies in the bosom of the Father. He became man, died, and rose again from the dead, extinguishing sin, death and the devil.

This is the true and thorough knowledge and way of thinking about God; it is called the knowledge of grace and truth, the "evangelical knowledge" of God.[7]

Nature and reason know nothing about this.

Reason has only a left-handed and a partial knowledge of God, based on the law of nature and of Moses; for the Law is inscribed in our hearts. But the depth of divine wisdom and of the divine purpose, the profundity of God's grace and mercy, and what eternal life is like—of these matters reason is totally ignorant. This is hidden from reason's view.[8]

What Luther calls "Christian knowledge" grasps the fact that all humankind is lost in sin and would be eternally condemned unless God had sent His Son, who washed our sins away on the cross with His blood. Human reason knows nothing of this. "Therefore the Scholastics should not debate the question whether man, of himself, can discover that there is a God. They have always striven to know God from the Law, which is inscribed in every heart."⁹ But in this way they will never know God as the saving God of grace and truth. "But the knowledge of God in His grace was revealed from heaven and was otherwise entirely hidden to man. . . . And the knowledge of God in His grace is the skill and wisdom which the Son alone has revealed to us."¹⁰

As Luther pursues his biblical studies with ever-increasing intensity, particularly in his Romans lectures, he comes to see more and more clearly the threat of this medieval synthesis of faith and reason, with human reason rising to challenge the dominion of faith in things spiritual. As the *via moderna* of the nominalists begins to crowd the *via antiqua* of the earlier scholastics off the center of the stage, Luther sees new hope on the theological horizon. He finds men like William of Occam and Gabriel Biel correcting the naturalistic theology of the earlier schoolmen, restoring to some degree at least the balance of faith and reason, giving final authority to Scripture as revelation, and the like. But he soon sees that they, too, fall short of the theology of grace alone. In exalting will over knowledge against the older scholastics, the nominalists emphasized the freedom of man's will to choose the good, to love God above all things, and to cooperate in his own salvation.

Luther is not slow to discover in all this the synergistic theology that has its roots in the false doctrine of original sin and free will. The two belong together. If man's will is free in spiritual things, then he is not spiritually dead, as St. Paul taught Luther. And it is at this point that he attacks both the scholastics, early and late, and the humanists, led by Erasmus.

> From the beginning of the world this key heresy of the freedom of the will and the merit of good works has continued. And this feud will never end. . . . The explanation of this: Reason is not able to surrender to faith alone. If anyone would believe solely and purely in God's word, it must be the work of the Holy Spirit in his heart.

Out of its own powers human nature holds onto the
merit of good works.[11]

Luther saw that it was this basic error that had cluttered the
Pauline doctrine of justification by grace through faith with the
whole machinery of merits, penances, pilgrimages, and meritorious works.

Luther's troubled heart found no solace as he continued to
cry, "How can I find a merciful God?" But in the crucible of
Anfechtung between the Law and the Gospel, between truth and
error, between grace and nature, the Reformer was being born.
Could the pope err? Could so many great theologians and popes
be wrong, and he, Brother Martin, alone be right? Eck puts the
question squarely to Luther at Worms.

Martin, how can you assume that you are the only one to
understand the sense of Scripture? Would you put your
judgment above that of so many famous men and claim
that you know more than they all? You have no right to
call into question the most holy orthodox faith, instituted by Christ the perfect lawgiver, proclaimed
throughout the world by the apostles, sealed by the red
blood of the martyrs, confirmed by the sacred councils,
defined by the Church in which all our fathers believed
until death and gave to us as an inheritance, and which
now we are forbidden by the pope and emperor to discuss lest there be no end of debate.[12]

This question of authority had been troubling Luther for
many years. It came to a head at Worms where, we recall, Luther
gave his answer—an answer without horns and without teeth.
"Unless I am convicted by Scripture and plain reason—I do not
accept the authority of popes and councils, for they have contra-
dicted each other—my conscience is captive to the word of God.
I cannot and will not recant anything, for to go against conscience
is neither right nor safe. God help me. Amen."[13]

It was undoubtedly the years of exegetical studies that had finally brought Luther to this conviction. He had already begun to question the scholastic and nominalist theology while he was lecturing on the *Sentences* of Peter Lombard. But as he threw himself into the exegesis of Genesis, Psalms, Romans, and Galatians, the errors of the schoolmen loomed larger.

As he began to move from the theology of glory of scholasticism and nominalism to his theology of the cross, Luther was challenged from another quarter. Erasmus, prince of humanism, raised his voice against corruption in the Church and called for reformation. He touched a sympathetic chord in Luther's heart: Return to the sources; whet your linguistic tools and examine Scripture in the original languages; correct the abuses in the Church and clean up the curia. This was all music in the ears of the nascent reformer.

But the flirtation was short-lived. This exaltation of man, this praise of reason, this sweet talk of the dignity of man who with free will could touch the stars—what did it all mean? It meant that man was not so bad after all. Original sin was not as bad as Luther made it out. The will of man was not really "at enmity with God," as Paul taught. Human beings were born free and the captains of their souls, free to choose their own destiny, free to step into the kingdom of God when they feel like it—with some help from God's grace, of course.

Luther's hopes were blasted again. Encouraged by Erasmus and his "Christian humanism," Luther's way to a theology of grace alone was barred by the same old roadblocks: free will, merit, and work righteousness. We can see Luther's disappointment in a letter to his friend John Lang, the humanist, in 1517:

> I have read our Erasmus and from day to day my estimation of him decreases. I am indeed pleased that he refutes, not less stoutly than learnedly, both the monks and the priests, and condemns their inveterate and lethargic ignorance. But I fear that he does not suffi-

ciently promote Christ and the grace of God, in which he
is more ignorant than Lefebre. The human prevails in
him more than the divine. . . . The judgment of someone
who attributes something to free will is very different
from that of one who knows nothing but grace.[14]

The failure of these two giants, Erasmus the humanist and
Luther the theologian, to join ranks in the Reformation struggle is
one of the great tragedies in the history of the Reformation. But
Erasmus, like Bucer and Zwingli, was "of another spirit," though in
a different way. Heinrich Bornkamm points out:

And, while Erasmus urged man to enhance his powers,
calling on all pedagogic means . . . Luther had learned to
tear man away from any kind of introspective reflection,
and to direct his trust exclusively toward the forgiving
and rejuvenating power of God's love. His interpretation
of the Bible was in keeping with his realistic concept of
man. For him the factual occurrence, the "flesh and
blood" of the Biblical story, was of final importance. He
rejected the devious moral-spiritual interpretation of
Erasmus as an arbitrary addition, as the mere exercise of
human thought. The intellectual realms of the two great
spiritual rulers of their time were bound to conflict
sooner or later.[15]

The significance of Luther's clash with humanism and of
his debate with Erasmus can hardly be overestimated. As Heinrich
Bornkamm puts it, "The epoch-making dialogue between Luther
and Erasmus is a prelude to the problems which have plagued
modern man since the time of the Reformation."[16]

How right Luther was that the feud surrounding "this key
heresy of the freedom of the will . . . will never end"! This ought to
serve notice on the Lutheran Church that Luther's *Bondage of the
Will* is as relevant for theology and life today as it was in the day
when he debated with Erasmus. As E. Gordon Rupp says, "This

book contains some excellent astringent medicine for modern Protestants in England and America."[17]

The winds of scholasticism, nominalism, and humanism had only increased Luther's spiritual agony and dissatisfaction with the medieval theology. No wonder he pricked up his theological ears when the soothing breezes of mysticism floated into his theological world. For a brief moment he thought this was it. He felt he had made a great discovery when he encountered John Tauler's *Sermons* and the *Theologia Germanica*, which he believed Tauler had written. He wrote to Spalatin in December 1516:

> If reading a pure and solid theology, which is available in German and is of a quality closest to that of the Fathers, might please you, then get for yourself the sermons of John Tauler, the Dominican. I am enclosing for you, so to speak, the essence of them all. I have seen no theological work in Latin or German that is more sound or more in harmony with the Gospel than this. Taste it and see how sweet the Lord is after you have first tried and realized how bitter is whatever we are.[18]

Born out of the school of the mystics who called themselves "Friends of God," there radiates from these works a Gospel of the cross and of grace that sends Luther into ecstasies.

Luther was well acquainted with Biel and Gerson, in whom mysticism and nominalism are ideal partners in a "wholesome 'mystical marriage.' "[19] But the theology Luther found in Tauler appeared to him to be much closer to the pure Gospel than what he had found in any of the nominalists. For here he found sin taken seriously. Here was no exaltation of man and his powers to cooperate with God in his salvation. Here was no emphasis on man's dignity and freedom to lift himself up to God. Instead, man's proud will must be mortified and the helpless sinner must throw himself at the mercy of God, and his will must be submerged completely in the will of God. The work-righteous mechanics and merits of the scholastic system could never lift despairing sinners to their goal: unity with God and peace of soul. All human efforts toward gaining righteousness before God only serve to swell the ego, and the ego must be mortified. When the will is stripped of its selfish ambitions and completely yielded to God, then comes union with God, and Christ comes alive in the heart. "Inebriated with salvation, the soul sinks into the sea of God."[20]

Suffering and cross-bearing are here recognized as the normal way of the Christian life and the necessary means of purging out self-dependence and of driving one to Christ, who suffered before us and for us. Here Romans 7 comes to life. The struggle between the flesh and the spirit must be so intense that it drives the sinner to the anguish of hell before Christ reaches down and lifts him up to union with Himself. Maybe this is where Luther learned for the first time what he so often proclaimed, that God brings the agony of conscience. "I have found in him [Tauler] more solid and true theology than is to be, or can be, found in all the scholastic doctors of the universities."[21]

But again the flirtation with another school of theology was short-lived. For Luther soon saw that the mysticism of Tauler and the Rhineland mystics fell short of the full Gospel. There was little emphasis on justification through faith. The old system of merits was not completely eliminated. The doctrine of God was hazy, like Meister Eckhart's "Perfect Being." Instead of Luther's emphasis on the Word of Scripture, here was talk of the "inner Word." With all his evangelical zeal, Tauler remained an obedient child of his Roman Mother, quite unaware of the inner corruption of the Church. Even the Pauline language of mortification of the flesh could not entirely escape the idea of a work that man had to perform to make himself ready for the entrance of God. As is so often the case, some of the mystics loved too well to tell of their *Anfechtungen* and their experience of release. It easily breeds a feeling of superiority and a sadistic satisfaction in suffering. In the last analysis Tauler's roots seem to run back to Scotus and Bonaventura.

Franz Lau wonders how Luther could be so blind to some of the features of German mysticism such as its "descents into pantheism."

> [B]ut that the humility and abasement, the reduction to sheer insignificance before God, and thus the acknowledgment that to God alone belongs glory, indeed, the experience of God even to the pangs of hell, bring one in truth to heaven—these are the stock of mystical ideas which helped to shape Luther, became a part of him, and may have assisted at the new birth which he experienced.[22]

We should hardly picture Luther as taking on these four movements and disposing of them one by one in rapid succession. The fact is that he was confronted by all four movements at once, and he never was finished with any one of them. The reformer emerged from late medieval theology, where these four schools all struggled for supremacy. Luther's reaction to them was not all negative. As a child of medieval theology he was constantly engaged in the sifting process, sloughing off what was bad, retaining what was good. He cannot be called a child of any one of the four schools, but his thinking was influenced by all of them. And they all contributed something to the theology of the Reformation. Aristotle taught him logic, which stood him in good stead in his many debates. Aquinas exemplified to him the danger of mixing theology and philosophy. The Occamists helped Luther see the Holy Scriptures as God's inspired revelation and to use it always as the final authority and absolute truth in theological debate. Mysticism strengthened him in his inner life with Christ and helped him recognize cross and suffering and *Anfechtung* as a normal part of Christian experience and growth. Erasmus and the other humanists drove him to sharpen the tools of his trade, without which he would never have become the great Bible interpreter and exegete that he was. And without Luther's exegesis we might well question whether there would have been a "Reformation."

But all the while that Luther was learning from these schools of theology he found himself suffocating spiritually and theologically. He was like a prisoner in chains, trying to free himself from the fetters of rationalism, moralism, legalism, and synergism. He climbed up as far as the papal church could lead him and beat against the sky, trying to break through the angry clouds to the light of the merciful God.

It was not Luther's nature to be a rebel. He honored the Church, the fathers, his teachers, and it was repugnant to him to set himself up against any of these. He proceeded slowly as he moved from teacher to teacher, from Lombard to Aquinas, from Bernard to Scotus, from Occam to Biel, from Gregory of Rimini to Tauler, then back to Augustine, and finally to St. Paul, from an infallible Church to an infallible Scripture. And as he became an obedient pupil of the Word, he learned to know the Church, not as a man-made organization that speaks through pope and priest with infallible authority but as the fellowship of believers and the body of Christ. Then the Church became to him the Holy Mother, who had been violated by priests and prelates and theologians, and who must be set free and cleansed by the Gospel of grace in Christ Jesus.

From now on Luther's struggle was not just the struggle of Brother Martin for his own peace of soul. As the reformer began to speak, he found that he was speaking for millions of other souls in distress. He was speaking, he felt, as a child of the Church and as a representative of the true Church in the midst of Babylon. For the Church was again in travail, as it had been at Nicaea. And the ferment and pain of the Church and of millions of Christians were focused in this awakened monk. Now the whole Church began to suddenly come alive once more around the eternal question, "How can a sinner be justified before God and saved?" The reformer had been born. Worms was the focal point of this experience of Luther, namely, that he was speaking for the Church. As he later looked back at Worms he said, *Tunc eram ecclesia*, "Then I was the church."

Luther's climbing and struggling had brought him nowhere. The theological skies remained clouded and he could not penetrate to the light of the merciful God. But Jesus had once spoken: "I have given them Your Word" (John 17:14). And now again God gave His servant the Word of truth and light and life. In complete submission of faith to this Word of God he began to see the error of all those ways by which he had been trying to climb to God. The way of scholastic theology was wrong because reason, too, was corrupted, together with the whole man, by the fall. The way of the Occamists had failed him, because good works could not justify, but could only flow in gratitude from a man justified by faith. Humanism could not help him because fallen man had no power to lift his sinful self to God, even with the help of original sources. And mysticism's demand that he mortify his own flesh was only a new kind of work righteousness, which expected miracles of grace apart from the means of grace.

The basic error that Luther saw in all the medieval schools of thought was the principle: *Facere quod in se est.* Man must do what is in him—do the best he can—to dispose himself to God's grace. Grace is only granted to the man who does what is in him, says Gabriel Biel. This Luther saw as a denial of the Pauline doctrine of justification by grace alone through faith. It maintained a certain capacity of free will to dispose one for grace.

Luther confronted this nominalist principle head on in his *Disputation Against Scholastic Theology* in 1517. Here the whole theology of a *free* will is turned into a theology of a *bound* will.

> THESIS 5. It is false to state that man's inclination is free
> to choose between either of two opposites. Indeed, the
> inclination is not free, but captive.

THESIS 15. Indeed, it is peculiar to it [the will] that it can only conform to erroneous and not to correct precept.

THESIS 21. No act is done according to nature that is not an act of concupiscence against God.

THESIS 30. On the part of man, however, nothing precedes grace except ill will and even rebellion against grace.

THESIS 33. And this is false, that doing all that one is able to do can remove the obstacles to grace.[23]

Luther's battle with this nominalist formula *Facere quod in se est* continued until the year 1518, and even from then on he never ceased to attack it. It comes again in the Heidelberg Disputation of 1518. Once more he finds the doctrine rooted in the doctrine of the free will, and he rejects the whole package.

THESIS 13. Free will, after the fall, exists in name only, and as long as it does what it is able to do, it commits a mortal sin.

THESIS 16. The person who believes that he can obtain grace by doing what is in him adds sin to sin so that he becomes doubly guilty.[24]

And now Luther summarizes the distinction he sees between the medieval theology and the theology of St. Paul:

THESIS 21. A theology of glory calls evil good and good evil. A theology of the cross calls the thing what it actually is.

It is quite evident that in these disputations of 1517 and 1518 Luther has arrived at his theology of grace alone and has finally rejected the medieval doctrine of free will and the principle *Facere quod in se est.* He has moved away from what he called the theology of glory to a theology of the cross. This did not happen overnight. It involved a struggle lasting many years. Exactly when it started no one can say. Certainly it got a good start in the monastery. When he pours out his heart to Staupitz, the intensity of his *Anfechtung* becomes more and more evident. Oberman pinpoints the period of transition between the years 1515 and 1516. He finds Luther adhering to the doctrine of *Facere quod in se est* in his exposition of Psalm 113. But in his lectures on Romans 14 in 1516 Luther has radically changed his position on the doctrine, rejecting it completely.[25]

This total break with the rational-natural theology of the late Middle Ages is simply the other side of the coin showing Luther's discovery of the Gospel of justification by grace alone through faith alone. The theology of glory has been replaced by the theology of the cross. How did it happen? Volumes have been written in an effort to answer this question. Luther scholars have tried to determine *when* it happened, and their answers have been spread all over the years from 1509 to 1519. Luther later often speaks about *that* it happened, but he does not have much to say about exactly *when* it happened. He says, "I did not learn my theology all at once, but I had to search deeper for it, when my temptations took me."[26] Luther's most detailed testimony regarding his discovery of the Gospel comes at the end of his life in his *Preface to the Complete Edition of Luther's Latin Writings*. It is worth quoting at length because of its unique importance.

> Meanwhile, I had already during that year [1519] returned to interpret the Psalter anew. I had confidence in the fact that I was more skilful [sic], after I had lectured in the university on St. Paul's epistles to the Romans, to the Galatians, and the one to the Hebrews. . . . I had been taught to understand philosophically regarding the formal or active righteousness, as they called it, with which God is righteous and punishes the unrighteous sinner.
>
> Though I lived as a monk without reproach, I felt that I was a sinner before God with an extremely disturbed conscience. I could not believe that he was placated by my satisfaction. I did not love, yes, I hated the righteous

God . . . I was angry with God, and said, "As if, indeed, it is not enough, that miserable sinners, eternally lost through original sin, are crushed by every kind of calamity by the law of the decalogue, without having God add pain to pain by the gospel and also by the gospel threatening us with his righteousness and wrath!" Thus I raged with a fierce and troubled conscience. Nevertheless, I beat importunately upon Paul at that place, most ardently desiring to know what St. Paul wanted.

At last, by the mercy of God, meditating day and night, I gave heed to the context of the words, namely, "In it the righteousness of God is revealed, as it is written, 'He who through faith is righteous shall live.' " There I began to understand that the righteousness of God is that by which the righteous lives by a gift of God, namely by faith. And this is the meaning: the righteousness of God is revealed by the gospel, namely, the passive righteousness with which merciful God justifies us by faith, as it is written, "He who through faith is righteous shall live." Here I felt that I was altogether born again and had entered paradise itself through open gates. There a totally other face of the entire Scripture showed itself to me. Thereupon I ran through the Scriptures from memory. I also found in other terms an analogy, as, the work of God, that is, what God does in us, the power of God, with which he makes us wise, the strength of God, the salvation of God, the glory of God.

And I extolled my sweetest word with a love as great as the hatred with which I had before hated the word "righteousness of God." Thus that place in Paul was for me truly the gate to paradise. Later I read Augustine's *The Spirit and the Letter*, where contrary to hope I found that he, too, interpreted God's righteousness in a similar way, as the righteousness with which God clothes us when he justifies us. Although this was heretofore said imperfectly and he did not explain all things concerning imputation clearly, it nevertheless was pleasing that God's righteousness with which we are justified was taught.[27]

It is clear from Luther's own testimony here that by 1519 the reformer had been born, with a clear grasp of the Gospel of grace alone, faith alone, Word alone. This does not change the fact that long before 1519 Luther had arrived at his Pauline understanding of the righteousness of God and justification by grace through faith. This new language appears already in his lectures on the Psalter in 1514, particularly in his comments on the seventieth and seventy-first psalms. His lectures on Romans in 1515–1516 indicate that his breakthrough is almost complete. True, he occasionally drifts into the old language of "infusion," "making righteous," and the like. But Luther's understanding of St. Paul's theology of justification by grace alone, through faith alone, without works shines forth with impressive splendor. The "righteousness of God" of Romans 1:17 is no longer the formal righteousness "with which God is righteous and punishes the unrighteous sinner." As revealed in the Gospel, it is "the passive righteousness with which a merciful God justifies us by faith." Here Luther pulls out all the stops of St. Paul's doctrine of justification. It is a "declaring righteous" rather than a "making righteous" in the sense of an inner ethical change. It is the imputation of Christ's righteousness, which is His obedience unto death. Justification is the forgiveness of sins, declared to us by God on the basis of Christ's atoning work. Man is given a new status before God where he is *simul justus et peccator*—at the same time righteous and sinner.

This justified man who is sinner and who is righteous before God lives in the tension of Romans 7, a tension between the flesh and the Spirit, between the Law and the Gospel. Like Paul he is never too good a Christian to suffer under this tension. If the time comes that he no longer does, he must ask himself if he is still a Christian. As in the life of St. Paul, Luther's *Anfechtung* was not limited to a few early years, in his case 1509–1519. It was a part of the lifelong struggle of a Christian living in the tension of Romans 7.

It is evident that through the years Luther had found the solution of his religious and theological problems through exhaustive searching of Holy Scripture, which to him was the inspired Word of God. Surely, if we regard the Reformation as an act of God, we must see the hand of God in Luther's appointment to the University of Wittenberg by Staupitz to lecture on the books of the Bible, particularly Genesis, Psalms, Romans, Galatians, and Hebrews.

We can speculate on the psychology of Luther's "conversion" from the medieval theology to the theology of the Reformation. How could it happen? How did it happen? How did God create the reformer? It happened the only way it could happen. Luther buried himself in the Word of God and out of this burial rose the reformer. "[S]o shall My word be that goes out from My mouth; it shall not return to Me empty, but it shall accomplish that which I purpose, and shall succeed in the thing for which I sent it" (Isaiah 55:11).

Finding Luther in spiritual and theological anguish, could any psychologist have given him a more perfect assignment than Staupitz gave him when he told him to go and exegete the Word of God? Digging deep into these basic books of Scripture, Luther found the answer to both his spiritual and his theological problems. And the evidence is inescapable that it was above all his intense study of Romans that brought him through to a clear understanding of the Gospel and to a peace of mind in the wounds of Christ. It was when Luther became a disciple of St. Paul that he really began to understand what it means to be a disciple of Christ.[28]

The theology of discipleship to Luther was a theology of the cross. From this high position he developed his concept both of man and of God. To try to say which came first would involve idle speculation. When God confronts a man and reveals Himself in

Christ, He at the same time shows a man what he is. And it is at the cross that he first comes to know God. When he is baptized, he is baptized into Christ and His death, even the death of the cross. If like St. Paul he meets the Lord on the Damascus Road, he is confronted by the risen Christ with the nail marks in His hands. And in due time he will say with the apostle, "But far be it from me to boast except in the cross of our Lord Jesus Christ" (Galatians 6:14). Then begins the life under the cross, where we learn to "count everything as loss because of the surpassing worth of knowing Christ Jesus my Lord . . . that I may know Him and the power of His resurrection, and may share in His sufferings, becoming like Him in His death" (Philippians 3:8–10). This is a theology to live by, and it is what Luther called the theology of the cross.

CHAPTER
THREE

THE THEOLOGY OF THE CROSS

What Luther calls the theology of the cross begs definition. And yet all mature Christians have this theology and live by it, even if they do not know what theology is. They know what St. Paul is talking about when he says, "But far be it from me to boast except in the cross of our Lord Jesus Christ" (Galatians 6:14). They know the heart of the Gospel that the Church preaches. "[B]ut we preach Christ crucified, a stumbling block to Jews and folly to Gentiles, but to those who are called, both Jews and Greeks, Christ the power of God and the wisdom of God" (1 Corinthians 1:23–24). And in humble, childlike faith, they sing with the Church, in the words of a later hymnist: "Nothing in my hand I bring, Simply to Thy cross I cling."[1]

Luther, in finding his tortuous way to St. Paul's theology of the cross, was like a photographer getting his object in exact focus. Looking through his scope he turns his finder back and forth until he has the object in the center where the lines cross. This is it. The finished picture shows the object as it is. So Luther, searching Scripture to get an accurate picture of its theology, turned his finder back and forth through its pages until he found it all centered in the cross. Then, and only then, did he grasp the meaning and the central message of Scripture. Then was born in him the theology of the cross. And it was the theology that he found most clearly and completely defined in the writings of the great apostle.

This theological stance of Luther was no flash in the pan. It was not, as sometimes pictured, a passing fad that he, like some twentieth-century theological students, picked up from a popular theologian, only to switch when a new scholar appeared on the horizon. Otto Ritschl is undoubtedly right when he says that Luther was helped by Augustine and Bernard on the way toward his theology of the cross.[2] But more recent Luther research has disproved Ritschl's intimation that Luther's theology of the cross was a monastic conception that Luther outgrew not long after his "conversion."[3]

An examination of Luther's works through the years shows very clearly that the theology of the cross was the dominant principle in all his theological thinking from possibly as early as 1509 to the end of his life. It begins to emerge in his studies of Augustine in 1509, at which time he says, "The crucifixion of Christ is a sacrament, because it signifies the cross of penitence (*poenitentiae*), in which the soul dies to sin; it is an example, because it incites us truly to offer our body to death or to the cross."[4]

Luther saw the theology of the cross in the Old Testament as well as in the New Testament. For to him the Bible was one book. Old and New Testaments alike bear witness to Christ. With our contemporary theology leaning over backward for fear of "reading into" the Old Testament the theology of the New Testament, the figure of Christ fades and sometimes all but disappears from the pages of the Old Testament. Our faith is restored and our spirits refreshed when we sit with Luther reading the Old Testament and with him see the figure of the Coming One, the Messiah, confronting us wherever we look. In his *Preface to the Old Testament*, first appearing in 1523, Luther says, "If you would interpret well and confidently, set Christ before you, for he is the man to whom it all applies, every bit of it."[5] And this Christ of the Old Testament is no half-Christ. He is the Christ, the Lamb of God, who "was wounded for our transgressions" and "crushed for our iniquities . . . and the LORD has laid on Him the iniquity of us all" (Isaiah 53:5–6). This is again the theology of the cross, which Luther saw as the dominant theology of the Old Testament. For the *Preface* continues:

> Make the High Priest Aaron, then, to be nobody but Christ alone, as does the Epistle to the Hebrews [5:4–5], which is sufficient, all by itself, to interpret all the figures of Moses. Likewise, as the same epistle announces [Heb. 9–10], it is certain that Christ Himself is the sacrifice— indeed even the altar [Hebrews 13:10]—who sacrificed Himself with His own blood. . . . He has gone in once for all through the curtain to God to make atonement for us [Heb. 9:12]. Thus you should apply to Christ personally, and to no one else, all that is written about the high priest.[6]

As early as 1513 Luther lectured on the Psalter at the University of Wittenberg. He did it again in 1532. In both courses the theology of the cross dominates his interpretation. In the earlier lectures the same idea appears of Christ as both the sacrifice and the altar, as well as the High Priest. Commenting on Psalm 84:3 ("at Your altars, O LORD of hosts"), Luther says, "The altar is the mystical Cross of Christ, on which all ought to be offered. Because 'he who does not take his cross and follow me is not worthy of me': for just as he was offered on the Cross: so also ought we in like manner to be offered on the cross."[7]

If we look at his later lectures of 1532 on the Psalter, it becomes clear that there has been no fading out of this theology of the cross, as Ritschl intimated. He uses the same language as he did in the earlier lectures. As he comments on Psalm 110:4, Luther says,

> But Christ is the only Priest whom God has assigned to the task of reconciling us to Him and obtaining the forgiveness of sins. He made His sacrifice in obedience to God's command, not as a venture of His own, moved by pious zeal. . . . However, it was His own blood, not the blood of a stranger. By His death on the cross He made such a sacrifice once for the sins of all the world (Heb. 7:27). The cross was the altar on which He, consumed by the fire of the boundless love which burned in His heart, presented the living and holy sacrifice of His body and blood to the Father with fervent intercession, loud cries, and hot, anxious tears (Heb. 5:7).[8]

Even more striking is Luther's statement in his *Preface to the Psalter*, published in 1545 shortly before his death:

> The Psalter ought to be a precious and beloved book, if for no other reason than this: it promises Christ's death and resurrection so clearly . . . that it might well be called a little Bible. In it is comprehended most beautifully and briefly everything that is in the entire Bible.[9]

Following his lectures on the Psalms at the University of Wittenberg, Luther took up the Epistle to the Romans in 1515. In these lectures he shows that he has made great strides forward in the understanding of the Gospel. He has discovered St. Paul's doctrine of justification by grace alone through faith alone in its basic elements. This makes his theology of the cross loom even larger than it did in the Psalms lectures. For the justification of the sinner is accomplished at the cross, and we are baptized into Christ and His death, justified in His blood. This is not to say that Luther in his Romans commentary has reached theological maturity. He will continue to grow in his grasp of the Gospel, and his theology of the cross will shine more brightly as the reformer emerges.

The most precise statement of the theology of the cross Luther gives us in the Heidelberg Disputation of 1518. There he makes it clear that according to Scripture we can know neither God nor man except through the cross. The theology of the cross is a theology of revelation. Through the ages man has sought to know God by rational speculation on His creation. In this way he tries to peer into the very majesty and power and glory of God. Philip, echoing this theology of glory, says to Jesus: "Show us the Father." Luther comments: "Christ forthwith set aside his flighty thought about seeing God elsewhere and led him to himself, saying, 'Philip, he who has seen me has seen the Father' [John 14:9]."[10] Luther rejects this theology of glory, this trying to see God where He has not chosen to reveal Himself. Man cannot bear to see God in His majesty. God told Moses he could not see God's face and live. "[W]hile My glory passes by I will put you in a cleft of the rock, and I will cover you with My hand until I have passed by. Then I will take away My hand, and you shall see My back, but My face shall not be seen" (Exodus 33:22–23). So Philip must learn to look for God where He has revealed Himself, and that, says Luther, is in the cross. "For this reason true theology and recognition of God are in the crucified Christ."[11] To Philip and all his speculating followers Luther says, "Now it is not sufficient for anyone, and it does him no good to recognize God in his glory and majesty, unless he recognizes him in the humility and shame of the cross. Thus God destroys the wisdom of the wise, as Isa. [45:15] says, 'Truly, thou art a God who hidest thyself.'"[12]

As Paul Althaus points out, the true knowledge of God is not found through Romans 1 but through 1 Corinthians 1.[13] The preaching of the cross is "foolishness." The theology of the cross means: "God lets Himself be known in that which according to natural judgment is the opposite to the Divine; His wisdom appears in foolishness, His glory in ignominy. His revelation is for natural man sheer hiddenness."[14]

Here Luther is confronting us again with his idea of the *Deus absconditus* (hidden God) and the *Deus revelatus* (revealed God). God hides Himself behind forms or signs or masks, which appear foolish to humans. Yet we will learn to know God only if we seek Him under these forms, particularly the Word and the Sacraments. In the Old Testament, God appeared to fallen Adam "in a gentle breeze as though enveloped in a covering." Later He manifested Himself in the tabernacle by the mercy seat. Moses speaks of the "faces of God" through which God showed Himself. No more can we recognize God without a covering. Therefore "God envelopes Himself in His works in certain forms, as today He wraps Himself up in Baptism, in absolution, etc. . . . Whoever desires to be saved and to be safe when he deals with such great matters, let him simply hold to the form, the signs, and the coverings of the Godhead, such as His Word and His works. For in His Word and in His works He shows Himself to us."[15] This theology of the cross, of Word and Sacrament, Luther opposes to the theology of glory of the scholastic theologians.

> But those who want to reach God apart from these coverings exert themselves to ascend to heaven without ladders (that is, without the Word). Overwhelmed by His majesty, which they seek to comprehend without a covering, they fall to their destruction. . . . Therefore, if we want to walk in safety, let us accept what the Word submits for our reflection and what God Himself wants us to know.[16]

This theology is no vague theory with Luther. It is a theology to live by. It is the theology of Christian experience. An adult comes to conversion and to faith like St. Paul on the Damascus Road. The apostle is brought to his knees in fear before the Lord he has been persecuting. But he is lifted up to faith by the wounded hands and the forgiving Word of the risen Lord, who sends him on to be baptized and to be commissioned for His service. This is the way one is brought to faith. According to Luther,

God brings agony of conscience, "So that man may learn to know himself and God; to know himself is to learn that all he is capable of is sinning and doing evil; to know God is to learn that God's grace is stronger than all creatures. Thus he learns to despise himself and to laud and praise God's mercy."[17]

This is not the kind of theology that is palatable to natural man. Nor is it palatable to many who sit in the pews of our churches. Even a good Christian must confess that even Jesus' "Take up the cross and follow Me" is a hard saying. Through the cross to the crown is not the way we like to go. Must we really go through the agony of conscience to reach a mature faith? We like to hear about the love of God. But who wants to hear about His wrath or even His righteousness? We love to hear about God's grace, but we are impatient when the preacher tells us about our sin. The hope of heaven is palatable preaching, but don't threaten me with the possibility of hell.

But is this cozy theology really a theology to live by? Has it anything to do with the Way to which Jesus calls us? Is it the Way the apostles laid out for the Christians of the Early Church, saying, "through many tribulations we must enter the kingdom of God" (Acts 14:22)?

Luther's theology of the cross presents a life lived in tension between the Law and the Gospel, between what Luther calls the foreign work and the proper work of God. Sinners who are to be brought to repentance and faith must hear the Law of God that tells them they are lost sinners, that they are "by nature sinful and unclean,"[18] that they have sinned against God "in thought, word, and deed," and that all their "righteous deeds are like a polluted garment" (Isaiah 64:6). This is what Luther calls the foreign work of God, which He must perform before He can accomplish His proper work, which is to save man through faith in Jesus Christ. This latter must be accomplished by the Gospel of God's grace in Christ.

Man, driven into fear and anxiety by the preaching of the Law, hears this Gospel message, which, instead of reminding him of God's demands, tells him what God has done for him. It points not to man's works, but to the works of Christ, and bids him confidently believe that for the sake of his Son God will forgive his sins and accept him as his child. And this message, when received in faith, immediately cheers and comforts the heart. The heart will no longer flee from God; rather it turns to him. Finding grace with God and experiencing his mercy, the heart feels drawn to him. It commences to call upon him and to treat and revere him as its beloved God. In proportion as such faith and solace grow, also love for the commandments will grow and obedience to them will be man's delight.[19]

This is the right use of the Law according to Luther: to bring people to see and confess their sin, so that they throw themselves on the mercy of God offered in the Gospel. There is a wrong use of the Law, namely, when men preach that we must obey the Law and do good works in order to be saved. Luther says there is a wrong preaching of the Law when men, "instead of making it tributary to faith in Christ, misuse it to teach work-righteousness."[20] "The Law," says Luther, "is that Word by which God teaches what we shall do, as, for instance, the Ten Commandments." But without God's grace it is impossible for human nature to keep the Law, for

man since the fall of Adam in Paradise is depraved and full of sinful desires, so that he cannot from his heart's desire find pleasure in the law, which fact we all experience in ourselves. . . . Thus the Law of God convicts us, even by our own experience, that by nature we are evil, disobedient, lovers of sin, and hostile to God's laws.[21]

The distinction between Law and Gospel and the necessity of both for our salvation are cardinal principles in Luther's theology of the cross, so that these two sermons must continue to be preached in Christendom, namely: the first, the teaching of the Law or of the ten commandments, and the second, the doctrine concerning the grace of Christ. For if either of these fall it pulls the other with it; while on the other hand, wherever the one remains steadfast and is faithfully put into practice, it brings the other with it.[22]

Luther then applies this to Christian life and says that "the doctrine [must] be observed by the Christians so that they may know what they have been, what they are still lacking and what they should again become." And this is to Luther "a glorious doctrine that teaches what we are to become."[23] But if it is to be realized, both Law and Gospel must be preached together. We must know what we were in Paradise, where Adam lived in perfect love to God and without sin. We must know that through Adam's fall we all became sinners and are under the wrath of God. Thus the Law drives me always to my knees, and I find no escape, for I cannot obey the Law perfectly as God demands. "Here the Prophets come now, and preach Christ, and say: One is coming who will give counsel how man may regain what he lost and again enter the state from which he fell, to which the Law points him. This is the other sermon that should and must be preached until the day of judgment." Thus the sinner in despair under the Law hears the Gospel of God's grace, that "Christ came and stepped between the Father and us, and prays for us: Beloved Father, be gracious unto them and forgive them their sins. I will take upon me their transgressions and bear them . . . shedding my blood for mankind. Moreover, I have fulfilled the Law and I did it for their welfare in order that they may partake of my fulfilling the Law and thereby come to grace." Through grace "man may find counsel and help to come to a perfect life. But the help offered us is, that Christ prays the Father to forgive us our sins against the Law, and not to impute what we are still indebted. Then he promises also to give the Holy Spirit, by whose aid the heart begins to love God and to keep his commandments."[24]

The Christian then lives by the Word of God, but only by the whole Word of God, by Law and Gospel together. The Law kills, the Gospel makes alive. I must die if I am to live, even as Christ went through the death of the cross to the resurrection. The Law must destroy all my pride and self-righteousness, and the Gospel must make me glory in nothing "save the cross of our Lord Jesus Christ." The Law makes me confess with the apostle, "For I know that nothing good dwells in me, that is, in my flesh. For I have the desire to do what is right, but not the ability to carry it out" (Romans 7:18). Here, as Luther points out in his commentary on Romans, the Christian is again caught in the tension of the Christian life, the tension between "flesh" and "Spirit." Insofar as the Christian is controlled by the Spirit, the Christian is spirit and wills the good and does the good. But insofar as he is controlled by the flesh, by old sinful nature, he is flesh and does the evil that he does not want to do. Luther comments,

> Because of the flesh, he is carnal and evil, for the good is not in him and he does evil; because of the spirit,[25] he is spiritual and good, for he does the good. . . . Just because one and the same man as a whole consists of flesh and spirit, he attributes to the whole man both of the opposites that come from the opposite parts of him. Thus there comes about a *communio idiomatum*: one and the same man is spiritual and carnal, righteous and sinful, good and evil.[26]

In this context Luther often likes to speak of *simul justus et peccator*. The Christian is a sinner, but justified through faith in Christ, declared righteous by God and clothed in the righteousness of Christ. As we noted above, Luther says that "one and the same man is spiritual and carnal, righteous and sinful, good and evil." This is one of the theological treasures Luther finds in Romans 7 particularly, but it appears frequently in his commentaries on both Romans and Galatians. "The saints in being righteous are at the same time sinners; they are righteous because they believe in Christ whose righteousness covers them and is imputed to them, but they are sinners because they do not fulfill the law and are not without sinful desires."[27]

This doctrine must receive further coverage in a later chapter. But we should not fail to see that here, too, is a theology to live by. How often does a Christian stand with St. Paul in Romans 7, confessing his defeat in the struggle between flesh and spirit and crying, "Wretched man that I am! Who will deliver me from this body of death?" Looking in upon himself he sees only failure, defeat, sin. "If You, O LORD, should mark iniquities, O LORD, who could stand?" (Psalm 130:3). David knew the answer: "But with You there is forgiveness, that You may be feared" (Psalm 130:4). The apostle, too, knew the answer: "Thanks be to God through Jesus Christ our Lord! So then, I myself serve the law of God with my mind, but with my flesh I serve the law of sin" (Romans 7:25).

This kind of theology is puzzling to the average Christian, who is apt to think that as he or she increases in Christian maturity, spiritual struggles and doubts will diminish. But we need only to look at the saints of God to see that the greatest saints are the ones who experience the greatest intensity in their struggle with sin and temptation and the "flesh." We remember the agony of David in Psalm 51. Isaiah cries, "Woe is me! For I am lost" (6:5). St. Paul sighs, "For I do not do what I want, but I do the very thing I hate. . . . Wretched man that I am!" (Romans 7:15–24).

Luther himself is probably the finest example of this thesis. When he says that God brings the agony of conscience, he is speaking from experience as well as from the testimony of Scripture. *Anfechtung* is the most real experience of the Christian who lives under the theology of the cross.[28] No English word or combination of words can fully express the meaning of this German word that appears so often in Luther. It covers everything that comprises the struggle of the serious Christian in tension between the flesh and the spirit, between Law and Gospel, between assurance and doubt. The agony of temptation is like that of our Lord in Gethsemane. Painful as it is, it is a normal part of the Christian life in Luther's estimation. Those who never experience it should ask themselves if they are still Christians.

A Christian in *Anfechtung* is simply experiencing the assaults of the devil. "This hurts beyond measure when men mock and laugh at those who are wretched and troubled, defying them and boasting against them. It constitutes a great and strong assault [*Anfechtung*] upon their faith in God and a powerful incentive to despair and unbelief."[29]

The devil launches his assaults from both the outside and the inside of a Christian.

> When a man would live an obedient life according to the teaching of the first book [Proverbs] and attend to his duty or office, then the devil, the world, and his own flesh put up so much resistance that he becomes weary and discouraged with his station in life and regrets everything he has begun, for things simply will not go as he wants them to. Everything becomes a struggle then; dissatisfaction, impatience, and murmuring arise until a man is ready to give up all hope and do nothing more. For if the devil cannot prevent obedience through covetousness and desire on the right hand, he will hinder it on the left hand through toil and trouble.[30]

But let this man be "patient and steadfast in obedience, in the face of unpleasantness and temptation [*anfechtung*], and ever to wait out the brief hour in peace and joy."[31]

When tempted to despair, Luther invariably turns back to the heart of the Gospel, that "justified by faith, we have peace with God through our Lord Jesus Christ" (Romans 5:1). But even the question of justification is "an elusive thing—not in itself, for in itself it is firm and sure, but so far as we are concerned."[32] As he so frequently does, Luther here turns to his own experience.

> I myself have had considerable experience of this, for I know how I sometimes struggle in the hours of darkness. I know how often I suddenly lose sight of the rays of the Gospel and of grace, which have been obscured for me by thick, dark clouds. In other words, I know how slippery the footing is even for those who are mature and seem to be firmly established in matters of faith.

Our mistake is that

> when in a struggle we should use the Gospel, which is the Word of grace, consolation, and life, there the Law, the Word of wrath, sadness, and death, precedes the Gospel and begins to raise a tumult. The terrors it arouses in the conscience are no smaller than was the tremendous and horrible spectacle on Mt. Sinai (Ex. 19:16). Thus even one passage in Scripture that presents some of the threats of the Law overwhelms and swamps any other comfort; it shakes our insides in such a way that it makes us forget justification, grace, Christ, and the Gospel.[33]

One of the deepest *Anfechtungen* that tortured Luther was caused by the question that would not be put down: How do you, Martin, a humble monk of Wittenberg, dare to question the authority of the pope and church councils and the teaching proclaimed by the Catholic Church for a thousand years? This question is constantly thrown at him, says Luther: "Are you, all by yourself, wiser than so many saints, wiser even than the entire church?"[34] This question, he believes, comes from the devil, who "disguises himself as an angel of light" (2 Corinthians 11:14). His opponents say, "But we are concerned that the authority of the holy catholic Church stand unimpaired. The Church has believed and taught this way for so many centuries; so have all the fathers of the primitive Church, who were saints, more ancient and more learned than you are. Who are you, then, to take it upon yourself to dissent from all these and to bring us an opposing doctrine?"

Luther cannot take this charge lightly. But the answer is always the same. He has his marching orders from God, and his final authority is Holy Scripture, the Word of God. "When Satan conspires with your flesh and your reason to argue this way, your conscience is terrified and despairs completely, unless you continually recover your sense and say: 'Whether it is St. Cyprian, Ambrose, or Augustine, St. Peter, Paul, or John, yes, or even an angel from heaven that teaches otherwise—I still know this for certain, that what I teach is not from men but from God.' "[35] Anxiety drives Luther to Matthew 6:34. "Anxiety about us is God's affair; our anxiety goes wrong anyhow, and produces nothing but wasted toil."[36]

Luther has found a way of life he pursues doggedly and methodically. It has three elements: *oratio, meditatio, tentatio.*[37] First, says Luther, we must know that the "Holy Scriptures constitute a book which turns the wisdom of all other books into foolishness." Despair of reason, "but kneel down in your little room [Matt. 6:6] and pray to God with real humility and earnestness, that he through his dear Son may give you his Holy Spirit, who will enlighten you, lead you, and give you understanding."[38]

"Secondly, you should meditate, that is, not only in your heart, but also externally, by actually repeating and comparing oral speech and literal words of the book, reading and rereading them with diligent attention and reflection, so that you may see what the Holy Spirit means by them." Luther here lays down a principle that has become a unique mark of Lutheranism and of Luther's theology of the cross. "For God will not give you his Spirit without the external Word."[39] Meditation on the Word of God is the prime business of the Christian and the very source of spiritual life. And for Luther and his theology of the cross, the central focus of this meditation is the Passion of our Lord Jesus Christ.

Then comes the third element, which Luther describes with that elusive word *tentatio,* adding the word *Anfechtung* as if to make them synonymous. This seems to refer to the testing or trial that the Christian must endure in the face of temptation. Luther points to David, who had to suffer this *tentatio* in the face of his enemies, "whom he must tolerate because he meditates, that is, because he is occupied with God's Word. . . . For as soon as God's Word takes root and grows in you, the devil will harry you, and will make a real doctor of you, and by his assaults will teach you to seek and love God's Word."[40]

When you have begun to live and study according to these three rules, then you can hope that "you have begun to become a real theologian." But beware of pride. And if you begin to flatter yourself with the idea that "you have made it . . . then take yourself by the ears, and if you do this in the right way you will find a beautiful pair of big, long, shaggy donkey ears."[41]

This is the picture of the man who through honest self-examination under the cross finds himself unmasked and naked with no cloak of faith, no adornment of love. How cold his faith, how shallow his love, when he stands beside Paul as he pours out his heart of love for Christ and his fellows: "For I could wish that I myself were accursed and cut off from Christ for the sake of my brothers, my kinsmen according to the flesh" (Romans 9:3). There must be very few saints who have dared to say this. For this must be the ultimate commitment to Christ and His will, the highest love for Christ and neighbor to which a Christian can attain. This is what Luther calls *resignatio ad infernum*, resignation to hell.

> Now this inverted love is the strongest and utmost kind of love: utter self-hatred becomes the sign of the highest love for another. . . . Yet no one can be purged unless he is resigned to hell.

> But the true saints actually achieve this resignation, because their hearts overflow with love, and they do this without great distress. For they are so completely dedicated to God that nothing seems impossible for them to do, not even the suffering of the pains of hell.[42]

This is indeed what it means to be Christlike.

> For even Christ suffered damnation and dereliction to a
> greater degree than all the saints. And his sufferings were
> not, as some imagine, easy for him. For he really and
> truly offered himself for us to eternal damnation to God
> the Father. . . . All his saints must imitate him in this. . . . [43]

This is a theology to live by because it is a theology of the cross and a theology of the Word. As such it penetrates not only the heart and mind of the Christian, but every phase of the Christian life. It drives us as Christians to prayer (*oratio*) in a life of worship in the communion of saints. We live in the Word of God according to the command of Jesus, and the vision of the Crucified One is ever before our eyes (*meditatio*). In our daily struggle against sin and Satan, the world and the flesh, we share in the fellowship of Christ's sufferings and conquering through the power of His resurrection (*Anfechtung*). Not for a moment does Luther pursue theology for the sake of theology alone. President McCord of Princeton Theological Seminary caught this spirit of Luther when he said recently: "One pursues truth but truth is for the purpose of life. . . . To regard theology as a closed system you stand off from—well that's what Kierkegaard was talking about when he said 'to be a theologian is to have crucified Christ.'" [44]

PART II

WHAT IS MAN?

Introductory Comments

B ehold the man!" said Pontius Pilate as he sent Him off to be crucified by evil men. Behold the man, "despised and rejected by men . . . smitten by God, and afflicted . . . wounded for our transgressions . . . crushed for our iniquities" (Isaiah 53:3–5). Then you will be ready to join Job on your knees before a holy and loving God, confessing and asking, "What is man, that You make so much of him, and that You set Your heart on him, visit him every morning and test him every moment? . . . If I sin, what do I do to You?" (Job 7:17–20). You will wail with Isaiah, "Woe is me! For I am lost; for I am a man of unclean lips, and I dwell in the midst of a people of unclean lips" (Isaiah 6:5). And with St. Paul, "Wretched man that I am! Who will deliver me from this body of death?" (Romans 7:24).

This is man as Luther finds him portrayed in Holy Scripture. This is man, created in the image of God, fallen from grace through disobedience, "by nature sinful and unclean,"[1] restored in the image of God through the incarnation, death, and resurrection of Jesus Christ, the Son of God, being justified by grace through faith in Him. This is the theology of man that is a fundamental element in Luther's theology of the cross.

Scholars sometimes speak of this as Luther's theology of man, sometimes as his theological anthropology. Whatever we call it, it has its source in Scripture and its confirmation in the Church fathers. It took Luther years to arrive at his theology of man. It followed as a part of the evolution of the reformer. He waded through the Scriptures, and through his resultant theology he sifted the theology of the Fathers and his whole theological heritage.

The Church already had a theology of man, and Luther, the theological student, was enveloped in this theology both in the monastery and in the university. Trained and steeped in the humanistic education of the medieval university, Luther knew how theologians and philosophers had wrestled with the problem of man up through the centuries. He knew Plato, the least damned among the pagan philosophers according to Augustine. He appreciated his ideal of the disciplined life where the three elements of man live in harmony: spirit, reason, and the appetites.[2] He knew Aristotle with his 12 moral virtues that characterize the life of man. But both of these, whom Luther honored as the greatest of philosophers, though he preferred Cicero, were pure rationalists who therefore could give us no true knowledge of either God or man. In fact, the answer to the question "What is man?" is not to be found in philosophy but only in theology, a theology based on revelation.

The relation between philosophy and theology is given serious treatment in Luther's *Disputation Concerning Man*. He tips his hat to philosophy, which defines man as "an animal having reason, sensation, and body."[3] And he recognizes reason as "the most important and highest in rank among all things. . . . the essential difference by which man is distinguished from the animals and other things."[4] But this does not enable man to know himself either in his origin or in his relation to God, his Creator. Only theology from its knowledge of Scripture and "from the fulness of its wisdom defines man as whole and perfect," namely, that he is created by God in His image, that by his sin he became "subject to the power of the devil, sin and death," that "[h]e can be freed and given eternal life only through the Son of God, Jesus Christ (if he believes in Him)."[5] Therefore, Luther concludes that "if philosophy or reason itself is compared with theology, it will appear that we know almost nothing about man."[6] Man can be known only by the revelation of God. "Philosophers and Aristotle are not able to understand or to define what the theological man is, but by the grace of God we are able to do it, because we have the Bible."[7]

This was Luther's mature estimate of philosophy after he had been thoroughly immersed in the prevailing medieval scholastic theology. The theology of Thomas Aquinas, which permeated this theology, Luther finds so contaminated by the rationalistic philosophy of Aristotle that it is leading the Church into error. "Thomas wrote a great deal of heresy," says Luther, "and is responsible for the reign of Aristotle, the destroyer of godly doctrine."[8]

Some scholars have tried to show that Luther did not know Aquinas.[9] But even though Occam and Biel get more attention from him than Aquinas, Luther's own testimony cannot be overlooked. Having criticized Thomas in the words just quoted, he continues: "I suppose that my judgment in these matters is not entirely ignorant, for I have been educated in them and have been tested [in debate] by the minds of my most learned contemporaries, and I have studied the best writings of this sort of literature."[10]

We have in a previous chapter traced Luther's gradual emergence from the scholastic theology of *facere quod in se est* to his theology of grace alone, faith alone, Word alone. It is time to look more specifically at his theology of man, which was a basic part of this theology of the cross.

In this segment of his theology, too, Luther owes much to Augustine. And here again we are confronted with the strange paradox that because of the contradictory elements in his theol-

ogy Augustine has been called the father of Roman Catholic theology on the one hand and the father of Luther's theology on the
other. Luther could stand on the sidelines and cheer when he saw
Augustine topple man from the throne on which Greek humanism had placed him, and saw him vanquish the synergism of
Pelagius and exalt the absolute sovereignty of God, the incapacity
of man, and the totality of grace. Proclaiming the bondage of the
will, he could quote Augustine, who said in his work *On the Spirit
and the Letter* (IV, 126), "The free will, without God's grace, can do
nothing but sin."[11] Luther calls him St. Paul's "most trustworthy
interpreter,"[12] and says, "no book except the Bible and St. Augustine has come to my attention from which I have learned more
about God, Christ, man, and all things."[13] Probably the highest
honor he ever paid the great Church father was when in challeng-
ing the authority of Church councils he called to witness "Paul,
Augustine, and even Christ himself."[14]

   If we examine a hundred references to Augustine in Luther's
writings, we shall probably find only one or two that do not have
Luther's approval. "[I]t is intolerable nonsense not to consider St.
Augustine one of the best fathers, since throughout all Christendom he is esteemed the highest of them."[15] Yet Luther did not hesitate to correct him or criticize him. In his treatise *Avoiding the
Doctrines of Men* Luther says, "Even if Augustine had said so, who
gave him the authority that we must believe what he says? What
Scriptures does he quote to prove this statement? What if he erred
here, as we know that he frequently did, just as did all the
fathers?"[16]

   It is evident from this that even with all his regard for
Augustine Luther had no compunction about subjecting him with
all the fathers to the superior authority of Holy Scripture. But
Luther's argument was far less with Augustine himself than with
those who claimed to be his disciples. He frequently charged the
scholastics with misinterpreting Augustine. "[T]hey not only
ascribe to Augustine an opinion he did not hold, but they also fal-

sify and pervert his words."[17] It is possible that this charge was not entirely justified in all cases. For it was Augustine himself who by his inconsistent and contradictory language made it possible for both sides to claim him as the "father" of their theology. This became particularly serious when it concerned the central doctrines of justification and free will. Luther himself said that Augustine spoke "imperfectly" about the righteousness of God, "and he did not explain all things concerning imputation clearly."[18] History shows that Augustine's attempt to combine Neoplatonism with Christianity led him to mingle the Greek *eros* with the Christian *agape*. While exalting grace, he could speak in the same breath of the "ascent" of the soul to God. Out of this could emerge the idea of *caritas*, which Luther felt he had to expunge from the doctrine of justification on the basis of St. Paul. The scholastic language about the "ascent" of the soul to God, which may be credited not only to mysticism but also to Augustine, Luther rejected as a synergistic denial of grace alone.[19]

The meandering stream of theological thought that emanated from Augustine's ambiguous language reached its watershed when Luther challenged the scholastic theology of man. The difference between the two grows from a crack to a chasm as the debate progresses from the image of God, to the Fall, to original sin, to free will, to justification. What is man? What natural powers, if any, lie in him to cooperate with God toward his salvation? Is man justified by grace alone through faith or by faith and works? The history, nature, and destiny of man can be written in four chapters: "Man in the Image of God," "Man in Sin," "Man in Grace," and "Righteous but Still a Sinner."

CHAPTER
FOUR

MAN IN THE IMAGE OF GOD

1. MAN WAS CREATED BY GOD

Creation looms large with Luther, and he can wax eloquent when
he contemplates the glory of it. "For this is undoubtedly the highest article of faith in which we say: I believe in God the Father
Almighty, Maker of heaven and earth."[1] This is faith in God
indeed. For when I believe this, then I know that I, together with
all creation, am a creature of God, created for God, subject to the
will of God, and embraced in His loving providence. Whom then
shall I fear but God? In whom shall I put my trust but in God? In
no one, especially not in myself. For when I look around at the
world and at everything God has created, then I recognize myself
as part of that creation. "From this must follow that it is not in my
power to move a hand, but that God alone does and works everything in me."[2]

Creation to Luther reveals both the sovereignty and the love
of God. For He alone has a free will to do what He pleases, to cre-

ate or not create.[3] He creates all things good, and when man spoils it by his fall into sin, God re-creates, restores, and renews. Thus creation and redemption hang together, and God the Creator is never divorced from God the Redeemer. "Luther's theology begins with the doctrine of creation, because for him redemption means not liberation from creation but its restoration and completion."[4]

God's creative activity did not end with the initial creation of the universe, but continues as He preserves and governs what He has made. Scripture teaches, says Luther, "that God created all things in order to prepare a house and an inn, as it were, for the future man, and that He governs and preserves these creatures by the power of His Word, by which He also created them."[5] This is a comforting fact for Christians. For we know not only that we are creatures of God, but that despite death in sin, God has re-created us in His image and restored us to life in Christ. "For we are His workmanship, created in Christ Jesus for good works" (Ephesians 2:10). Then we can be sure that our salvation is completely in the hands of God. For it is God who has given us faith and life. "And I am sure of this, that He who began a good work in you will bring it to completion at the day of Jesus Christ" (Philippians 1:6).

While humans are the supreme creation of God, Luther will not let us forget the glory of all God's creation. It shows us that God is God and that He is a God of love and beauty and order. "And God saw everything that He had made, and behold, it was very good" (Genesis 1:31). It is man who by his sin has marred the beauty of God's creation and continues to do so.

> O, if Adam had not sinned, how man would have seen God in all His creatures, lauded, loved, and praised Him, seeing and contemplating His omnipotence, wisdom, and goodness in the tiniest flower! For who can truly fathom how God out of dry earth created a variety of little flowers of such beautiful color and lovely fragrance that no painter or apothecary could match it. God can still bring green, yellow, red, blue, brown and all kinds of colors out of the earth.[6]

We in our indifference and blindness are like cows and dumb animals that trample under foot the loveliest flowers and lilies. Luther has been quoted as saying, "If a man could make a single rose, they should give him an empire."[7]

The highest creation of God, however, is man. For it is only of man that Scripture says, "So God created man in His own image, in the image of God He created him; male and female He created them" (Genesis 1:27). Created by God, man belongs to God. In the Garden man walked with God in a relation of intimate fellowship and perfect sonship, "completely engulfed by the goodness and justice of God. As a result, there was between them a single union of hearts and wills. No other beautiful sight in the whole world appeared lovelier and more attractive to Adam than his own Eve."[8] His joy was to do the will of his Creator and thus fulfill the purpose of his creation.

When man rebelled against God and fell into sin, he broke this perfect relationship and established enmity between himself and God. But in His mercy God bought him back at the price of His own blood. So through atonement and redemption divine sonship is restored, and again man belongs to God, his Creator. He may proudly deny God's ownership when God claims him through the Gospel and invites him to the enjoyment of it. God's ownership is no forced allegiance, and man is free to follow the voice of the devil, as his first parents were free to do and did. Thus man belongs to God by virtue of creation and redemption.

Then let twentieth-century man, stewing in the muck of his own dechristianized anthropology, claiming to be the captain of his own soul and riding for destruction, be reminded by the Church that he is a creature of Almighty God. Let him hear that he is answerable to God, so that he may repent. Let him know that he is created with infinite possibilities for joy and accomplishment, so that he may have hope. Let him learn again that God has a great purpose and a glorious destiny for him, made possible of fulfillment through the sacrifice of Jesus Christ, so that he may believe

in Him. For those who believe and acknowledge that they belong
to God by virtue of creation and redemption will by the grace of
God have their whole life directed into the channel of God's eternal purpose. And thus will attain the highest goal of living, which
is to glorify God. For "[n]o higher goal can he reach, no nobler
end aim at, than to become conscious of his function in the plans
of God. For then the image of God will be restored in him. By the
assistance of Christ, he will then do what God Himself is doing."[9]

> I believe that God has made me and all creatures ... that
> He provides me richly and daily with all that I need ...
> protects me from all danger, and guards me and pre-
> serves me from all evil; and all this out of pure, fatherly,
> divine goodness and mercy, without any merit or wor-
> thiness in me; for all which I owe it to Him to thank,
> praise, serve, and obey Him.[10]

Man was created "a living soul," for "the LORD God formed
the man of dust from the ground and breathed into his nostrils
the breath of life, and the man became a living creature" (Genesis
2:7). Here it is made plain that man was exalted above all other
creatures of God.

Man was formed of the dust of the ground. He is earthy. He
is called Adam. He is from the earth and of the earth. This is the
"animal life" of man, where the unbelieving evolutionist is content
to stop. Stopping here would indeed seem to explain the bestial
behavior of twentieth-century man, leading the world into chaos
by way of hate, murder, and suicide. For, says Luther, "[i]f you
consider the animal life about which Moses is speaking here, there
is no difference between man and the donkey."[11] But this is not all
there is to man. He is not only earthy, not only flesh, not only animal. He is spirit. He is "a living soul." In this way Moses so exalts
the life of man "that he says about him alone that he was made a
living soul—not simply like the other animals but an eminently
living soul, because he was created after the image of God."[12]

Luther faces the problem raised by the words *body*, *soul*, and *spirit*, which are used in Scripture, but he does not make it a bone of theological contention. In his 1527 sermons on Genesis he comments on Genesis 2:7 ("man became a living creature"), saying that the Scripture calls the soul "everything that lives in the five senses." So the term must be understood to mean "that man was created into bodily life, what we call natural life."[13] Luther then comments on St. Paul's use of the verse in 1 Corinthians 15:45 ("Thus it is written, 'The first man Adam became a living being'; the last Adam became a life-giving spirit."):

> We must understand the word of Paul thus, that the first man is created into natural life. For there he contrasts bodily life and spiritual life. . . . Hence Adam is created into natural life; but Christ, who is the last Adam, says Paul, into spiritual life, that is, He has a spiritual body, so that He no longer eats or drinks, sees or hears as we do, does any bodily thing or work, but is altogether another being and yet true man, as we also shall be in that life.[14]

Luther discusses this problem at length in his 1521 work, *The Magnificat*. There he harmonizes the apparent conflict in terminology. For Scripture sometimes divides man into two parts, spirit and flesh, at other times into spirit, soul, and body. He examines 1 Thessalonians 5:23: "Now may the God of peace Himself sanctify you completely, and may your whole spirit [*pneuma*] and soul [*psyche*] and body [*soma*] be kept blameless at the coming of our Lord Jesus Christ." There is no conflict here, says Luther. For when we speak of man as spirit and flesh, this is a division, not of the nature of man but of his qualities. The nature of man consists of the three parts—spirit, soul, and body; and all of these may be good or evil, that is, they may be spirit or flesh. In this trichotomy Luther calls the spirit "the highest, deepest, and noblest part of man. By it he is enabled to lay hold on things incomprehensible, invisible, and eternal. It is, in brief, the dwelling place of faith and the Word of God."[15]

Coming to the soul, the trichotomy seems to shrink to a virtual dichotomy. For Luther says, "The second part, the soul, is the same spirit, so far as its nature is concerned, but viewed as performing a different function, namely, giving life to the body and working through the body."[16] This is the position followed by the great Lutheran dogmaticians, beginning with Johann Gerhard, who says "there are but two parts of man. . . . The term spirit is sometimes put exegetically for the soul itself, since the soul is a spirit."[17] The soul is the seat of life. In fact, says Luther: "In the Scriptures it is frequently put for the life; for the spirit may live without the body, but the body has no life apart from the spirit. Even in sleep the soul lives and works without ceasing."[18] In its nature the soul differs from the spirit, in that while the spirit deals with the incomprehensible, invisible, and eternal things, the soul embraces "not incomprehensible things but such things as the reason can know and understand. Indeed, reason is the light in this dwelling."[19]

And now Luther shows the place of reason in human life. While it is "the light" of the soul, reason does not hold the preeminent position in man's make-up. For above it stands the spirit, "which is lighted with the brighter light of faith." And unless this controls the light of reason, "it cannot but be in error" because reason is "too feeble to deal with things divine."[20] For that reason Scripture puts them in their right relation by ascribing to the spirit, wisdom, and to the soul, knowledge.

Luther is careful to avoid every philosophic approach to the problem. Like the other problems of theology, it must not be a cold-blooded analysis of man's nature, which makes a pretty exhibit on the laboratory shelf but has no relation to life. On Romans 8:19 Luther says, "[A]nyone who searches into the essences and functionings of the creatures rather than into their sighings and earnest expectations is certainly foolish and blind. He does not know that also the creatures are created for an end."[21]

The place of the body "is only to carry out and apply that which the soul knows and the spirit believes."[22] The whole picture is beautifully illustrated by the example of the tabernacle in Exodus, with its three compartments. The holy of holies is God's dwelling place, and in it there is no light. The holy place is illuminated with the seven-branched candlestick and the seven lamps. The outer court is out in the open sunlight. Here is a good picture of the Christian, says Luther. "His spirit is the holy of holies, where God dwells in the darkness of faith, where no light is; for he believes that which he neither sees nor feels nor comprehends. His soul is the holy place, with its seven lamps, that is, all manner of reason, discrimination, knowledge, and understanding of visible and bodily things. His body is the forecourt, open to all, so that men may see his works and manner of life."[23]

The spirit then is the seat of faith and holiness; and "the holiness of the spirit is the scene of the sorest conflict and the source of the greatest danger." For here are the issues of life determined: the invisible and the eternal. Here must be faced the attacks of false teachers who endanger not only the body and the mind, but the immortal soul and the whole man.[24]

Man can be compared to the Person of Christ, whose "words and works must always be attributed to the whole Person and are not divided, as though He were not true God or not true man. . . . Similarly, body and soul present two distinct entities in a natural and sound person; yet the two constitute but one person, and we ascribe the functions, activities, and offices of each to the whole person."[25] It is the whole man who was created in the image of God. He was created all good. And when he fell, the whole man fell, and the whole man was corrupted and came under the curse of God. It is still the whole man who lives and moves, believes and acts.

Luther applies his anthropology to the life of worship. He has learned it not only from the psalmist but also from Mary, who says, "My soul magnifies the Lord" (Luke 1:46). That means, says Luther, that

> my whole life and being, mind and strength, esteem Him highly. She is caught up, as it were, into Him and feels herself lifted up into His good and gracious will. . . . How much more will such a lively inclination be awakened in us when we experience the favor of God, which is exceeding great in His works. All words and thoughts fail us, and our whole life and soul must be set in motion, as though all that lived within us wanted to break forth into praise and singing.[26]

Here again we see how Luther's theology is a theology to live by. For it leads to the most sublime activity in life, which is the worship of God. Whether Luther was preaching or writing or enjoying his evening meal together with his family and friends, all was part and parcel of the life of worship. "This is the unique and most precious service of God in the New Testament, to glorify and praise the Son of God in singing, writing, and preaching."[27] But theology and worship will claim our attention later.

2. MAN WAS CREATED IN THE IMAGE OF GOD

Luther is very modest about trying to explain all that Scripture means by the term "image of God." How can sinful man possibly comprehend the glory and perfection of man in the Garden? For "through sin this image was so obscured and corrupted that we cannot grasp it even with our intellect. Although we utter the words, who is there who could understand what it means to be in a life free from fear, without terrors and dangers, and to be wise, upright, good, and free from all disasters, spiritual as well as physical?"[28]

In trying to describe the image of God, Luther shows the influence of Augustine. He says the image of God according to which Adam was created was a thing of beauty and excellence, "since obviously no leprosy of sin adhered either to his reason or to his will. Both his inner and his outer sensations were all of the purest kind. His intellect was the clearest, his memory was the best, and his will was the most straightforward—all in the most beautiful tranquility of mind, without any fear of death and without anxiety."[29] The body, too, shared in the glory and perfection of the image of God.

> To these inner qualities came also those most beautiful and superb qualities of body and of all the limbs, qualities in which he surpassed all the remaining living creatures. I am fully convinced that before Adam's sin his eyes were so sharp and clear that they surpassed those of the lynx and eagle. He was stronger than the lions and the bears, whose strength is very great; and he handled them the way we handle puppies.[30]

Knowledge and trust are important elements in this image of God, for Adam "had it in his being." He knew God. He believed that He was good. And he lived a life that was "wholly godly." He was "without the fear of death or any other danger, and was content with God's favor." Luther paraphrases the words of the Lord to our first parents: "Adam and Eve, now you are living without fear; death you have not experienced, nor have you seen it. This is My image, by which you are living, just as God lives. But if you sin, you will lose this image, and you will die."[31]

The noblest qualities of the Paradisiac man according to Luther are knowledge and love. "In Adam there was an enlightened reason, a true knowledge of God, and a most sincere desire to love God and his neighbor, so that Adam embraced Eve and at once acknowledged her to be his own flesh."[32]

It is easy to lose oneself in unprofitable philosophical speculation about the physiological nature of man in Paradise. It is much more important to know what the image of God means for man's relation to God, then and now. The apostle indicates that it is something wonderful that man had in the Garden, which we now have lost with him, and which is restored in Christ.

Luther's indiscriminate use of "image of God" and "original righteousness" caused the Formula of Concord, as well as the Lutheran dogmaticians after him, to use these terms inter-changeably. In defining original righteousness Luther uses the same terminology used by Philip Melanchthon in the Apology of the Augsburg Confession: "to know God, to trust in God, and to fear God."[33]

Luther realized that out of the meager positive material in Scripture it is impossible to draw a complete picture of man in the image of God. A great deal of our information must come from what we know of the opposite side of the picture. For when we consider what we have lost, according to Scripture, we begin to realize how glorious was man in his original condition. "All these things [perfect trust, purity, obedience, etc.] we have lost through sin to such an extent that we can only conceive of them only in a negative and not in a positive way. From the evil which we have with us we are forced to infer how great the good is that we have lost."[34]

The whole discussion of the image of God may appear to be futile and of no practical value. Yet to man in his present state of corruption it has in it, like the cross itself, both Law and Gospel. For in it man sees what he was and was meant to be in the plan of God. He is thereby brought to the shocking realization of what he has done to the perfect work of God. On the other hand, there lies in that contemplation a note both of hope and of inspiration. For this is what man can again become through Christ, who is the perfect image of God, Himself God and man. For we are predestinated "to be conformed to the image of His Son" (Romans 8:29), and "we all, with unveiled face, beholding the glory of the Lord, are being transformed into the same image from one degree of glory to another" (2 Corinthians 3:18). The whole life of the Christian is to be a putting on of the image of God. For the believer has "put on the new self, which is being renewed in knowledge after the image of its creator" (Colossians 3:10).

So in the last analysis our believing contemplation of the image of God points us to Christ. He shows us in Himself the image of God. It is only in Him we can hope to have the lost image restored and to regain our lost righteousness. For He is our righteousness. By faith we are clothed with it, even here and now. And "when He appears, we shall be like Him, because we shall see Him as He is" (1 John 3:2).

Right at this point in Luther's theology of the cross the contemplation of the crucified Christ looms large in our devotional life. And we Lutherans may well ask ourselves if we have completely surrendered the life of contemplation to the Roman Church. A daughter who for 20 years adores her mother is sure to become more like her as the years pass. What of the Christian who takes time to adore the living Christ, to contemplate His person in living and dying, and to see in Him the love and the holiness of God? Will the Christian not grow more like Him through the years of contemplation? And He is the image of God in the full sense. We were created to be like Him. The highest compliment we can pay a Christian is to say he or she is Christlike. Our contemplation of Christ on the cross can thus take on new meaning if we take time to concentrate on the image of God that is perfectly embodied and exemplified in the Crucified One.

> The heavenly image is Christ, who was a man full of love, mercy, and grace, meekness, patience, wisdom, light, and all good, whose very nature was to serve all men and harm none. This image we must also carry; we must be like Him. In this image belongs also how He died and suffered and everything that is in Him and everything that is His: His resurrection, life, grace, and virtue, all so planned that we should put on the same image. Of this kind are all heavenly men, i.e., all believers. So you see what the image is.[35]

It is evident from this that Luther regards "the image of God" as a valid concept, relevant to the life of the Christian and the Church. Aquinas found it a basic concept in his doctrine of man. In discussing the relation between individuality and personality Maritain interprets Aquinas as finding that

> the deepest layer of the human person's dignity consists in its property of resembling God—not in a general way after the manner of all creatures, but in a *proper* way. It is the *image of God.* For God is spirit and the human person proceeds from Him in having as principle of life a spiritual soul capable of knowing, loving, and of being uplifted by grace to participation in the very life of God so that, in the end, it might know and love Him as He knows and loves Himself.[36]

MAN IN SIN

1. THE CAUSE OF THE FALL

When God created man in His image, He graciously endowed him with a free will. No other kind of man could possibly have glorified God through loving service and worship. If this is remembered, we shall not be tempted to blame God for the fall of man into sin. This very freedom was perhaps the highest of God's gifts to man. It must have been important in God's sight. For God could so easily have created a man who could do nothing but obey, do nothing but go the way God directed him. Man would then have been a robot. Can anyone imagine a robot created in the image of God? There is something to what D. R. Davies says, namely, that "it is in his freedom to will that man is most like God."[1]

Luther lays the fall at the door of Satan himself. "But then, alas, Satan interfered and within a few hours ruined all this." The Curious will inquire, he says, "why God permitted so much to

Satan as to tempt Eve."[2] But it is not our business to demand that God give an account of why He does things as He does. We might as well insist that God tell us why the grass is not green all year round. But by the fact that God gave man a free will, He thereby permitted Satan to tempt Eve. For "it pleased the Lord that Adam should be tempted and should test his powers."[3] Satan attacked. Man, in the exercise of his freedom, chose to disobey God and give heed to the suggestion of Satan.

2. The Nature of the Fall

It was Satan who caused the fall. But it was man who sinned. His sin was a simple transgression of God's command. It was disobedience, rebellion. But at the bottom lay unbelief. Luther traces the steps in the fall.

> Thus we see Adam and Eve so fallen and sunk in sin that they cannot sink deeper. After unbelief follows the disobedience of all of man's powers and parts. After this disobedience follows later on the excuse and defense of sin; and after defense, the accusation and condemnation of God. This is the last step of sin, to insult God and to charge him with being the originator of sin.[4]

Thus man's unbelief is turned into blasphemy, and disobedience into reproach against his Creator![5]

Luther presents the whole doctrine of the fall just as simply and literally as he does the whole Christian faith in the Small Catechism. He has no patience with "man's rosewater dream about human nature."[6] He refuses to handle the devil with kid gloves or to excuse man, as Rousseau did when he said blandly that "man is naturally good and . . . our social institutions alone have rendered him evil."[7] Luther, with an intellect great enough to debate with Erasmus, had a faith humble enough to accept the biblical account of the fall, apple and all, rather than lose the fact in vague words like myth, allegory, fable, saga, symbolism, and the like. "Adam did indeed put his teeth into the fruit, but actually he put his teeth into a sting. This God had forbidden; this was disobedience to God. This is the true cause of the evil, namely, that Adam sins against God, disregards His order, and obeys Satan."[8]

This unfaltering, childlike obedience to the Word, which Luther manifests in this very discussion, is exactly the point at which he finds Eve guilty. For Eve's sin lay not in the outward act, but "Eve sinned against . . . God Himself and His Word . . . she casts aside the Word of God and offers her whole self to Satan as his pupil."[9] It is not necessary, Luther feels, to say exactly what the sin of Eve was. "It is, therefore, vain for us to discuss this or that sin. Eve is simply urged on to all sins since she is being urged on against the Word and the good will of God."[10] But unbelief is basic. And so the devil's strategy with Eve and with us is to create distrust of God's Word. "Unbelief is the source of all sins; when Satan brought about this unbelief by driving out or corrupting the Word, the rest was easy for him."[11] From Luther's interpretation of the fall, Julius Köstlin draws a definition of sin.

> In thus portraying the first sin, Luther has already expressed the idea as to what is the essential [NATURE OF SIN IN GENERAL]. Sin is the transgression of the divine Law—everything which is not in conformity with the Law of God. The Scriptures, he [Luther] declares, never employ the word sin in any other sense. The fundamental sin is unbelief, which is a violation of the fundamental commandment, and thus of the entire Decalogue. The impelling force in unbelief is exaltation of self, in which man seeks himself to be God, and would have God be nothing.[12]

3. THE CONSEQUENCES OF THE FALL

The fall of Adam brought sin into the world. His sin became the sin of the whole human race. "Here we must confess, as Paul says in Rom. 5:11, that *sin originated from one man Adam, by whose disobedience all men were made sinners,* subject to death and the devil.

This is called original or capital sin."[13] The basic character of original sin for theology and for life is expressed in a classic statement of Luther. He calls "original sin, or natural sin, or personal sin, the real chief sin; if this were not, there would be no real sin. This sin is not committed like all other sins, but it is, it lives, and it commits all sins, and is the essential sin, which does not sin for an hour or for a time; but where and for how long the person is, there, too, is the sin."[14]

Luther's reference here to the person emphasizes his idea of the whole man (*totus homo*). The whole man is corrupt and utterly sinful. Hence everything he does and thinks and desires and wills is sinful, and in this state he can do nothing good. When he sins, it is not the body that sins, but the whole man; for the whole man is sinful. It is the person, with his center in what the Bible refers to as the heart. The whole person is *sarx*, flesh, i.e., man apart from God through sin. Commenting on Romans 5:12, Luther says, following Augustine, that "original sin is the very first sin, namely, the transgression of Adam. For this, 'all have sinned,' he [Augustine] understands concerning the real act and not concerning the transfer of guilt (*Schuldverhaftung*)." Luther includes both in the entire context. And when St. Paul in v. 19 says, "For as by one man's disobedience the many were made sinners," it is the same as saying, "All have sinned in the sin of one. . . . While one sinned, all sinned." Luther uses Isaiah 43:26–27 "[S]et forth your case, that you may be proved right. Your first father sinned," and he interprets, "You cannot be justified, because you are a son of Adam who was the first to sin. Therefore you too are a sinner because you are the son of a sinner; a sinner cannot but beget a sinner like himself."[15]

The negative consequence of the fall was the loss of the image of God or of man's original righteousness. This is sometimes spoken of as a total loss, sometimes as a partial loss. There is no conflict here, even though Luther uses both kinds of language. He can speak of the image being "almost completely lost"[16] when he is talking about man's dominion over other creatures. He even goes so far as to say in regard to the knowledge of God that "we have feeble and almost completely obliterated remnants. The other animals, however, completely lack this knowledge."[17] In other words, we are by the grace of God not left mere animals after the fall. In fact, the image of God in the wider sense, as the Lutheran dogmaticians spoke of it, regarding everything that marks man as a rational being, was not wholly lost. For man does retain his reason. He even has a remnant of a free will in regard to the things of reason, to things in the realm of civil righteousness. He still has some freedom, "not in respect of those things which are above him, but in respect only of the things which are below him . . . God-ward, or in things which pertain unto salvation or damnation, he has no free will, but is a captive, slave, and servant, either to the will of God, or to the will of Satan."[18] But we leave the question of the free will for later consideration.

While these "remnants," relics, or vestiges of the image of God—reason, dominion over nature, and the like—are not said to be wholly lost, nevertheless they are wholly corrupted. But lost is the image of God in the specific sense of original righteousness, holiness, fear, love, trust in God. It has "disappeared."[19] Man can only bear one image. It is either God's image or it is the devil's.[20]

When we think of Luther's definition of righteousness as "the righteousness that avails before God," this is really what man lost in the fall, namely, everything that avails before God for righteousness. He has lost his sense of direction. He is averted (*aversus*) from God, and in all his affections, will, and understanding he is opposed to God. For everything that he has left is totally corrupted, and he is left completely incapacitated to move "God-ward," or to will or do the good. Thus it is evident that "original sin is the loss or deprivation of sight."[21] Blindness is a favorite concept of Luther in describing the nature and result of the fall and original sin. Those of the street think that if God is just, He will punish the wicked and reward the good. These naive folks don't know that their eyes have been "bewitched"; "they are looking through blue glasses and cannot see God as anything else than what they think He ought to be. For they do not see what misery and evil original sin has brought upon us all, and how it has destroyed our righteousness (*iudicium*)."[22]

The positive side of the fall was man's complete corruption and total depravity. It would take volumes to contain all that Luther has to say about the utter sinfulness of fallen man. With all his tremendous vocabulary he still seems unable to find words to express the depth of depravity to which man has fallen and in which all are born. "Everything that man is, by virtue of his birth and his reason, is only sin and corruption, by which he has brought upon himself the wrath of God."[23] Too often, says Luther, this corruption is thought of in terms of lust or concupiscence alone. "But original sin is in truth the entire fall of the whole human nature." With that summary statement he goes on to show how intellect, will, and conscience have all been corrupted. "The intellect is so darkened that he can no longer understand God and His will, nor perceive or acknowledge the works of God."[24] From Aristotle to John Dewey, men have glorified reason as the light of man, "the cause of all virtues."[25] It is an attractive philosophy Marcus Aurelius Antoninus gives us when he says, "To reverence and honor thy own mind will make thee content with thyself, and in honor with society, and in agreement with the gods, that is, praising all that they give and have ordered."[26]

Luther has no such praise to give the mind or human reason. It was indeed a great gift to man in the beginning. And a gracious God has left us in possession of reason and will, "but how depraved in many ways! Just as reason is overwhelmed by many kinds of ignorance, so the will has not only been confused but has been turned away from God and is an enemy of God."[27] There is no contradiction in Luther's alternating exaltation and condemnation of human reason. In the things where reason has a judgment, it "directs and leads to what is honorable and useful in respect to the body or the flesh." But this is not true in "higher matters." "How can a reason which hates God be called sound? How can a will which resists God's will be called good?" How is it that when the Gospel is preached in order to restore reason, "then those who are the ablest and, so to speak, are endowed with a better reason and will hate the Gospel all the more bitterly"? Hence the bitter conclusion Luther reaches is that "in theology" we must maintain "that reason in men is most hostile to God, and that the respectable will is most opposed to the will of God. From this source arise the hatred of the Word and the persecution of godly ministers."[28]

Lest someone should misunderstand Luther's criticism of reason, as John Wesley did, it might clarify the issue to quote a paragraph from Philip S. Watson:

> "How does he . . . decry reason, right or wrong, as an irreconcilable enemy to the Gospel of Christ!" John Wesley exclaims after turning the pages of Luther's *Galatians.* "Whereas," he continues, "what is reason . . . but the power of apprehending, judging, and discoursing? Which power is no more to be condemned in the gross, than seeing, hearing, or feeling." With this last statement Luther would whole-heartedly agree; but he would strongly and rightly protest that he has never decried reason "right or wrong", nor condemned it "in the gross". In fact, as "the power of apprehending, judging, and discoursing," he never condemns it at all, but praises it most highly as one of the best of all God's gifts to men. It is by virtue of his reason, Luther holds, that a man is worthy to be called, and is, a man. Reason is a "natural light" that is kindled from the "divine light," and "above all other things of this life, it is something excellent and divine". It is the discoverer and governor of all arts and sciences and "whatever of wisdom, power, virtue, and glory is possessed by men in this life". About reason in this sense of the term, Luther can wax almost lyrical. What he con-

demns is the use men commonly make of their reason,
when they apprehend, judge, and discourse about matters pertaining to God and their own relationships with
Him.[29]

John Wesley is neither the first nor the last theologian to be
offended at Luther's idea of the corruption of human reason. This
doctrine of original sin, which says that the sin of Adam has contaminated the whole man in his very nature, including his reason
and will, is probably the most offensive doctrine in the Bible,
where Luther finds it. Protestant and Roman Catholic theologians
alike rise up to charge that it destroys both man's dignity and his
sense of responsibility. Reinhold Niebuhr decries this "pessimistic" note in Augustinian-Lutheran theology. "Therefore, if
man is totally corrupt he is not sinful at all. At any rate, sin has
been stripped of the connotation of guilt, or guilt has been
divested of the implication of moral responsibility."[30] Emil Brunner's "sense of responsibility" forbids him to accept the strict doctrine of original sin as he finds it in Augustine and in Luther. "If
there is one element in the Biblical message which from time
immemorial has been clear and beyond all doubt, it is this: sin and
responsibility are inseparably connected, and there is no ascrip-
tion of responsibility, no verdict of guilt, without accusation and
proof of responsibility, that is, no one is pronounced guilty for
something which he has not done."[31]

Paul Tillich recognizes man's "estrangement" from God, but
"the notion of a moment in time in which man and nature were
changed from good to evil is absurd. . . . "[32] The "paradise story" in
its literal interpretation must be rejected. "There was no 'utopia' in
the past, just as there will be no 'utopia' in the future."[33] Man's
estrangement does indeed have the character of

universal human destiny. However, the combination of
man's predicament with a completely free act by Adam is
inconsistent as well as literally absurd. . . . Adam must be
understood as essential man and as symbolizing the

transition from essence to existence. Original or hereditary sin is neither original nor hereditary; it is the universal destiny of estrangement which concerns every
man.[34]

Rudolf Bultmann in discussing original sin under Romans 5 calls
verse 13 "completely unintelligible" and declares that in verse 19,
"in describing the curse that lies upon Adamitic mankind, Paul is
unquestionably under the influence of the Gnostic myth."[35] Just as
through Christ "there was brought about no more than the *possibility* of life," so it is reasonable to "assume by analogy that
through Adam there was brought about for Adamitic mankind
the *possibility* of sin and death—a possibility that does not
become reality until individuals become guilty by their own
responsible action."[36]

It is unnecessary to go further in showing the almost universal rejection of the Augustinian-Lutheran doctrine of original
sin by leading contemporary Protestant theologians. Tillich
reduces the fall to a "cosmic myth," but declares that "of all the
aspects of the cosmic myth of Genesis, the doctrine of 'original
sin' has been most violently attacked since the early eighteenth
century. This concept was the first point criticised by the Enlightenment, and its rejection is one of the last points defended by
contemporary humanism."[37] The point is that this "negative eval-
uation of man" expresses a theology of "pessimism" that would
"inhibit the tremendous impulse of modern man . . . to transform
world and society." Therefore, says Tillich, theology "must join
classical humanism in protecting man's created goodness and naturalistic and existential denials of his greatness and dignity."[38]

This resistance of modern Protestant theology to the doctrine of original sin in Luther and Augustine thus seems to be
rooted in a humanistic approach rather than a theological
approach to the problem. The dignity of man, that is, of sinful
unregenerate man, must not be tampered with, not even by man's
Creator. And if St. Paul teaches such a doctrine as Luther says he

does, then St. Paul is "wrong," "unintelligible," or "under the influence of the Gnostic myth," as Bultmann says. Luther met this
resistance in Erasmus, the greatest humanist of them all. And the
battle has been going on ever since between Augustine and Luther
and the Lutheran Confessions on the one side and the humanistic
Protestant and Catholic theology on the other.

Luther yielded to no one in his exaltation of the dignity of
man, the crown of God's creation. But the real dignity of man lay
in his creation in the image of God. Of man in the garden thus
created Luther says that he "is a unique creature and that he is
suited to be a partaker of divinity and of immortality. For man is
a more excellent creature than heaven and earth and everything
that is in them."[39] He was "an extraordinary creature of God,"[40]
created to "to take possession of heaven."[41] He was "a creature far
superior to the rest of the living beings that live a physical life,
especially since as yet his nature had not become depraved."[42] But
the thing that made man set apart and superior to all other creatures, says Luther in the same paragraph, was that God made him
in His own image. This was reflected in a "keen intellect," and
"accurate knowledge of all the creatures"; he was "righteous and
upright . . . endowed with extraordinary perception." All this was
lost in the fall, and "the name 'original sin' is correctly given to
whatever was lost of those conditions which Adam enjoyed while
his nature was still unimpaired."[43] What a glorious creature was
man before he began to play God! "But who can describe in words
the glory of the innocence we have lost?"[44]

Here lies the true "dignity" of man: his creation in the image
of God. "Attention should, therefore, be given to the text [Gen.
1:26] before us, in which the Holy Spirit dignifies the nature of
man in such a glorious manner and distinguishes it from all other
creatures."[45] Man spoiled all this through disobedience in the garden. He does indeed remain the supreme creation of God, still
towering above all other creatures. For he is still a man, retaining
his *humanitas*—everything that makes him a man. He is still in

possession of reason, "the most important and the highest in rank among all things," marking "the essential difference by which man is distinguished from the animals and other things."[46] But this "most beautiful and most excellent of all creatures, which reason is even after sin, remains under the power of the devil." Therefore it must be concluded that "the whole man and every man, whether he be king, lord, servant, wise, just, and richly endowed with the good things of this life, nevertheless is and remains guilty of sin and death, under the power of Satan."[47]

But do not both the psalmist and the author of Hebrews proclaim the dignity of man? "[W]hat is man that You are mindful of him, and the son of man that You care for him? Yet You have made him a little lower than the heavenly beings and crowned him with glory and honor" (Psalm 8:4–5; cf. Hebrews 2:6–7). Luther finds no reason here to boast of man's dignity. For this passage, he says, refers to Christ. "Therefore those who think that this verse refers to the dignity of human nature, which is very close to that of the angels, follow an improper understanding, which is the death of true understanding. . . . This verse says nothing about the dignity of our nature." It speaks of Christ. "What a man He is!" is a better translation, says Luther.[48]

This is all a part of his theology that his critics refer to as Luther's "pessimism." But they seem to know only half of Luther, the half that proclaims the utter sinfulness and helplessness of man to save himself or to cooperate in his salvation. Man has indeed lost his dignity. But then comes the glorious Gospel that through the cross and resurrection of Christ the image of God is restored to the one who believes, and thus dignity is regained. Forgiveness becomes the great triumphant note in Luther's theology. "For where there is forgiveness of sins, there is also life and salvation."[49]

4. LAW AND GOSPEL

The charge of "pessimism" leveled at Luther's theology by some theologians probably has its roots in a misunderstanding of his doctrine of Law and Gospel. In Luther it is total sinfulness on man's side and total grace on God's side. You can't have the one without the other. If man is not altogether sinful, but has the capacity to cooperate with God in his salvation, then it is no longer grace alone that saves him. Luther insisted on *sola gratia*, grace alone, precisely because there was not one iota of power in man to cooperate in his justification or salvation. Therefore, to Luther the Law gives no quarter, shows no mercy, but puts natural man under the curse and condemnation of God. "All our righteous deeds are like a polluted garment" (Isaiah 64:6); "they are dragged out of the mud."[50] When the Law thus declares natural man as utterly sinful and under the wrath of God, Luther takes it at face value, whether in the Old Testament or in the New Testament, whether in Isaiah or in St. Paul. When the apostle says that all men "are under sin" (Romans 3:9), Luther comments that this "does not deal with men as they appear in their own eyes and before other men but as they are before God, where they are all under sin, both those who are obviously evil even in the sight of men and those who appear to be good to themselves as well as to other men."[51]

This doctrine of Law and Gospel is extremely distasteful to natural man. We like to hear about the love of God. We feel comfortable hearing about His fatherly goodness, His forgiving grace, and His promise of heaven. It is good to cast our cares on Him who, as Jesus says, knows our needs better than we know them ourselves. But who wants to hear, "Your sins will find you out," and, "The wages of sin is death"? The love of God? Yes. But the righteousness of God or the wrath of God? No. How many congregations are lulled to sleep every Sunday with the assurance that there is nothing to worry about for God is love, but never hear the call to repentance? Who takes seriously Luther's word from the apostle that God kills in order to make alive?

> The wrath of God is necessary because of "the body of sin" spoken of in Rom. 6:6 and because of "the law of my members" (Rom. 7:23). For it is necessary that "the body of sin" and the law of the flesh or the members "be destroyed" (Rom. 6:6), since it is impossible for "anything unclean to enter the kingdom of heaven" (cf. Rev. 21:27). But such destruction comes about through crosses, sufferings, deaths, and disgraces. Therefore God kills in order to make alive; He humiliates in order to exalt, etc.[52]

Luther uses a unique terminology to explain this twofold activity of God in convicting of sin by the Law and granting forgiveness through the Gospel. God's *opus proprium* (proper work) is saving and sanctifying and blessing men, and this He does through the Gospel. But before He can do His proper work, He must do His *opus alienum* (alien work), which is to convict of sin, to make man aware that he is a lost and condemned creature under the wrath of God. This alien work God performs through the Law. It is by the Law He kills. By the Gospel He makes alive. "Therefore the proper function of the Law is to make us guilty, to humble us, to kill us, to lead us down to hell, and to take everything away from us." This is the so-called "pessimistic" side of Luther's theology. But we dare not stop there, for there is only despair and death. But this convicting, killing process of God has a divine purpose, which is carried out through the Gospel. And the purpose is "that we may be justified, exalted, made alive, lifted up to heaven, and endowed with all things. Therefore it does not merely kill, but it kills for the sake of life."[53]

Luther is wrestling here with one of the most profound doctrines in the entire theology of the cross.[54] It is not a mere theory for theologians to play with, but it is a matter for everyone who would be saved and live a daily Christian life. In other words, here is a theology to live by.

> The knowledge of this topic, the distinction between the
> Law and the Gospel, is necessary to the highest degree;
> for it contains a summary of all Christian doctrine.
> Therefore let everyone learn diligently how to distin-
> guish the Law from the Gospel, not only in words but in
> feeling and in experience; that is, let him distinguish well
> between these two in his heart and in his conscience.[55]

Let everyone understand this basic principle of Jesus: "Those who
are well have no need of a physician, but those who are sick"
(Matthew 9:12). A man must know that he is sick before he will
seek a cure. The problem is that natural fallen man does not know
that he is sick, sick unto death under sin. But God wants to save
man, every man (Cf. 1 Timothy 2:4). To do this, He uses His Word
that is "living and active, sharper than any two-edged sword"
(Hebrews 4:12). This Word is both Law and Gospel, and God
must use them both to accomplish His saving work. The theology
of the cross means that Christ had to go through cross and death
to resurrection, victory, and lordship. So the way to life for everyone goes through crucifixion to resurrection, through death to
life. Through the Law "God kills in order to make alive." He must
do His alien work before He can do His proper work. His proper
work is "to create righteousness, peace, mercy, truth, patience,
kindness, joy, and health."[56] Luther continues,

> But he cannot come to this his proper work unless he
> undertakes a work that is alien and contrary to himself.
> . . . His alien work, however, is to make men sinners,
> unrighteous, liars, miserable, foolish, lost. . . . Therefore,
> since he can make just only those who are not just, he is
> compelled to perform an alien work in order to make
> them sinners, before he performs his proper work of jus-
> tification. Thus he says. "I kill and I make alive; I wound
> and I heal" [Deut. 32:39].[57]

This is the way we are brought from unbelief to faith, from
death in sin to life in Christ. Conviction, confession, and death

come through the Law, faith, forgiveness, and life through the Gospel. It is evident then, as St. Paul says, that no one is saved by the Law or by one's own efforts to keep the Law. Anyone who seeks salvation in that way is under slavery to the Law. We must be brought to realize that we cannot free ourselves from this slavery. The Gospel tells us that Christ has won freedom for us. For by His perfect life He has fulfilled the Law for us, and by His cross He has suffered the Law's penalty for our sin. This is the Gospel, the proper work of God, by which He kindles faith in the man's heart. Like St. Paul, he is baptized into Christ and into the Church, which is the body of Christ. He has become a Christian. Now he grasps the meaning of the alien and proper work of God. Now he begins to live in the tension between the Law and the Gospel. For though his sin is forgiven, he is still a sinner. Though he now lives "in the Spirit," the "flesh" clings to him (Romans 7). The Law keeps him awake to the presence of sin and Satan, and he often finds himself crying out with the apostle, "For I do not do what I want, but I do the very thing I hate. . . . For I know that nothing good dwells within me, that is, in my flesh. For I have the desire to do what is right, but not the ability to carry it out. . . . Wretched man that I am! Who will deliver me from this body of death?" But St. Paul knows where to turn from these accusations of the Law. He knows the Gospel. "Thanks be to God through Jesus Christ our Lord!" (Romans 7:15, 18, 24–25).

Thus the Christian, like the apostle, has to know that there is in the daily Christian life a time for Law and a time for Gospel, a time to confess sin and helplessness, and a time to lay hold of forgiveness in the crucified and risen Christ.

Therefore when the Law terrifies you, sin accuses you, and your conscience is crushed, you must say: "There is a time to die and a time to live" (Eccl. 3:2). There is a time to hear the Law and a time to despise the Law. There is a time to hear the Gospel and a time to know nothing about the Gospel. Let the Law go away now, and let the Gospel come; for this is the time to hear the

Gospel, not the Law. But you have nothing good; in fact, you have sinned gravely. Granted. Nevertheless, I have forgiveness of sins through Christ, on whose account all my sins are forgiven.[58]

So the Gospel has the last word. It is there the sinner flees for refuge and forgiveness. He must not let the Law drive him to despair, but let it do its work and bring him to see his sin and his need of help. "Sins are remitted only to those who are dissatisfied with themselves, and this is what it means to repent. But only those are dissatisfied with themselves who know this. But only those know it who understand the law. But no one understands the law unless it be explained to him. This, however, the gospel does."[59] So when I have become a Christian, the Law has become my friend, and I must not let it become my enemy by enslaving me to fear. Luther said it beautifully if not shockingly in his Table Talks: "I won't tolerate Moses because he is an enemy of Christ. If he appears with me before the judgment I'll turn him away in the name of the devil and say, 'Here stands Christ.' In the last judgment Moses will look at me and say, 'You have known and understood me correctly,' and he will be favorably disposed to me."[60]

From all this it appears that in Luther's thinking there is a certain parallel between Law-Gospel on the one hand and reason-faith on the other. A man who even in the spiritual realm is dominated by reason is living under the Law in what Luther would call slavery. He will know the freedom of the Gospel only as his life comes to be dominated by faith. This does not mean that he despises reason, but that he accepts its limitations in the realm of the spiritual as laid down in Holy Scripture.

5. FREE WILL

With the dethronement of reason in the spiritual realm must go the deposition of the free will. It did not take Luther long to find that truth in Scripture. Already in his lectures on Romans in 1516–17 he denies that natural man has a free will in matters spiritual. "The power of free decision in so far as it is not under the sway of grace has no ability whatsoever to realize righteousness, but is necessarily in sins. Hence, Blessed Augustine is right, when, in his book against Julian, he calls it 'the enslaved, rather than free, will.' "[61] By the year 1521 Luther had become so completely nauseated by the talk about a free will that he exploded with the declaration:

> I would wish that the words, "free will," had never been invented. They are not found in Scripture and would better be called "self will" which is of no use. But if anyone wishes to retain these words, he ought to apply them to the newly created man, so as to understand by them the man who is without sin. He is truly free, as was Adam in Paradise, and it is of him that Scripture speaks when it deals with our freedom. But those who are involved in sins are not free, but prisoners of the devil. Since they may become free through grace you can call them men of free will, just as you might call a man rich, although he is a beggar because he can become rich.[62]

In the Heidelberg Disputation in April 1518 Luther had already begun to debate the question of the free will. He had evidently reached clarity at that time, as is shown by thesis 13: "Free will, after the fall, exists in name only, and as long as it does what it is able to do, it commits a mortal sin." This means that "free will is captive and subject to sin. Not that it is nothing, but that it is not free except to do evil."[63] He cites Augustine, who said that "the free will without grace has the power to do nothing but sin."

The real debate on the freedom of the will, however, came when the great Erasmus in his *Discourse on Free Will*[64] challenged Luther's teaching of the bondage of the human will.[65] Erasmus states the problem: "By freedom of the will we understand in this connection the power of the human will whereby man can apply to or turn away from that which leads unto eternal salvation."[66]

Erasmus is very humble in his attack on Luther. "Here some will surely close their ears and exclaim, 'Oh prodigy! Erasmus dares to contend with Luther, a fly with an elephant?' " But Erasmus considers it no outrage "to dispute over one of his dogmas, especially not, if one, in order to discover truth, confronts Luther with calm and scholarly arguments. . . . We are not two gladiators. . . . I want to argue only against one of Luther's teachings. . . . I am quite aware that I am a poor match in such a contest . . . and I have always had a deep-seated aversion to fighting."[67]

Thus it is clear from the very start of the debate that Erasmus is no crusader for truth like Luther. Concerned, yes; involved, no. Erasmus is the cool, scholarly humanist, seeking honestly for the truth with the tools of his trade. But he has none of the passionate involvement of Luther fighting for the truth not only as a matter of conscience but also as a matter of life and death—yes, of eternal salvation. This detached attitude of Erasmus appears in his initial attack on Luther's *Assertions*. He dislikes "assertions," in fact, the entire stance of Luther, who presumes to speak with both certainty and authority. "So great is my dislike of assertions that I prefer the views of the sceptics wherever the inviolable authority of Scripture and the decision of the Church permit. . . ."[68]

Erasmus admits that Luther's knowledge of Scripture is far superior to his own. So he throws the weight of a galaxy of Church fathers against him, from both the early and the Medieval Church, to prove that the human will is free to make all choices also in matters concerning our salvation.

It is in answer to this *Diatribe* of Erasmus that Luther composes his monumental work, *The Bondage of the Will*. Thus the two giants are locked in combat, and one of the great theological debates in history is under way.[69] Before examining the argument it is well to be aware that we are dealing with one of the most important of Luther's theological works. Probably because we have a natural aversion to this idea that man's will is not free in spiritual matters, some writers have dismissed this treatise as a work of "the early Luther," implying that he changed his position later in life. This is contrary to Luther's own testimony and the findings of the best Luther scholars. In a letter to Capito in 1537 Luther acknowledges only two of his writings to be important: *The Small Catechism* and *The Bondage of the Will*.[70] Strange, then, that this latter work should find more resistance in modern American Protestantism than anything Luther has written. When Dietrich Bonhöffer had spent a year at Union Seminary he wrote, "A seminary in which it can come about that a large number of students laugh out loud in a public lecture at the quoting of a passage from Luther's *De Servo Arbitrio* on sin and forgiveness because it seems to them to be comic has evidently completely forgotten what Christian theology by its very nature stands for." The shock is softened when Harvey Cox adds, "I doubt if these students, after thirty-five years of rediscovering Reformation theology, would laugh now. But the fact that American and Continental theologians labor in very divergent vineyards is just as true today."[71]

After more than half a century of Luther research, theologians have begun to discover the profound theology that Luther packed into this great treatise.[72] Sigurd Normann, the Norwegian Luther scholar, has pointed out the importance of this work of Luther in the history of the Church. "As Luther's struggle with Erasmus marks one of the most decisive chapters in the history of the Reformation, so *The Bondage of the Will* stands for all time to come as the great monument of the mighty spiritual battles of that period and as the center of the theological thought and spiritual development of the entire Lutheran Reformation."[73]

Luther was quite aware that he was in the ring with no second-string opponent. He recognized Erasmus as a most learned scholar who wanted to direct all knowledge and art and culture into the service of the Church. At first Luther thought he had found an ally in the work of reformation when he saw Erasmus attacking corruption in the clergy, calling for an open Bible among the laity, and fighting superstition and the philosophy of ignorance in the Church. But he soon realized that Erasmus was at heart a humanist and a child of the Renaissance. He was more at home in philosophy than in theology. He was more at home in the classics than in the Bible. What to Luther was a matter of life and death was to Erasmus a subject for speculation. This strange combination of philosopher and theologian was an ordained priest, yet he never served as priest. He seemed more interested in composing heroic poems or a Sapphic ode to the archangel Michael than preaching the Gospel. He rarely celebrated Mass and seems to have lived pretty much without the blessed Sacrament and to have died without asking for it. This separation of theological thinking from the sacramental life and piety of the Church was as destructive to the life of the Church then as it is today. And as the eminent Catholic Luther scholar Joseph Lortz says, "For this kind of theology which barely stands within the sacramental life of the Church, Erasmus is the most important individual example of ecclesiastical history.... He wrote much on piety and instructed a great deal on religion, but it is painfully evident that his pious expositions give frequently the impression of a cultural religiosity."[74] This helps to explain why Erasmus, with all his desire for a reformation of the Church, could never become "the reformer." Not only Luther saw the seriousness of the threat of humanism and Erasmus to the Church. It was the papal delegate to the Diet in Worms who warned the pope that Erasmus was doing more harm to the Church than Luther could ever do. But it was Luther, according to Lortz, "who banished the danger that threatened from humanism. With the tremendous force of his one-sidedness he led the way from the cultural religiosity of Erasmus back to the faith religion of Paul."[75]

Heinrich Bornkamm, the distinguished German Luther scholar, has neatly summarized the character of this "cultural religiosity" of Erasmus.

> In the pedagogically oriented religion which he initiated
> a wealth of disparate themes lingers on: skepticism and

an ensuing indifferent tolerance, an awareness of tradition and a need for security, a reduction of Christianity to an easily grasped morality, faith in education as a factor of basic importance to man, disregard for ecclesiastical institutions and high esteem for the Church as a political and moral authority, a tendency to resolve Biblical statements into allegory and metaphor, and in spite of all this, almost aesthetic respect for traditional forms and dogmas.[76]

No one, least of all Luther, could fail to recognize the greatness of Erasmus as a thinker, scholar, and man of letters. And his contribution to the Reformation cannot be overlooked. His publication of the Greek New Testament and his incisive literary and linguistic studies inspired Luther to discipline himself to thorough and exact scholarship not only in his translation of the Bible but in all his writing, teaching, and debating. His *Diatribe* was undoubtedly a fine literary work, superior to Luther's answer in literary style. Adolf Harnack calls it "the crown of his literary work," but adds: "It is entirely worldly, at bottom an irreligious work."[77] So Luther must regard the *Diatribe* as more than an attack on one basic doctrine of the Church. As Franz Lau of Leipzig says,

Luther attacked Erasmus with vehemence because the latter regarded religion as something human, as a human striving, a human obedience, a fulfillment of the love commandment, however it may be expressed; Luther, on the contrary, wished to proclaim not a religion of which Christianity is only a special form, but God's work in man. . . . In other words, this struggle also centered upon the theme of the righteousness of men and the righteousness of God. The Luther who could show himself so perfectly open to everything great and important that humanism had produced shut himself off from the humanist world at the point where he saw the gospel of the glory and grace of God impugned by it. At the crucial

point neither a capitulation to humanism nor a compromise with it was possible for him.[78]

Luther's *De Servo Arbitrio* was no Don Quixote assault on
theological windmills. It was a down-to-earth attack on the semi-
Pelagianism and synergism of Rome and on the so-called Christian humanism whose prophet was Erasmus. It is essential for a
Christian to know that God "foresees, purposes and does all things
according to His immutable, eternal and infallible will. By this
thunderbolt, 'Free-will' is thrown prostrate and utterly dashed to
pieces."[79] Erasmus protests the futility of proclaiming to the world
the paradox "that whatever is done by us, is not done by Free-will,
but from mere necessity."[80] Who will then try to amend his life?
Luther replies, "The reason of the divine will is not to be inquired
into, but simply to be adored, and the glory given to God.... With
this answer those that fear God are content." Gratuitously, however, Luther adds, "There are two causes which require such things
to be preached. The first is the humbling of our pride, and the
knowledge of the grace of God. The second is the Christian faith
itself." A man will never be thoroughly humbled until he learns
that "his salvation is utterly beyond his own powers . . . and
absolutely depending on the will, counsel, pleasure, and work of
another, that is, of God only."[81] Furthermore, this all belongs to the
nature of faith. For

> faith is in things not seen. Therefore, that there might be
> room for faith, it is necessary that all those things which
> are believed should be hidden. But they are not hidden
> more deeply than under the contrary of sight, sense and
> experience. Thus, when God makes alive, He does it by
> killing; when He justifies, He does it by bringing in
> guilty; when He exalts to Heaven, He does it by bringing
> down to hell.... Thus He conceals His eternal mercy and
> loving-kindness behind His eternal wrath; His righ-
> teousness behind apparent iniquity. This is the highest
> degree of faith—to believe that He is merciful, who saves

so few and damns so many; to believe Him just, who according to His own will makes us necessarily damnable. If, therefore, I could by any means comprehend how that same God can be merciful and just, who carries the appearance of so much wrath and iniquity, there would be no need of faith. But now, since that cannot be comprehended, there is room for exercising faith, while such things are preached, and openly proclaimed.[82]

Thus in the face of the mystery of the hidden God of predestination, Luther finds the only answer in faith on man's side, and God's Word and purpose on the other. When Erasmus cries, "Determinism!" Luther answers, "But, by necessity, I do not mean compulsion, but (as they term it) the necessity of immutability, not of compulsion, that is, a man void of the Spirit of God does not evil against his will as by violence . . . but he does it spontaneously, and with a desirous willingness. And this willingness and desire of doing evil he cannot, by his own power, leave off, restrain, or change; but it goes on still desiring and craving." Such a man might be compelled to do good by force, but he would still hate it because of his perverse will. But his will would not hate it "if it were changed, and made willing to yield to a constraining power. This is what we mean by the necessity of immutability:—that the will cannot change itself, nor give itself another bend; but rather the more it is resisted, the more it is irritated to crave."[83] This is the apostle's idea of the Law coming that sin might "abound" (Romans 5:20).

What hope is there for man then? None at all in the powers he has within himself. He must abandon his pride and look outside himself. He must be changed. He must be made a new creation by God. His will must be changed by God. His will, which is in complete bondage, must be set free. For his will shares in the total corruption of the whole human nature. And here again it is no mere languishing or dormant disease. It is a will in rebellion against God and His Law, actively hostile against God and against everything that concerns God, His will, and His salvation. Go from one to another of Luther's great works and we find the same picture of a will that is at war with God and a captive of Satan.[84] This is the enemy who has spoiled all the natural faculties of man until "the will and reason have become depraved through sin, and man not only does not love God any longer, but flees from Him, hates Him, and desires to be and live without Him."[85] This is the active hate of a will that is completely turned against God and is in the service of the archenemy.

But are we not magnifying the depravity of the will beyond all proportion? Luther, on the contrary, insists that "this manifold corruption of our nature should not be minimized; it should rather be emphasized. From the image of God, from the knowledge of God . . . man has fallen into blasphemies, into hatred, into contempt of God, yes, what is even more, into enmity against God."[86] And the heart of this enmity is the will of fallen man. For it is not the works that a man does that are good or evil. It is the disposition of his will. And because man's natural will is evil, everything that he does is evil, even what the world calls good works.

Herein lies the cosmic dimension of this doctrine, and the tragic hopelessness of humankind. We are drawing up reams of peace pacts, treaties, charters, and constitutions aiming at a just and peaceful world. And all of them are on a high moral plane. But what use are they all unless the hearts and wills of all are changed so that they love the good and will the good because their wills have been brought into harmony with the will of God? D. R. Davies has given the answer in the simplest terms: "The way out of the present crisis of civilization . . . is to change the belief in man into belief in God and dependence upon Him."[87] Luther saw it so plainly when he said, "The most exalted virtues among the nations, the highest perfections of the philosophers, and the greatest excellencies among men, appear indeed in the sight of men to be meritoriously virtuous and good, and are so called; but . . . in the sight of God they are in truth 'flesh,' and subservient to the kingdom of Satan: i.e., ungodly, sacrilegious, and in every respect evil!"[88]

With this attitude in the will, and this corruption permeating our very nature, it is easy to see how there will flow forth from original sin all the actual sins that are spoiling human life. Put all these together: the loss of original righteousness, the blight of original sin, and the transgressions of God's Law that are our sins, and you have piled up a mountain of guilt that throws human beings into the terrible shadow of God's wrath.

6. Man Is Guilty and Under the Wrath and Judgment of God

The breach of God's Law brings with it guilt and the righteous judgment of an angry God, whether it be the Law in its primitive form in the garden, the Law written in men's hearts (Romans 1:18–23), or the Ten Commandments. Luther knows only one Law of God, and whether the theologians want to speak of a *lex naturae*, a *lex scripta*, or a *lex evangelica*, they are all part and parcel of the one Law of God. "[T]here is one law which runs through all the ages, is known to all men, is written in the hearts of all people, and leaves no one from the beginning to the end with an excuse . . . this one, which the Holy Spirit dictates unceasingly in the hearts of all men."[89]

Law and conscience belong together. "*Ego peccavi; tum venit mala conscientia, quia lex steckt ym in hertzen drinnen*."[90] And the penalty for the breach of this Law is death. "For the wages of sin is death" (Romans 6:23). Adam learned it, and all men are under the same condemnation. For "one trespass led to condemnation for all men" (Romans 5:18). "Hence all under the wrath of God are condemned to death, and must be forever separated from God. In this way God manifests His strong and terrible wrath against all men, which we bring upon us through sin, so that all of us must be overcome by death; because we are born of flesh and blood and in consequence must bear the guilt of our parents, and thus have become sinners and worthy of death."[91] And now Luther over-throws every attempt to blame God for it all, as he was accused of doing. For quoting Psalm 90:7, he says, "It is the wrath of God he says; hence it is not an accidental thing, or because man has been so created by God; but it is our fault that we commit sin. For since there is wrath, there must also be guilt, which causes such wrath. This wrath is not a mere ordinary thing, but such a serious affair that no one can endure it, and under which all succumb."[92]

Thus by the fall of Adam all men are sinners, guilty under the righteous wrath and judgment of God, and under the con-demnation of death. Man, created in the image of God, has lost his original righteousness. He is dead in trespasses and sin. And worst of all, the world does not know "how one may be freed from all this misery, nor can it accomplish this by its own wisdom and power." And being under the wrath of God, "the world is so blind that it does not see nor regard this wrath of God."[93] With a will perverted and turned against God, how can man appease Him? In death, how can he bring himself to life? For his will is "bound in error, in a lie, in death."[94]

What a key place the doctrine of the bondage of the will holds in Luther's theology is beautifully illustrated in his discus-sion of the dispute between Peter and James recorded in Acts 15. "From the beginning of the world this key heresy of freedom of the will and the merit of good works has continued. And this feud will never end. . . . The explanation is this: reason is not able to surrender to faith alone. If anyone would believe solely and purely in God's Word, it must be the work of the Holy Spirit in his heart. Out of its own powers human nature cannot do so. No matter what one says, human nature holds on to the merit of good works."[95]

"A pessimistic theology indeed," has to be the reaction of the optimistic humanism of Erasmus and his disciples. This is like saying that the Gospel of the cross is a pessimistic Gospel because it portrays sinful man at his worst, crucifying the Lord of life. But the theology of the cross, like the Gospel itself, is a theology of death and life, of cross and resurrection. Salvation is salvation from all evil, from sin, from death, from Satan, and from hell. And the sinner will never embrace in faith the good news of his salvation unless he is aware of his enslavement under these enemies. Heinrich Bornkamm's answer to this charge is worth quoting at length.

> Luther was anything but a pessimist. The boundless, exuberant joyousness which breaks forth from him despite all sadness has nothing in common with the rather sour humor of a melancholy person. But he uncovered sin in man so unmercifully as no one else in New Testament days only because God demands unrestricted recognition of reality from us. Here unsparing honesty is the best policy; it is the most merciful because man can be helped only in this way. This is the only course that points to freedom. A sick person cannot be helped by the physician so long as he imagines that he is well and requires no cure. With a penetrating eye Luther recognized this spasmodic claiming to be well before God as humanity's most dangerous sickness, the conviction that one is not so bad after all as its vilest sin. When Luther spoke of humankind's hopeless abandonment to sin, he was far from envisaging mankind as a band of criminals. No, but the worst thing was the fact that we human beings feel insulted when we are called sinners and that we appear to be far too respectable in our own sight to require repentance. Privately we are too prone to measure ourselves according to how far we surpass others, whom we regard as our inferiors, not by the distance that separates us from our God and His Commandments. So long as we do this we will not understand a single word about God. For what He says about us men always has a double message: "Ye shall be holy; for I the

Lord, your God, am holy!" and "For there is no difference; for all have sinned and come short of the glory of
God!" This is reality. If we recognize God as reality, then
we also see our own reality. The two are indissolubly
connected. That we have lost our contact with the real,
living God so alarmingly is undoubtedly due to the fact
that we have lost sight of our true selves and, in place of
our human reality, behold a man of straw clothed in our
wishes and illusions. To recognize God also means to
recognize our sins. And to see one's sins also means to
behold the holiness of God. Whoever speaks about God
and does not know that in His sight he is a very guilty
person has not felt a trace of God's reality. It is impossible to have the one half without the other. God's majesty
and our sin, the two together constitute the entire reality.
Luther's faith was a real faith because it comprised both
halves.[96]

The point is that Luther's theology of the cross does not
leave the sinner in his hopeless captivity under the wrath of God.
It shows him the way out, yes, it actually brings him out of his captivity into the freedom of faith in the Christ of the Gospel. But the
experience of repentance, of sorrow for sin, is part of "the Way"
and cannot be bypassed. David had to face the accusing finger of
Nathan saying: "Thou art the man." And it was only from his
knees of contrition that he cried out in repentance, "Have mercy
on me, O God . . . blot out my transgressions. . . . Against You, You
only, have I sinned" (Psalm 51:1–4).

This operation of crushing the proud, smug, self-righteous
sinner cannot be performed with kid gloves. "Insensate sinners,
who in spite of their great sins live day by day without the slight-
est apprehension of danger, must be hounded" until they recognize the power and the righteousness and the wrath of God. Yes,
"they must, as it were, be clubbed with hammers. They must learn
to know the true nature and greatness of Him whom they are pro-
voking to anger with their sins and compelling to inflict punish-

ment. They must be made to see the flashes of lightning and to hear the peals of thunder on Mount Sinai (Ex. 19:16, 18)."[97] When this time comes, then the hour of the Law is ended, and the hour of the Gospel has arrived.

> At this moment all the trumpery of philosophy of religion . . . at this moment all the preventives and relics the church has to offer against punishment for sin, against temporal and eternal destruction—all this is gone and forgotten. From an object of meditation, from a paragraph in a book on dogmatics, God has suddenly become a Person who calls to me personally. And this Person calls to me to tell me that my time has run out. At the sight of this every prayer for delay is frozen. The will to live dies—the will to live the life one has led up to this time. Time stands still.[98]

It is zero hour, the brink of conversion. The sinner has reached the end of his rope. "Wretched man that I am! Who will deliver me . . . ?" The hour of the Law is ended. Enter the Gospel. The despairing sinner is confronted by the God of grace in Jesus Christ assuring him: "What you could not do, I have done. What you should have suffered for your sin and guilt, I have suffered on the cross. The enemies you could not defeat, I have defeated in the Resurrection. The righteousness you could not attain, I have attained for you. Your sin is forgiven."

7. GOD SAVES MAN BY A MIRACLE OF GRACE

"God himself had to have compassion on our misery and to conceive a plan for our deliverance. . . . This had to be done by Christ, the Son of God himself, and he therefore became man, that is, took upon himself death and its cause, sin and the wrath of God, in order that He might free us from these and bring us to life and righteousness."[99]

Luther would undoubtedly have liked to end the debate with Erasmus right here in the Gospel of the atonement, the heart of his *theologia crucis*. But the debate on the freedom of the human will does not end there. Erasmus will not let Luther side-step the next question: How does man become a partaker of this finished work of Christ? "Don't you see," Erasmus would say, "that in the last analysis it is man who must choose whether or not he will accept this salvation which God has prepared for him? And this must be a decision of man's own free will." This power of the will to choose for or against his salvation Luther categorically denies.[100] For the will is not free. It is a captive of Satan, to do his will. "God-ward, or in things which pertain unto salvation or damnation he has no 'Free-will,' but is a captive, slave, and servant, either to the will of God, or to the will of Satan."[101] The man who has not Christ has nothing. Without Christ he can do nothing (John 15:5). "Outside of the faith of Christ there is nothing but sin and damnation."[102]

Luther presses the Gospel on Erasmus. For he is at all times aware that he is dealing with a humanist who believes he can find the solution to the mystery of conversion in man and in his "free will." Luther insists that the same God who accomplished man's salvation at the price of His own Son wills also to make that salvation available to all men. Those two truths together form the heart of the Gospel. God has done the first. He must do the second. But He must not only make it available, Erasmus, He must actually bring it to man, give it to him, and persuade him to believe it and to stake his life on it. He must bring life to the dead and sight to the blind. "Therefore this work of life has been accomplished in such a manner that without our effort or work we attain it, just as we became subject to death without our effort and work. . . . It means, therefore, that now all men can be delivered from sin and death and be made alive, not by nor through their own efforts, but apart from themselves through the righteousness and life of this Lord Jesus Christ, namely, if he touches them with his hand and through his Word imparts to them his work and power to destroy sin and death, and provided they believe his Word."[103]

The mercy of God is revealed to us in the fact that all His will, power, and love are bent toward restoring the lost image of God in man, restoring man in his manhood as created by God. That is what the Word of God tells Luther, and tells him further that it is through that very Word He purposes to perform this miracle of grace. But Erasmus, with his Channing-like reverence for the dignity of man, will not let Luther rob man of his responsibility for his own salvation. God Himself, declares Erasmus, ascribes to man a free will to choose the good or the evil, to choose life with God or death without Him. For in Ecclesiasticus 15:14–17 He says, "God made man from the beginning, and left him in the hand of his own counsel. He added his commandments and precepts. If thou wilt observe the commandments and keep acceptable fidelity forever, they shall preserve thee. He hath set water and fire before thee; stretch forth thine hand for which thou wilt. Before man is life and death, good and evil; that which he shall choose shall be given him."[104] This is all foolishness, says Erasmus, unless man is able to choose of his own free will. This is the answer of every man who does not know the nature and purpose of God's Law. Luther answers that words like these, "If thou wilt," do not mean, "therefore thou art able." On the contrary, "this and similar expressions man is warned of his impotence, which in his ignorance and pride, without these divine warnings, he would neither acknowledge nor be aware of. . . . that this and similar passages—'If thou wilt, if thou shalt hear, if thou shalt do,'—show not what men can do but what they ought to do."[105]

Such is the purpose of the Law in the salvation of man.

The words of the law are spoken, therefore, not to affirm the power of the will, but to enlighten blind reason and make it see that its own light is no light and that the virtue of the will is no virtue. "Through the law," says Paul, "comes knowledge of sin" [Rom. 3:20]. . . . The

whole meaning and purpose of the law is simply to fur-
nish knowledge, and that of nothing but sin; it is not to
reveal or confer any power whatever. For this knowledge
. . . shows that there is no power there, and how great a
weakness there is.[106]

The word "return" in Scripture is a stumbling block to the
modern theologian, as it was to Erasmus. "If you return, I will
restore you," says Jeremiah (15:19). Why call man to return if he is
not able to return? Luther says, "If thou wilt" is language of Law.
But

the word "return" has two uses in the Scriptures, one
legal, the other evangelical. In its legal use it is an expression of exacting and imperious command, which
requires not merely an endeavor but a change of the
whole life. Jeremiah frequently makes this use of it, as
when he says: "Return every one of you from his evil
way" [Jer. 18:11; 25:5; 35:15] and "Return to the Lord"
[Jer. 4:1]; for there it quite plainly involves obedience to
the demands of all the precepts. In its evangelical use it is
an expression of divine comfort and promise, by which
nothing is demanded from us, but the grace of God is
offered to us, as, for instance, in Psalm 15[14:7]: "When
the Lord turns the captivity of Zion," and Psalm 22:
"Return, O my soul, to your rest." Zechariah, therefore,
has given us the briefest possible epitome of both kinds
of preaching, both of law and of grace; for it is nothing
but law, law at its peak, when he says "Return to me," and
it is grace when he says, "I will return to you."[107]

This whole error of the sinner, at enmity with God, having
a free will to choose to be converted—this "decision" theology—
is therefore rooted in a misunderstanding of the distinction
between Law and Gospel. "It is therefore the mark of a discerning
reader of Scripture to notice what are words of law and what of
grace, so as not to have them all jumbled up as the filthy Sophists
. . . "[108] Why insist on robbing God of all the glory by saying that

man must do his share before God will save him? God *has* saved him, and by the Gospel He brings that truth home to the sinner who stands condemned before the Law. Erasmus confuses the whole way of salvation at this point by making Law out of the Gospel. Ezekiel says, "Have I any pleasure in the death of the wicked, declares the Lord God, and not rather that he should turn from his way and live?" (18:23). Erasmus says: Then it is up to man to exercise his free will and turn. Luther says, "It is an evangelical word and the sweetest comfort in every way for miserable sinners" when Ezekiel speaks.[109] And God "lifts up and comforts the sinner from his affliction and despair, so as not to quench the smoking flax and break the bruised reed [Isa. 42:3], but to give hope of pardon and salvation, so that he may rather be converted (by turning to salvation from the penalty of death) and live."[110]

But man's pride will not down, and proud reason demands an explanation of God's dealing with different men. Reasonable man wants to know "why some are touched by the law and others are not, so that the former accept and the latter despise the offered grace." Here, says Luther, we are trying to search out the will of the "hidden God," who

> ordains by his own counsel which and what sort of persons he wills to be recipients and partakers of his preached and offered mercy. This will is not to be inquired into, but reverently adored, as by far the most awe-inspiring secret of the Divine Majesty, reserved for Himself alone. . . . To the extent, therefore, that God hides himself and wills to be unknown to us, it is no business of ours. For here the saying truly applies, "Things above us are no business of ours."[111]

"What is man, that thou art mindful of him?" "But who are you, O man, to answer back to God? Will what is molded say to its molder, 'Why have you made me like this?' Has the potter no right over the clay, to make out of the same lump one vessel for honored use and another for dishonorable use?" (Romans 9:20–21). These questions all come out of a wavering faith that is not quite willing to yield, with Luther, to St. Paul's principle of grace alone. If God must change our will to save us, why does He not change everybody's will? Luther answers,

> But why that majesty of his does not remove or change this reflect of our will in all men, since it is not in man's power to do so, or why he imputes this defect to man, when man cannot help having it, we have no right to inquire; and though you may do a lot of inquiring, you will never find out. It is as Paul says in Romans 11[9:20]: "Who are you, to answer back to God?"[112]

But is not this maddening to intelligent men? What becomes then of the "dignity of man," that phrase with which the Unitarian Channing has forever saddled modern Protestantism? Is not this something to drive men to despair? That is exactly what it is. That is the convicting work of the Law, the "foreign" work of God, which He must do before He can save a man by His Gospel.

Thus prostrated, overcome by his own helplessness to escape the wrath of God, the lost sinner lies there like the wounded man on the Jericho road. And here Luther paints one of the finest of all his word-pictures in showing how God raises up the lost sinner. Preaching on that story in Luke 10:23–37, he shows the futility of the Law to save the fallen sinner.

> The dear sainted fathers saw very well that the people lay in their sins over their ears, and also felt the anguish of sin, but what could they do to remedy it? They could make it only worse, but not better. These were the preachers of the law, and showed what the world was, namely, full of deadly sins, and it lay there half dead, and could not help itself, notwithstanding all its powers, reason or free will. Go then, thou beautiful painted rogue, and boast of thy free will, of thy merits and holiness![113]

The answer is not in the Law, or in man's obedience to the Law. He
has no power for that. He must be lifted up by a power outside
himself. Then comes

> Christ, the true Samaritan, takes the poor man to himself
> as his own, goes to him and does not require the helpless
> one to come to him; for here is no merit, but pure grace
> and mercy; and he binds up his wounds, cares for him,
> and pours in oil and wine, this is the whole Gospel from
> beginning to end. He pours in oil when grace is
> preached, as when one says: Behold, thou poor man,
> here is your unbelief, here is your condemnation, here
> you are wounded and sore. Wait! All this I will cure with
> the Gospel. Behold, here cling firmly to this Samaritan,
> to Christ the Savior, he will help you, and nothing else in
> heaven or on earth will. You know very well that oil soft-
> ens, thus also the soft loving preaching of the Gospel
> gives me a soft, mild heart toward God and my neigh-
> bor.[114]

In that way Luther illustrates his principle that "the law discovers
the disease, the Gospel ministers the medicine."[115]

It is Christ who must save the sinner, who must deal with his
sins, who must soften his hard heart. It is God who must take his
hostile, God-hating will and change it. When that miracle of grace
has been performed, "when God works in us, the will, being
changed and sweetly breathed on by the Spirit of God, desires and
acts, not from compulsion, but responsively, from pure willingness, inclination, and accord."[116]

This is Luther's theology of grace alone, God reaching out to
raise up the fallen and condemned sinner. And where has this theology been more simply and beautifully stated than in Luther's
own explanation to the Third Article of the Apostles' Creed? "I
believe that I cannot by my own reason or strength believe in Jesus
Christ, my Lord, or come to Him; but the Holy Ghost has called
me by the Gospel, enlightened me with His gifts, and sanctified
and kept me in the true faith."[117] This humble confession tells the

whole story of fallen man rescued by God's grace. It is God who calls man through a Gospel that has the power in it to draw the man it calls. It is God who enlightens the darkened understanding, which to Luther means the same as to kindle faith. It is God who sanctifies the man whom He has brought to faith, and who preserves him in that faith to the end.

Here belongs also that great sentence in the Fifth Article of the Augsburg Confession, "Through the Word and sacraments, as through instruments, the Holy Ghost is given, who works faith, where and when it pleases God, in them that hear the Gospel."[118]

Luther praises God for his unspeakable gift of faith. "'This faith, in which is contained all good, is a gift of God. I do not by reason thereof boast myself superior to others, but I think the more on what I may give the Lord in return. It is the nature of the proud to ascribe to themselves the gifts which they have above others. . . . The way of the humble is . . . to consider how they may repay God; and to confess that they have received those things from His hand."[119] "The Spirit makes alive and gives strength." For God "must inspire and teach man, and give both grace and fire."[120]

CHAPTER
SIX

MAN IN GRACE

"That is why it depends on faith, in order that the
promise may rest on grace." (Romans 4:16)

*T*hrough this faith, which is worked by the Holy Spirit
through Word and Sacrament, man is justified. He who has
no righteousness of his own, nor any power to attain it,
has been declared righteous by God. He has been led by the Law
and the Gospel out of darkness into light, out of death into life.
Through it all he has been a conscious, thinking person, reflecting, feeling, experiencing that something is happening, yes, suddenly, that something has happened. Luther will let no Erasmus
nor any other humanist psychologize this experience of conversion, the coming of faith. This is a divine miracle of grace, nothing less! You can cast a veil over the glory of Christ, join the
doubting Nicodemus and stammer, "Lord, how can this be?" But
you only get the answer, "You must be born again." A miracle! Or
you can join the Pharisees in taunting the man who said Jesus had

healed his blindness, and you get the answer of faith, "One thing I know, that though I was blind, now I see." Or you can give the neat answer of Erasmus and his modern disciples, "You see, this man exercised his free will and chose to believe in Christ."

Luther is nauseated with this kind of humanism that presumes to rationalize the miracle of the birth of faith. "Is not this a perverted and blind people? They teach we cannot do a good deed of ourselves, and then in their presumption go to work and arrogate to themselves the highest of all the works of God, namely faith, to manufacture it themselves out of their own perverted thoughts." For "true faith . . . cannot be manufactured by our own thoughts, for it is solely a work of God in us, without any assistance on our part. As Paul says to the Romans, 5:15, it is God's gift and grace, obtained by one man, Christ."[1]

Luther has never put this more bluntly than he did against Latomus, the theologian from Louvain University, in 1521: God "has justified us through the gift of faith."[2] This shows beautifully how Luther insists that justification by faith alone is justification by grace alone. It is not possible then to talk about faith as a condition man must fulfill before God will justify him. We can understand now why Luther could never speak of justification as dependent upon man's decision. God is not a far off spectator, Luther tells Erasmus, who sits twiddling His thumbs waiting for man's free will to come to a decision. "God has not gone off to an Ethiopian banquet,"[3] as E. Gordon Rupp paraphrases Luther's words, while man is left to come to a decision with his free will either for or against faith.

No, justification by faith is God's act of grace from beginning to end. "A man cannot be thoroughly humbled until he comes to know that his salvation is utterly beyond his own powers, counsel, endeavours, will and works and absolutely dependent upon the will, counsel and pleasure of another."[4] And yet it is man who believes. Luther calls faith "a work, and of all works the most excellent and the most difficult to do. Through it alone you will be saved, even if you should be compelled to do without any other works. For it is a work of God, not of man, as Paul teaches [Eph. 2:8]. The other works He works through us and with our help, but this one He works in us without our help."[5]

You can hear the protesting refrain of the free-will cult: "See how you rob man of all responsibility!" But haven't we seen enough of Luther's preaching to recognize in it always a scorching indictment of sin and a passionate call to repentance? Those who rejected the call in unbelief he convicted with the Lord's own "Ye would not." But those who believed the Gospel he left to praise God with him for His great gift. He never spoiled his Gospel by arguing with people how much they had to do or had done to be saved. "For neither you nor I could ever know anything of Christ or believe on Him, and obtain Him for our Lord, unless it were offered to us and granted to our hearts by the Holy Ghost through the preaching of the Gospel. The work is done and accomplished."[6]

The content of this faith is Christ. And therefore it is justifying faith. He is the very form and perfection of faith. "Therefore the Christ who is grasped by faith and who lives in the heart is the true Christian righteousness, on account of which God counts us righteous and grants us eternal life."[7]

Read a few paragraphs like this from Luther and you begin to see the many brilliant facets reflecting the breadth and depth of his great overriding doctrine of justification. We theologians have made the doctrine so complex that even a world council of Lutheran scholars found it impossible to come up with a clear unified definition of the Reformation doctrine of justification.[8] True, Luther also found here a profound mystery. For years he struggled in sweat and tears and agony of conscience with the question: How can I gain the righteousness that avails before God? We have seen how all his efforts failed and how his conscience told him that all his good works did not cause God to declare him righteous. But when through his study of the Scriptures the

Gospel had done its work, Luther found the complete answer to his question in Jesus Christ, crucified and risen, "who was delivered up for our trespasses and raised for our justification" (Romans 4:25). Now he could talk about the righteousness of God and justification in a language that a child could understand. The righteousness that enables me to stand before God is not something I can earn by my own efforts. It is an "alien" righteousness, which must come to me from the outside. It must be given to me by God. He has won it for me and presents it to me in Jesus Christ. The simple word of Jeremiah, "the LORD is our righteousness" (23:6), is echoed again and again in Luther. Christ—all that He is, all that He has done for our justification and salvation—this is our righteousness. Luther frequently speaks of this as the obedience of Christ, namely, that by His life He fulfilled the Law for us[9] and "by His obedience and sacrifice in suffering and death appeased and removed the wrath of God, which we deserved, won for us and granted us forgiveness of sins and eternal life, so that we for His sake when we believe in Him are acceptable to God and heirs of life eternal."[10] This righteousness of Christ becomes mine when I come to faith. It is imputed to me. As Scripture says, "Abraham believed God, and it was counted to him as righteousness" (Genesis 15:6; Romans 4:3; Galatians 3:6). So when the Holy Spirit brings me to faith through Word and Sacrament, He bestows on me this righteousness of Christ, declares me to be righteous, justifies me, forgives me my sin.

Luther, in accord with Scripture, puts this in another way, namely, that faith is our righteousness, faith justifies. "Therefore faith alone is the righteousness of a Christian and the fulfilling of all the commandments."[11] But this is not a "virtue," as some scholastics called it, not a good work that merits God's favor and justification. It is justifying faith only "because it takes hold of and possesses this treasure, the present Christ."[12]

In this way faith is seen as the instrument or channel by which God identifies us with Christ, so that when I believe in

Him, everything that He has done is mine. His obedience is mine. His righteousness is mine. His fulfillment of the Law is mine. His payment for sin is mine. His satisfaction of God's wrath is mine. His victory over sin, death, and hell is mine. And God looks at me in Christ as though I had not sinned.

> Here it is to be noted that these three things are joined together: faith, Christ, and acceptance or imputation. Faith takes hold of Christ and has Him present, enclosing Him as the ring encloses the gem. And whoever is found having this faith in the Christ who is grasped in the heart, him God accounts as righteous. This is the means and the merit by which we obtain the forgiveness of sins and righteousness. "Because you believe in Me," God says, "and your faith takes hold of Christ, whom I have freely given to you as your Justifier and Savior, therefore be righteous." Thus God accepts you or accounts you righteous only on account of Christ, in whom you believe.[13]

This idea of the identification of the sinner with Christ through faith has probably never been put more beautifully than in Luther's treatise *The Freedom of a Christian*.

> The third incomparable benefit of faith is that it unites the soul with Christ as a bride is united with her bridegroom. By this mystery, as the Apostle teaches, Christ and the soul become one flesh [Eph. 5:31–32]. And if they are one flesh and there is between them a true marriage—indeed the most perfect of all marriages . . . it follows that everything they have they hold in common, the good as well as the evil. Accordingly the believing soul can boast of and glory in whatever Christ has as though it were its own, and whatever the soul has Christ claims as his own. Let us compare these and we shall see inestimable benefits. Christ is full of grace, life, and salvation. The soul is full of sins, death, and damnation. Now let faith come between them and sins, death, and

damnation will be Christ's, while grace, life, and salvation will be the soul's; for if Christ is a bridegroom, he
must take upon himself the things which are his bride's
and bestow upon her the things that are his. If he gives
her his body and very self, how shall he not give her all
that is his? And if he takes the body of the bride, how
shall he not take all that is hers?[14]

It is evident that Luther has gained a profound insight into
St. Paul's doctrine of justification. In one breath he can speak of
Christ as our righteousness, in another that it is faith that God
reckons as righteousness. The apostle can say of Christ, He is "our
righteousness" (1 Corinthians 1:30). But he can also declare that
"to one who does not work but trusts in him who justifies the
ungodly, his faith is counted as righteousness" (Romans 4:5). And
whichever way he says it, he is saying that we are justified by grace
and not by our works. Hence he adds, "That is why it depends on
faith, in order that the promise may rest on grace" (Romans 4:16).
We have already seen the importance of this emphasis in Luther's
theology. For a theology of the cross is a theology of grace. And
justification by faith alone (*sola fide*) is still justification by grace
alone (*sola gratia*).

Luther has another way of emphasizing this fact. He
declares that "faith justifies because it renders to God what is due
Him; whoever does this is righteous." Justifying faith "attributes
glory to God, which is the highest thing that can be attributed to
Him. To attribute glory to God is to believe in Him." And what is
it to believe? It is to "regard Him as truthful, wise, righteous, merciful, and almighty, in short, to acknowledge Him as the Author
and Donor of every good. . . . To be able to attribute such glory to
God is wisdom beyond wisdom, righteousness beyond righteousness. . . . From this it can be understood what great righteousness faith is and, by antithesis, what a great sin unbelief is."[15]

Luther has no interest in the specious arguments of theologians who declare, "Faith is to believe in some one, not in some

thing. Faith is to believe in a person, not in a word or a proposition. Faith is not believing that something is true." To Luther all of this belongs to faith. To believe in God means to believe in His Word. To put my trust in God means I put my trust in His Word and promises. I believe what He says is absolute truth, and I stake my life on it as well as on Him. His Word in which I trust is what He says in Holy Scripture. Luther's faith is the simple faith of the Church as expressed in the ancient creeds, believing who God is and also believing what He has done, and believing that He has done it all *for me* (*pro me*). In the ancient creeds a Christian confesses not only *whom* he believes in but *what* he believes, and this all belongs to "believing." His simplest expression of this faith is in his explanations to the three articles of the Creed.

> I believe in God the Father. . . . What does this mean? I believe *that* [!] God has made me . . . *that* He . . . provides . . . protects . . . guards me and preserves me.

> And in Jesus Christ, His only Son, our Lord; who . . . suffered . . . was crucified . . . descended . . . ascended . . . and sitteth . . . from thence He shall come to judge the quick and the dead.

> What does this mean? I believe *that* Jesus Christ, true God . . . and also true man . . . is my Lord, who has redeemed me . . . purchased and won me from all sins . . . with His holy, precious blood . . . in order that I may be His own, and live under Him . . . and serve Him. . . . [16]

In the same manner in the explanation to the Third Article of the Apostles' Creed Luther is saying that to believe means not only to trust in God but also to believe in the factuality and efficacy for him of God's redemptive work in Christ and to stake his eternal salvation on it, in accordance with God's Word in Holy Scripture.

Certainly, faith to Luther is a personal relationship to Jesus Christ.

God in his grace has provided us with a Man in whom
we may trust, rather than in our works. For although he
has justified us through the gift of faith, and although he
becomes favorable to us through his grace, yet he wants
us to rely on Christ so that we will not waver in ourselves and in these his gifts, nor be satisfied with the righteousness which has begun in us unless it cleaves to and
flows from Christ's righteousness. . . . But he does not
want us to halt in what has been received, but rather to
draw near from day to day so that we may be fully transformed into Christ . . . to have faith is to cleave to him, to
presume on him, because he is holy and just for you.
Observe that this faith is the gift of God, which the grace
of God obtains for us, and which purging away sin,
makes us saved and certain—not because of our works,
but because of Christ's—so that we can stand and
endure in eternity, even as is written: "His righteousness
endures forever" [Ps. 112:3].[17]

Jesus Christ is always the principle object and content of
faith with Luther. "As I have said, faith grasps and embraces Christ,
the Son of God, who was given for us, as Paul teaches here [Gal. 2,
20]. When He has been grasped by faith, we have righteousness
and life. For Christ is the Son of God, who gave Himself out of
sheer love to redeem me."[18] Here again it is evident that Luther will
not allow Christ and His redemptive work to be separated, but
both together are the object and content of faith. Faith is indeed to
believe in Christ, but in the Christ of the cross and the empty
tomb, the Christ with the wounds in His hands.

This faith in Christ is an extremely personal faith. Luther
warns against a general faith that merely confesses that Christ died
for the sins of the world. Even the devil believes that. But justifying faith believes that He died *for me* (*pro me*). Commenting on
Gal. 2:20, Luther says,

Now these words, "who loved me," are filled with faith.
Anyone who can speak this brief pronoun "me" in faith

and apply it to himself as Paul did, will, like Paul, be the best of debaters against the Law. For He did not give a sheep or an ox or gold or silver for me. But He who was completely God gave everything He was, gave Himself for me—for me, I say, a miserable and accursed sinner. I am revived by this "giving" of the Son of God into death, and I apply it to myself. This applying is the true power of faith.[19]

Now the exegete and theologian becomes the pastor and the soul curate, deeply concerned about the salvation of his hearers and readers, whether in the classroom or in the assembled congregation.

Therefore read these words "*me*" and "*for me*" with great emphasis, and accustom yourself to accepting this "*me*" with a sure faith and applying it to yourself. Do not doubt that you belong to the number of those who speak this "*me*." Christ did not love only Peter and Paul and give Himself for them, but the same grace belongs and comes to us as to them; therefore we are included in this "*me*." ... For He did not die to make the righteous righteous; He died to make sinners into righteous men, the friends and sons of God, and heirs of all heavenly gifts. Therefore since I feel and confess that I am a sinner on account of the transgression of Adam, why should I not say that I am righteous on account of the righteousness of Christ, especially when I hear that He loved me and gave Himself for me?[20]

While faith is principally this personal relationship with God in Christ through the Holy Spirit, Luther easily picks up the language of Scripture and speaks about believing the Word, believing the Gospel, believing the forgiveness of sins, and the like. Luther sums it all up when he says, like Jesus preaching in Galilee, "repent and believe in the gospel" (Mark 1:15). To believe in Jesus means to believe in the Gospel and the whole story of Jesus Christ presented there: to put your trust in Him and in the promises of the Gospel. "*Inasmuch as the faith in Christ by which we are justi-fied consists in this, that one believe not only in Christ* (or in the per-son of Christ) *but in all that belongs to Christ, the proud and the heretics deceive themselves in the conviction it pleases them to hold that they believe in Christ while they refuse to believe in what belongs to him.*"[21] This totality of the faith that is believed (*fides quae creditur*) is emphasized still more in Luther's comment on James 2:10, "Whosoever stumbles in one point is become guilty of all." Luther explains, "For faith consists of something indivisible: it is either a whole faith and believes all there is to believe, or it is no faith at all if it does not believe one part of what there is to believe. . . . (For Christ is not divided; therefore, one either denies him in his totality when one denies him with respect to one point or one affirms him in his totality. But one cannot at the same time deny and confess him now in this, and then in that, word.)"[22]

Included in faith is the knowledge that I am a sinner, lost and condemned under the Law of God. "Even if we recognize no sin in ourselves, we must yet believe that we are sinners. . . . There-fore, we must stand in the judgment of God and believe him when he says that we are sinners, for he cannot lie." Faith "rests content with the words of God alone."[23] Likewise faith rests in the Word of forgiveness in the Gospel. On Romans 3:4 Luther comments, "God, then, is justified in his words when one believes him in what he says in the gospel about the fulfillment of the promise and thus regards him as righteous and truthful. For his words are the word of the gospel. He is justified in them when one believes that he speaks the truth in them and that what is prophesied in this word of the psalmist will come to pass." This is the "trusting belief in his word" that Luther so often speaks of.[24] He sums it up when he says of Romans 1:17, "Here, too, '*the righteousness of God*' must not be understood as that righteousness by which he is righteous in him-self, but as that righteousness by which we are made righteous (justified) by Him, and this happens through faith in the gospel."[25]

So faith to Luther means believing in someone and in something. It involves knowledge and assent and trust, even though Luther does not formulate the definition of faith in these terms as formally as the later orthodox theologians did. We have already encountered Luther's use of these three elements of faith. It bears repeating in this context. "But if it is true faith, it is a sure *trust* and firm *acceptance* in the heart. It takes hold of Christ in such a way that Christ is the object of faith, or rather not the object but, so to speak, the One who is present in the faith itself. Thus faith is a sort of *knowledge* or darkness that nothing can see. Yet the Christ of whom faith takes hold is sitting in this darkness. . . . "[26] But the knowledge alone is not enough. With it must be joined trust. "We should note that there are two ways of believing. One way is to believe *about* God, as I do when I believe that what is said of God is true. . . . This faith is knowledge or observation rather than faith. The other way is to believe *in* God, as I do when I not only believe that what is said about Him is true, but put my trust in Him, surrender myself to Him and make bold to deal with Him, believing without doubt that He will be to me and do to me just what is said of Him."[27]

CHAPTER
SEVEN

RIGHTEOUS BUT STILL A SINNER

Righteous, justified by grace through faith in Jesus Christ, I am still a sinner. But I am a forgiven sinner, a sinner clothed in the righteousness of Christ. "Blessed is the one whose transgression is forgiven, whose sin is covered" (Psalm 32:1). *Simul iustus et peccator* (at the same time righteous and sinner) did not originate with Luther, but it has become one of the hallmarks of his Pauline theology of the cross. Forgiveness is central here as it is in the entire doctrine of justification. I am not righteous before God because I have attained to a sufficiently high moral standard of life, but because He has forgiven my sin and declared me righteous through faith in Christ, which is also His gift. I can boast of no adequate piety before God. "Our piety before God consists entirely in the forgiveness of sins. . . . For this reason, I say, one must understand that the righteousness of a Christian is nothing that can be named or imagined but the forgiveness of sins. . . . "[1]

Simul iustus et peccator is as basic in Luther's theology as the doctrine of justification by faith itself. The Christian is righteous, clothed with the righteousness of Christ, whose righteousness, or perfect obedience, is imputed to him (Romans 4:24). But he remains a sinner still, though his sin is covered through forgiveness in Christ. Original sin was not done away in Baptism. Its guilt was forgiven.

Here is a basic element in the doctrine of original sin that the Church is in danger of losing. Who in the waning twentieth century cares about original sin? Preachers, if they preach sin at all, preach about our *sins*, particularly our social sins: materialism, sex madness, greed, oppression, repression; and it is well that they do. But to lay open the natural wickedness and deep corruption of man's heart, how many preachers dare to throw this charge at a respectable congregation of "good" people? We often quite glibly confess our many sins, but how many of us beat our breast with the publican and cry, "God, be merciful to me, a sinner"? The historic Confession of Sins in the Lutheran liturgy reads, " . . . we poor sinners confess unto Thee that *we are* by nature sinful and unclean and that *we have* sinned. . . . "[2] The new rite published for trial by the Inter-Lutheran Commission on Worship reads, " . . . we confess . . . that *we have* sinned both in our actions and in our failure to act."[3] The General Confession in the Book of Common Prayer has the phrase, " . . . there is no health in us." An experimental liturgy by Cope, Davies, and Tytler, reads: "We confess . . . that *we have* sinned. . . . "[4]

Examine the new suggested liturgies the churches are experimenting with, and the accent is consistently on our actual sins and not at all on our innate sinfulness. *Services for Trial Use* contains alternatives to Prayer Book services, authorized by the 63rd General Convention of the Episcopal Church in 1967.[5] The First Service of the Holy Eucharist reads: "We confess that we have sinned. . . . " The Eucharistic Prayer does have " . . . we are sinners in your sight." The Services of Morning and Evening Prayer in the

Confession of Sin follow the Book of Common Prayer saying, " . . . we have erred and strayed. . . . We have offended. . . . And we have done those things which we ought not to have done." But here is omitted the crucial sentence of the old Prayer Book: "And there is no health in us."

These examples indicate that the concept of original sin, which was so real to Luther and the Church fathers, seems to be fading out of the life and consciousness of the Church. But if the Christian is to have a theology to live by, Luther insists that he must know who he is and what he is in relation to God. "Those who are well have no need of a physician, but those who are sick" (Matthew 9:12). It is not enough to acknowledge before God that I have today lied or cursed or cheated or failed to love as I should. I must lay open before Him my innermost heart and thoughts that cause me to do those things the Bible calls sins. The eyes of God probe deeper than my outward acts and peccadilloes. Luther insists that I must face the fact that "original sin really means that human nature has completely fallen; that the intellect has become darkened, so that we no longer know God and His will . . . that the will is extraordinarily depraved, so that we do not trust the mercy of God. . . . "[6] This means that in my daily Christian living I don't play the Pharisee before God, thanking Him that I don't do those bad things that my neighbor does but do the good things that the Law commands. Rather I let God be God, and I approach Him humbly with a sense of my own unworthiness and sinfulness, praying, "God, be merciful to me, a sinner."

The above is simply another way of stating Luther's thesis that original sin is not done away in Baptism, but its guilt is forgiven. Concupiscence remains, the evil inclination that Paul calls *epithumia*, which is inclining a man to actual sin. And this evil inclination, or lust, is sin, even in the man who is born again in Baptism. We must at all times "call upon God against original sin. For as long as we are here, we are not without sin, but there remain always the evil lust and desires in us which drag us into sin, against which we must struggle and fight."[7] Luther quotes here the classic statement of Augustine, "Original sin is indeed forgiven in Baptism, not in such a way that it no more exists, but that God no longer imputes it to you." Hence Luther says that as often as you feel yourself being drawn into uncleanness and other sins, then you know that you are experiencing the deadly darts of original sin, which the devil shot into Adam's flesh, from which you are born.[8]

This marks the struggle between the old man and the new man, the flesh and the spirit, which make up the whole man (*totus homo*). Parallel with man's justification, and simultaneous with it, is his regeneration. He is born again, born into the kingdom of God; he is a new man, and the Holy Spirit dwells in him. By adoption he is made a son of God. But here again in this whole man the old nature persists, the old Adam, the flesh.

Here Luther finds the trichotomy of flesh, soul, and spirit to be confusing. For, he says, "the flesh experiences no desire except through the soul and spirit, by virtue of which it is alive. By spirit and flesh, moreover, I understand the whole man, especially the soul itself."[9] He is like the man on the Jericho road, left with healing by the Good Samaritan, but not yet altogether healed.

> Thus we in the church are indeed in the process of being healed, but we are not fully healthy. For the latter reason we are called "flesh"; for the former, "spirit." It is the whole man who loves chastity, and the same whole man is titillated by the enticements of lust. There are two whole men, and there is only one whole man. Thus it comes about that a man fights against himself and is opposed to himself. He is willing, and he is unwilling. And this is the glory of the grace of God; it makes us enemies of ourselves. For this is how it overcomes sin, just as Gideon overcame Midian. . . .[10]

This inner struggle of flesh and spirit is a paradox and a mystery. St. Paul says, "For I do not do what I want, but I do the very thing I hate" (Romans 7:15). "For one and the same person is spirit and flesh; thus what the flesh does the whole man is said to do. And yet what resists is not the whole man but is rightly called a part of him. Both then are true: it is he that acts and yet it is not he."[11] It is the mystery that "our life is a life in the midst of death."[12]

Luther makes it clear that in all this discussion of man as body, soul, and spirit, as "new man" and "old man," he rejects any atomistic view of man and insists on the oneness of the whole man. This has serious ethical implications. For if we press the idea that man is "flesh" and "spirit," or "old man" and "new man," and that the one is striving against the other, it is easy to draw the wrong ethical conclusions. The apostle himself says, "[I]t is no longer I that do it" (Romans 7:17). But he does not thereby excuse himself, as though he were not altogether responsible for his sin or his innate sinfulness. Neither can I say when I sin, "It is not I who do it, but the 'old man' in me, therefore I am not responsible, not guilty." On the contrary, I must say with St. Paul that "I see in my members another law waging war against the law of my mind and making *me* captive to the law of sin. . . . Wretched man that *I* am! Who will deliver *me*?" (Romans 7:23–24, *emphasis added*). Hence Luther would emphasize that it is the whole man who sins and the whole man who is guilty and must stand before God to be judged by Him. Luther says you cannot distinguish "spirit" and "flesh" as two "substances," since "the whole man is spirit and flesh, spirit insofar as he delights in the law of God, flesh insofar as he hates the law of God."[13] As Karl Holt says, the man who wants to measure his worth before God cannot simply push into the background that part of his nature which is "painful" to him; "he must take himself as a whole undivided man."[14]

Luther's whole interpretation of Romans 7 thus moves in the frame of his concept of man as *simul iustus et peccator*. It is not the "old man" who is sinner and the new man righteous. But the whole man is a sinner, yet he is wholly covered by the righteousness of Christ.

Luther applies this thinking to verses 18 and 15 of Romans
7, where the apostle says "I will" and "I hate."

> Just because one and the same man as a whole consists of
> flesh and spirit, he attributes to the whole man both of
> the opposites that come from the opposite parts of him.
> Thus there comes about a *communio idiomatum*: one
> and the same man is spiritual and carnal, righteous and
> sinful, good and evil. Just so the one person of Christ is
> at the same time both dead and alive, both suffering and
> blessed, both active and inactive, etc., because of the
> *communio idiomatum*, even though there belongs to nei-
> ther of his two natures what is characteristic of the other,
> for, as everyone knows, they differ absolutely from each
> other.[15]

For "because flesh and spirit are so closely connected with each
other that they are one, although they feel differently, he attributes
to himself as a whole person what both are doing, as if he were at
one and the same time wholly flesh and wholly spirit."[16]

It is within the frame of this doctrine of *simul iustus et peccator* that Luther confronts one of the critical problems that
plague modern New Testament scholars. Who is speaking in
Romans 7:13–25, the unconverted Saul of Tarsus or the converted
Paul the Christian? Luther answers unequivocally that it is Paul
the Christian. He is in good company, for he is following the traditional interpretation of both Augustine and Ambrose. Luther
tells how Augustine struggled with this problem, first thinking
that it was the unconverted Saul speaking, but after further study
concluding that it must be the converted Paul.

Luther examines the passage and finds it full of hatred of the
flesh and love of the good and of the Law. "Now such an attitude
is not characteristic of a carnal man, for he hates and laughs at the
law and follows the inclinations of his flesh. . . . and bemoans the
fact that he cannot do as he wills. But a carnal man does not fight
with it but yields and consents to it."[17] When Paul says in Romans

7:14, "But I am carnal," Luther says this is a spiritual man speaking, "[B]ecause it is characteristic of a spiritual and wise man that he knows that he is carnal, that he is dissatisfied with himself and hates himself, and that he praises the law of God because it is spiritual."[18] The carnal man, on the other hand, thinks he is spiritual. He is satisfied with himself and he loves his life here in the world. The language of the entire chapter, says Luther, could only be used by a spiritual man. Only he could hate sin, could grieve because he doesn't do what he wants to do, could confess that in his flesh there is no good. And he winds up the argument with the conclusion: "As everyone knows, one never hears of such a conflict or of a complaint about such a conflict in the carnal man."[19] The climax, of course, is in verse 24: "Wretched man that I am! Who will deliver me from this body of death?" This, says Luther—and now the pastor is speaking—shows even more clearly than the foregoing that the spiritual man is speaking here, for he sighs and grieves and longs to be delivered. Certainly no one will declare himself wretched except one who is a spiritual man. Therefore, says Luther, "It is astonishing that it could have entered anyone's mind that the Apostle speaks these words in the person of the old and carnal man, words which reflect such remarkable perfection. . . . Indeed it is a great consolation to us to learn that such a great apostle was involved in the same grievings and afflictions in which we find ourselves when we wish to be obedient to God."[20]

Out of this whole argument emerges Luther's unique doctrine of *simul iustus et peccator*, and here we encounter one of his best statements of the case.

> The saints in being righteous are at the same time sinners; they are righteous because they believe in Christ whose righteousness covers them and is imputed to them, but they are sinners because they do not fulfill the law and are not without sinful desires. They are like sick people in the care of a physician: they are really sick, but healthy only in hope and in so far as they begin to be bet-

ter, or, rather: are being healed, i.e., they will become healthy. Nothing can harm them so much as the presumption that they are in fact healthy, for it will cause a bad relapse.[21]

In this last statement of Luther we again meet the idea of imputation, so basic in St. Paul's doctrine of justification. Luther treated this concept earlier, as we have seen, in his comments on Romans 4:7–8, "Blessed are those whose lawless deeds are forgiven, and whose sins are covered; blessed is the man against whom the Lord will not count his sin." Here the idea of imputation appears as central in the doctrine of *simul iustus et peccator*, as it is central in the whole doctrine of justification. The Christian is a sinner, but the righteousness of Christ is imputed to him and thus covers his sin. So he is a sinner indeed, but a forgiven sinner, hence righteous by imputation.

> For inasmuch as the saints are always aware of their sin and implore God for the merciful gift of his righteousness, they are for this very reason also always reckoned righteous by God. Therefore, they are before themselves and in truth unrighteous, but before God they are righteous because he reckons them so on account of this confession of their sin . . . by virtue of the reckoning of a merciful God they are righteous; they are knowingly righteous and knowingly unrighteous, sinners in fact but righteous in hope.[22]

In this day of ecumenical concern some theologians have yielded to the temptation to minimize the forensic element in Luther's doctrine of justification. For this is one of the less palatable elements in the Lutheran position. But every such effort collapses before this idea of *simul iustus et peccator*. For the latter doctrine does not make sense outside the frame of a forensic idea of justification. You are a sinner, but God declares your sins forgiven.

Here, too, is a theology to live by. And Luther as pastor uses it to comfort and encourage the struggling Christian. Every Christian, he says, must be constantly aware of his double character as sinner and righteous.

> The reason why God leaves us in sin . . . in the "tinder," in concupiscence, is that he wants to keep us in fear of him and in humility so that we may always keep running to his grace, always fearful that we may sin, i.e., always praying that he does not impute our sin to us and that he does not let it get dominion over us.[23]

By the year 1521 Luther could see that much of the Roman Catholic opposition to his theology centered in this very idea of *simul iustus et peccator*. The conflict exploded when the University of Louvain in Belgium, led by a professor named Latomus, condemned Luther's writings.

The first proposition attacked by Latomus was Luther's declaration that every good work is sin; even the good work of a Christian is tinged with sin. This is a revolting idea at first blush, even to the intelligent Christian. It is hard to believe that when a good Samaritan helps a sufferer, his action is contaminated with sin. But here again the secret lies in the fact that the Christian is *simul iustus et peccator*. He is still a sinner, and therefore what he does is poisoned with sin. As the tree, so are the branches. Doesn't Isaiah say that "all our righteous deeds are like a polluted garment" (64:6)? This was a man of God speaking. Then our only salvation is that God deals with us not in judgment but in mercy. "Therefore, if he judges, we all sin before him, and perish if he is angry; and yet if mercy covers us, we are innocent and godly before him and all creatures."[24] This is what Isaiah is saying. "[W]hen the covering cloud of grace is removed, a good work is by its nature unclean, and it is pure and worthy of praise and glory only through forgiving mercy."[25] Luther appeals to Ecclesiastes 7:20, "Surely there is not a righteous man on earth who does good and never sins." Then a Christian cannot glory in his good works.

Even "the saints of God are ashamed of their works before him and glory in him alone."[26] St. Paul says in 1 Corinthians 1:31, "Let the one who boasts, boast in the Lord."

Luther asks Latomus to imagine St. Paul boasting of any good work of his as being perfect and without sin.

> Let us take St. Paul or Peter as they pray, preach, or do some other good work. If it is a good work without sin and entirely faultless, they could stand with appropriate humility before God and speak in this fashion: "Lord God, behold this good work which I have done through the help of Thy grace. There is in it neither fault nor any sin, nor does it need Thy forgiving mercy. I do not ask for this, as I want Thee to judge it with Thy strictest and truest judgments. In it [my work] I can glory before Thee, because Thou canst not condemn it, for Thou art just and true. Indeed, I am certain that Thou canst not condemn it without denying Thyself. The need of mercy which, as Thy petition [in the Lord's Prayer] teaches, forgives the trespass in this deed is canceled, for there is here only the justice which crowns it." Latomus, doesn't this make you shudder and sweat?[27]

The one who is baptized has all his or her sins forgiven. Nevertheless, sin remains as an evil inclination and quality in man that makes him guilty of what he is and what he does unless it is covered by God's mercy. "Even after forgiveness there is still sin, but it is not imputed."[28] So Luther repeats his thesis "that all good work is sin unless it is forgiven by mercy.... The fruit exhibits the nature of the tree.... The Commandments are fulfilled by the forgiving mercy of God, not by the works which are done. But what is forgiven if not sin?"

Is there then no such thing as good works? Or have they lost their importance in the Christian life? The answer again lies in the theology of the cross, the theology of grace.

> It is through mercy, not through your efforts, that your works are good. You will therefore judge yourselves one

RIGHTEOUS BUT STILL A SINNER

way in accordance with the severity of God's judgment, and another in accordance with the kindness of His mercy. Do not separate these two perspectives in this life. According to one, all your works are polluted and unclean on account of that part of you which is God's adversary; according to the other, you are genuinely pure and righteous. As testimony that you are thus purified, you have the symbol of baptism, through which all sins are most truly forgiven you—entirely forgiven, I say, but not wholly abolished. We believe that the remission of all sins has been without doubt accomplished, but we daily act in the expectation of the total removal and annihilation of all sin. It is those who labor toward this who do good works.[29]

Luther repeatedly comes back to the illustration that our Lord used so effectively.

As is the tree, so is the fruit. Thus he will not boast before God of the cleanliness which he has in himself, but will rather glory in the grace and gift of God, and in the fact that he has a gracious God on his side who does not impute this sin and, besides this, has given the gift through which it is purged away. He therefore confesses the truth that if he must be judged according to the nature of his works apart from grace, he cannot stand before His face; but now, because he relies upon grace, there is nothing which can accuse him.[30]

The rationale of Luther's emphasis here is clear, and it all falls in place as an integral part of his doctrine of justification by grace alone. It is the same old story: We must learn to trust in Christ and His finished work for our justification and salvation and not in our own works. For our works are simply "polluted garments" if we try to present them to God as worthy of reward. "The reason why there is no condemnation is not that men do not sin, as Latomus in lying fashion suggests, but because—as Paul says—they are in Christ Jesus; that is, they repose under the shadow of His righteousness as do chicks under a hen."[31]

Simul iustus et peccator, the fact that a Christian is at the same time both sinner and righteous, is undoubtedly one of the brightest spots in Luther's theology. When Christians really get hold of this fact, they will find themselves in possession of a theology on which and by which they can live day by day in what the psalmist calls "the joy of Thy salvation." But there may be need for a caveat at this point. *Simul iustus et peccator*—this is no static doctrine. I find rest and comfort in it, but I do not go to sleep on it. God still calls me to Christian living, to the fruits of faith, to the works of love. The Spirit's work of sanctification must go on. Just because my good works do not merit the pleasure of God, this is no excuse for not doing them.

PART III

THE CHRISTIAN LIFE—ITS DYNAMIC AND DESTINY

CHAPTER EIGHT

THE LIFE WE LIVE—
UNDER THE CROSS

Luther believed that this theology of the cross was a theology to live by. He never put a theological system on a pedestal for people to analyze and criticize, to praise or to damn. From pulpit and podium, from platform and printed page came his passionate plea: Here is a theology to live by; now go and live it!

This life is born under the cross, and it can only be lived under the cross. Then the Christian life is no cozy Sunday School picnic. It is a life in tension. Calvary was no picnic ground. As our Lord hung in tension between life and death, between heaven and earth, between humiliation and glory, so the Christian lives his life in tension between sin and grace, guilt and forgiveness, wrath and mercy, fear and assurance, flesh and spirit, life and death, heaven and hell. And this is only another way of saying that he lives his life in tension between Law and Gospel. It all begins in Baptism, where the sinner is baptized into Christ and into the forgiving love of God. Sin is forgiven, but "Paul calls that which remains after baptism, sin."[1] The "flesh" is still present, and the Holy Spirit given in Baptism is busy the rest of your life putting down the flesh and preventing it from taking dominion over the spirit, which is really the Holy Spirit in you. "From that hour [of baptism] he begins to make you a new person. He pours into you his grace and Holy Spirit, who begins to slay nature and sin, and to prepare you for death and the resurrection at the Last Day." But for you it continues to be a life in tension. For in Baptism you pledge yourself "to slay your sin more and more as long as you live, even until your dying day. This too God accepts. He trains and tests you all your life long, with many good works and with all kinds of sufferings. Thereby he accomplishes what you in baptism have desired, namely, that you may become free from sin, die, and rise again at the Last Day, and so fulfill your baptism."[2]

Here again the Christian can draw comfort from Luther's idea of *simul iustus et peccator*. For although sin remains to trouble you, God "pledges himself not to impute to you the sins which remain in your nature after baptism, neither to take them into account nor condemn you because of them. He is satisfied and well pleased if you are constantly striving and desiring to conquer these sins and at your death to be rid of them."[3]

So the Christian must carry on the good fight all his life. But this is his consolation, that he is carrying on a winning battle with Christ, who has triumphed over the enemy. The enemy is not dead, but he is beaten. Whether we are thinking of Satan, sin, or flesh, they are strong, but Christ is stronger.

> And so if we look at the flesh, we are sinners; if we look at the Spirit, we are righteous. . . . Yet our righteousness is more abundant than our sin, because the holiness and righteousness of Christ, our Propitiator, vastly surpasses the sin of the entire world. Consequently, the forgiveness of sins, which we have through Him, is so great, so

abundant, and so infinite that it easily swallows up every sin, provided that we persevere in faith and hope toward Him.[4]

This all serves notice on the Christian to be vigilant, to keep on his toes, to stay spiritually awake. He should not resent but welcome the pricking of the Law, which keeps him sensitive to his sinfulness and need of forgiveness in Christ. "And so it is very beneficial if we sometimes become aware of the evil of our nature and our flesh, because in this way we are aroused and stirred up to have faith and to call upon Christ."[5] So let the good law of God drive me to my knees to cry with St. Paul, "Wretched man that I am! Who will deliver me from this body of death?" But let the saving Gospel raise me up again with the assurance of the apostle, "Thanks be to God through Jesus Christ our Lord!" Thus the experience of daily repentance maintains the tension and at the same time the supremacy of the Spirit over my flesh, of grace over my sin, of righteousness over my unrighteousness. Christus Victor!

Then I am free—free from sin, from its guilt, its power, its penalty! For through the blessed Gospel I know that my sins are forgiven in Christ. And as Luther says, those with a clear conscience are most free.[6]

With our freedom from sin goes, as St. Paul says in Romans, our freedom from the Law. The Law has become our friend, even while it is pricking and hurting us.

> Here we must point out that the entire Scripture of God is divided into two parts: commandments and promises. Although the commandments teach things that are good, the things taught are not done as soon as they are taught, for the commandments show us what we ought to do but do not give us the power to do it. They are intended to teach man to know himself, that through them he may recognize his inability to do good and may despair of his own ability.[7]

But he is not left in despair. For at this point comes the blessed Gospel to remind him that he is free, for the demands of the Law have been satisfied by Christ.

> Here the second part of Scripture comes to our aid, namely, the promises of God which declare the glory of God, saying, "If you wish to fulfil the law and not covet, as the law demands, come, believe in Christ in whom grace, righteousness, peace, liberty, and all things are promised you. If you believe, you shall have all things; if you do not believe, you shall lack all things." That which is impossible for you to accomplish by trying to fulfil all the works of the law . . . you will accomplish quickly and easily through faith. . . . This is that Christian liberty, our faith. . . . Therefore faith alone is the righteousness of a Christian and the fulfilling of all the commandments, for he who fulfils the First Commandment has no difficulty in fulfilling all the rest.[8]

This Christian liberty that is our faith is not a static, inactive sort of thing that lies hidden and useless like the talent hidden in the ground. It does not "induce us to live in idleness or wickedness."[9] No, it is "a living, busy, active, mighty thing, this faith. . . . Faith is a living, daring confidence in God's grace, so sure and certain that the believer would stake his life on it a thousand times. This knowledge and confidence in God's grace makes men glad and bold and happy in dealing with God and with all creatures. And this is the work which the Holy Spirit performs in faith."[10]

Luther has here moved us from the realm of justification to that of sanctification, terms the theologians have snatched right out of St. Paul's Epistles. The question is no longer: How can I become righteous before God? Having been declared righteous, the question now is: How do I live the Christian life? Luther will not let the two questions be divorced from one another. Nor can he talk about sanctification without constant reference to justification. For we live in the forgiveness of sins and in the consciousness of that forgiveness. This is that tension we have talked about in the Christian life. The Christian knows that he is a sinner. But in the experience of daily repentance the Holy Spirit reminds him that in Christ he is a forgiven sinner. And it is through this constantly renewed assurance of forgiveness that the Holy Spirit spurs him on to live the free Christian life.

The Christian exercises this freedom of faith in two directions. On the one hand, it means mortifying the flesh and contending against evil within and without. On the other, it means serving God and the neighbor in love.

Again Luther's teacher is St. Paul. "We know that our old self was crucified with Him in order that the body of sin might be brought to nothing, so that we would no longer be enslaved to sin. . . . Let not sin therefore reign in your mortal bodies, to make you obey their passions" (Romans 6:6, 12). "To destroy the body of sin means, therefore, to break the desires of the flesh and of our old man by exertions of penitence and the cross, and so to decrease them from day to day and to put them to death."[11] Hence this Christian freedom is no invitation to license. Are we to sin because we are not under Law but under grace? "By no means!" says St. Paul (Romans 6:15). Instead, he calls us to live a disciplined life in the midst of our freedom. "Let not sin therefore reign in your mortal bodies, to make you obey their passions" (v. 12). We live not in fear but in loving thankfulness, "as those who have been brought from death to life" (v. 13).

And do not carry on this battle against sin and the flesh with a defeatist attitude! "For sin will have no dominion over you, since you are not under law but under grace" (v. 14). The man of God who has tasted forgiveness in the fellowship of Christ hates sin. He is living in the brave tradition of Moses, who chose "rather to be mistreated with the people of God than to enjoy the fleeting pleasures of sin" (Hebrews 11:25). The Law no longer drives him to a slavish obedience of fear but to the loving obedience of one who has tasted the forgiving love of God in Christ. The Law has become his friend. When we have entered into the freedom of the

Gospel, says Luther, "we are changed and from enemies of the Law are made friends of the Law."[12]

Man's sinfulness and consequent guilt, then, cannot be minimized in terms of dividing man into parts and blaming the "old man," any more than we can lay the blame on Adam alone, any more than we can call original sin merely the loss of superadded gifts. It is the whole man who is "altogether sinful and unclean," as the sacred liturgy says. "Flesh and spirit are one and the same man. That is why the 'new man' must reckon to himself also the sins of the old Adam."[13]

The mystery of the grace of God shows itself here—here, too, according to Luther's theology. For even as the whole man is by nature sinful and utterly under the wrath of God, so the whole person is completely clothed in the righteousness of Christ. God looks at him in Christ as though he had not sinned (Romans 4).

But we must not lose ourselves in what Protestant theologians have frequently called Luther's pessimistic theology. There is also a great and beautiful, positive side to this life of liberty in faith. It is the glorious position of the man Luther describes in his *Treatise on Christian Liberty*, the man who is "a perfectly free lord of all, subject to none," and a "perfectly dutiful servant to all, subject of all." The prototype is Christ, who, "although he was Lord of all, was 'born of a woman, born under the law' [Gal. 4:4], and therefore was at the same time a free man and a servant, 'in the form of God' and 'of a servant.' "[14]

As lord of all, man is free from the chains of legalism, and his life is at all times guided by a new motive, the motive of love, grounded in faith. "For though I am free from all, I have made myself a servant to all" (1 Corinthians 9:19). The relation between faith and love has perhaps never been described more beautifully outside of Holy Writ than in those immortal words of the *Treatise* already quoted: "[A] Christian lives not in himself, but in Christ and in his neighbor. Otherwise he is not a Christian. He lives in Christ through faith, in his neighbor through love. By faith he is caught up beyond himself into God. By love he descends beneath himself into his neighbor. Yet he always remains in God and in His love."[15]

The Christian, having experienced the *agape* of God in Christ, is always moved by that love to a life of love toward God and neighbor. And love for God shows itself preeminently in loving service to the neighbor. Like Christ, man empties himself, takes upon himself the form of a servant, "to serve, help, and in every way deal with his neighbour as he sees that God through Christ has dealt and still deals with him." The man

> ought to think: "Although I am an unworthy and condemned man, my God has given me in Christ all the riches of righteousness and salvation without any merit on my part, out of pure, free mercy, so that from now on I need nothing except faith which believes that this is true. Why should I not therefore freely, joyfully, with all my heart, and with an eager will do all things which I know are pleasing and acceptable to such a Father who has overwhelmed me with His inestimable riches? I will therefore give myself as a Christ to my neighbor, just as Christ offered himself to me; I will do nothing in this life except what I see is necessary, profitable, and salutary to my neighbor, since through faith I have an abundance of all good things in Christ."[16]

Gratitude, love, joy are the fruits of faith, the hallmarks of the Christian life of freedom. The Christian's whole life and attitude toward his neighbor is determined by love. And in the free and willing service of the neighbor there is no thought of "gratitude or ingratitude, of praise or blame, of gain or loss."[17] He serves friend and enemy alike.

This kind of a life of love can only come from one thing, namely, that a man remembers the great gift God has bestowed on him. Here again it is the love of God revealed in the Gospel that reaches down and sheds abroad in our hearts "the love which makes us free, joyful, almighty workers and conquerors over all tribulations, servants of our neighbors and yet lords of all."[18] Love, *agape*, thus flows from the heart of God through His children to bring help, comfort, and blessing to men. "Hence, as our heavenly Father has in Christ freely come to our aid, we also ought freely to help our neighbor through our body and its works, and each one should become as it were a Christ to the other that we may be Christs to one another and Christ may be the same in all, that is, that we may be truly Christians."[19]

At this point Luther can become a crusader, an evangelist for social action. The temperature of his pulpit rises and he preaches with an intense passion. Luther is pictured as a preacher of justification, of forgiveness, of faith, and rightly so. But when he sees signs of people going to sleep on the doctrine of justification, and failing to follow through in a life of love and good works, his righteous wrath thunders from the pulpit. Ensconced in the security of the Wartburg, he hears that his followers in Wittenberg have fallen into just such a slumber. The members of his congregation sit twiddling their thumbs and thanking God for the Gospel that has come to them through his preaching. But where are the changed lives going out into the community to help the poor, to feed the hungry, to visit the sick, and to convert the unbeliever? Luther, at the risk of his life, bursts out of the Wartburg, goes to Wittenberg, mounts his pulpit, and preaches eight fiery sermons in eight days. In the seventh sermon he excoriates his people for reveling in their new Gospel freedom but failing to exercise it in loving service to people who need help. "It is true, you have the true gospel and the pure Word of God, but no one as yet has given his goods to the poor, no one has yet been burned, and even these things would be nothing without love."[20]

Preaching on Romans 13, Luther pours out a burning appeal to Christians to turn their faith loose in lives of love and service to those in need. He echoes the language of the apostle when he says,

Love is the chief virtue, the fountain of all virtues. Love gives food and drink; it clothes, comforts, persuades, relieves and rescues. What shall we say of it, for behold he who loves gives himself body and soul, property and honor, all his powers inner and external, for his needy neighbor's benefit, whether it be friend or enemy; he witholds nothing wherewith he may serve another. There is no virtue like love. . . . Love does all things. It will suffer in life and in death, in every condition, and that even for its enemies.[21]

Great compassion and deep social concern radiate from Luther's preaching. Suffering humanity weighs heavily on his heart, and his idea of love is deeply colored by compassion for the afflicted. "Such love is most active and powerful in serving the poor, the needy, the sick, the wicked, the simple-minded and the hostile; among these it is always and under all circumstances necessary to suffer and endure, to serve and do good." There can be no separation of love to God and love to the neighbor. Luther finds that St. Paul "makes love to God and love to our neighbor the same love. . . . In these lowly ones we are to find and love God, in them we are to serve and honor Him, and only so can we do it. The commandment to love God is wholly merged in that to love our neighbors."[22]

The love that characterizes the Christian life is no mere matter of feeling. Love means action, good works. "Note, Paul terms love not only an affection, but an affectionate good act."[23] And here Luther relates faith and love in one of his classic statements: "Faith is ever the actor, and love the act." "For faith loves and works, as said in Galatians 5, 6, 'Faith worketh through love.' " Faith and life, justification and sanctification are always together. "Love and works do not change us, do not justify us. We must be changed in person and justified before we can love and do good works. Our love and our works are evidence of justification and of a change, since they are impossible until the individual is free from sin and made righteous."[24]

This interlaced relationship between faith and life, between justification and sanctification, between faith and love and works gets the full treatment in another great treatise of Luther, the *Treatise on Good Works*. A Christian does good works; otherwise he is not a Christian. He performs them neither in a slavish obedience of fear nor to gain justification or any merit whatsoever. He does them as a free expression of faith, an offering of love and thanksgiving to Him who loved him and gave himself for him and still loves him. "[A] Christian man living in this faith has no need of a teacher of good works, but he does whatever the occasion calls for, and all is well done."[25] The emphasis is again on freedom. Luther had come out of a long enslavement to the theology of work-righteousness. We have already noted his years of struggle to gain righteousness before God by way of good works, penances, satisfactions, self-mortification, and strict obedience to the rules of the church. Now that he has tasted the free grace of God through faith, he never tires of preaching this happy Gospel of freedom. "Thus a Christian man who lives in this confidence toward God knows all things, can do all things, ventures everything that needs to be done, and does everything gladly and willingly, not that he may gather merits and good works, but because it is a pleasure for him to please God in doing these things. He simply serves God with no thought of reward, content that his service pleases God."[26]

Here Luther cannot resist a gibe at the poor man who still persists in trying to get right with God by his own efforts.

> He runs off to St. James, to Rome, to Jerusalem, hither and thither; he prays St. Bridget's prayer, this prayer and that prayer; he fasts on this day and that day; he makes confession here and makes confession there; he questions this man and that man, and yet finds no peace. He does all this with great effort and with a doubting and unwilling heart, so that the Scriptures rightly call such

works in Hebrew *aven amal* [Ps. 90:10], that is, labor and
sorrow. And even then they are not good works and are
in vain. Many people have gone quite crazy with them
and their anxiety has brought them into all kinds of misery.[27]

Many readers are offended, as Latomus was, when Luther
says, "Every good work of the saints while pilgrims in this world is
sin."[28] The recognition of this is part and parcel of faith. "Yes, this
confidence and faith must be so high and strong that a man knows
that all his life and works are nothing but damnable sins in the
judgment of God, as it says in Psalm 143 [:2], 'For no man living
is found righteous before thee.' "[29] As the tree, so the fruit. As a
man, so his works. What I do bears the brand of what I am. "For I
meant and now [expressly] say . . . that sin, as long as we live,
inheres essentially in good works, just as the ability to laugh
inheres in a man. . . . a man does good and therefore sins, because
a man doing good is a subject which has sin as its attribute. . . ."[30]

We are tempted to ask with the disciples, "Who then can be
saved?" (Matthew 19:25). Luther's answer is: No one except
through the mercy of God and faith. "Our good works are not
good unless His forgiving mercy reigns over us."[31] Another way to
put it is that "faith alone makes all other works good, acceptable,
and worthy because it trusts God and never doubts that everything a man does in faith is well done in God's sight. . . . For the
works are acceptable not for their own sake but because of faith."[32]
"They are good because of faith, which abandons itself to this
same mercy."[33]

This is the Christian life about which Luther is concerned. It
is the fruit of what we have called a theology to live by. It is faith
active through love in the service of our fellow men to the glory of
God. Now let the Christian beware! In his struggle to rise to this
kind of Christian living, he is liable to fall into the very error that
Luther was fighting: If I will only do what lies within me, per-
chance I can gain the favor of God and thus be sure of my justifi-

cation. Here and every step of the way Luther reminds the Christian that his faith and his Christian living, his justification and his sanctification, all are the work of the Holy Spirit, all are the gift of God. He is the one who justifies us, declares us righteous through faith in Jesus Christ. He is the one who sanctifies us, "makes us holy," as Luther says.

This work of the Holy Spirit, which Luther according to Scriptural terminology calls *sanctification*, receives the full treatment in his explanation of the Third Article of the Apostles' Creed. This article, he says, deals with sanctification, teaching that the Holy Ghost

> makes holy. . . . For as the Father is called Creator, the Son Redeemer, so the Holy Ghost, from His work, must be called Sanctifier, or One that makes holy. . . . Just as the Son obtains dominion, whereby He wins us, through His birth, death, resurrection, etc., so also the Holy Ghost effects our sanctification by the following parts, namely, by the communion of saints or the Christian Church, the forgiveness of sins, the resurrection of the body, and the life everlasting; that is, He first leads us into His holy congregation, and places us in the bosom of the Church, whereby He preaches to us and brings us to Christ.[34]

And this bringing us to Christ is not only the initial work of regeneration or justification in Baptism, but it marks the continuing work of the Holy Spirit in the justified man. "For now we are only half pure and holy, so that the Holy Ghost has ever [some reason why] to continue His work in us through the Word, and daily to dispense forgiveness, until we attain to that life where there will be no more forgiveness, but only pure and holy people. . . ."[35]

Possibly the best description Luther ever gave of the Holy Spirit's work of sanctification is the one he gives in his treatise *On the Councils and Churches.*

For Christian holiness, or the holiness common to
Christendom, is found where the Holy Spirit gives people faith in Christ and thus sanctifies them, Acts 15 [:9],
that is, he renews heart, soul, body, work, and conduct,
inscribing the commandments of God not on tables of
stone, but in hearts of flesh, II Corinthians 3 [:3]. Or, if I
may speak plainly, he imparts true knowledge of God,
according to the first table, so that those whom he
enlightens with true faith can resist all heresies, overcome all false ideas and errors, and thus remain pure in
faith in opposition to the devil. He also bestows strength,
and comforts timid, despondent, weak consciences
against the accusation and turmoil of sin, so that the
souls do not succumb or despair, and also do not
become terrified of torment, pain, death, and the wrath
and judgment of God, but rather, comforted and
strengthened in hope, they cheerfully, boldly, and joyfully overcome the devil. He also imparts true fear and
love of God, so that we do not despise God and become
irritated and angry with his wondrous judgments, but
love, praise, thank, and honor him for all that occurs,
good or evil. This is called new holy life in the soul, in
accordance with the first table of Moses. It is also called
tres virtutes theologicas, "the three principal virtues of
Christians," namely, faith, hope, and love; and the Holy
Spirit, who imparts, does, and effects this (gained for us
by Christ) is therefore called "sanctifier" or "life-giver."[36]

Luther's emphasis here is clearly on the spiritual life that the
Spirit creates and maintains. But this inner life must be reflected
in the life we live in the physical world. This, too, is the work of the
Spirit.

In accordance with the second table, He also sanctifies
the Christians in the body and induces them willingly to
obey parents and rulers, to conduct themselves peace-
fully and humbly, to be not wrathful, vindictive, or mali-
cious, but patient, friendly, obliging, brotherly, and lov-

ing, not unchaste, not adulterous or lewd, but chaste and
pure with wife, child, and servants, or without wife and
child. And on and on: they do not steal, are not usurious,
avaricious, do not defraud, etc., but work honorably,
support themselves honestly, lend willingly, and give and
help wherever they can. Thus they do not lie, deceive,
and backbite, but are kind, truthful, faithful, and trustworthy, and do whatever else the commandments of
God prescribe. That is the work of the Holy Spirit, who
sanctifies and also awakens the body to such a new life
until it is perfected in the life beyond. That is what is
called "Christian holiness."[37]

Faith, love, good works, all this is the work of the Holy Spirit
in us. We believe, we love, we serve, all by the power of the Spirit.
"And being accepted and justified as to our person, love is given us
in the Holy Spirit and we delight in doing good."[38] The Law
demands this, says Luther, but "we cannot do good works without
the Spirit and love." Justification, forgiveness, and faith always lie
in the background of this good life. "We must be changed in person and justified before we can love and do good works. Our love
and our works are evidence of justification and of a change, since
they are impossible until the individual is free from sin and made
righteous." Or, looking at it from another side, "Faith, when it
comes, creates a nature capable of accomplishing the works the
Law demands. Thus is the Law fulfilled." Lest this statement be
misunderstood, it must be balanced by what Luther says immediately afterwards, that Law, faith, and love each have their own
"mission," and we must rightly "understand the Scripture declara-
tions in their harmonious relations that while faith justifies, it
does not fulfil the Law, and that while love does not justify, it does
fulfil the Law. . . . So love in its fulfilment of the Law after faith
intervenes is a sign and a proof to the individual of his faith and
righteousness."[39]

In his study of Galatians Luther is constantly aware of the
apostle's threefold appeal. It is a call to faith, to love, and to good

works. And while faith is always the starting point of the Christian life, Luther never lets it be divorced from its fruits: love and good works. St. Paul's call to social action naturally reaches its climax in the later chapters of the Epistle. But Luther does not wait that long in his commentary. After an intensive discussion of faith under Galatians 2:16, he pauses to emphasize the social implications of this faith.

> When we have taught faith in Christ this way, then we also teach about good works. Because you have taken hold of Christ by faith, through whom you are righteous, you should now go and love God and your neighbor. Call upon God, give thanks to Him, preach Him, praise Him, confess Him. Do good to your neighbor, and serve him; do your duty. These are truly good works, which flow from this faith and joy conceived in the heart because we have the forgiveness of sins freely through Christ.[40]

Through all of this shines the theology of the cross. The Epistle to the Galatians rises gradually to a powerful call to social action. "Let us not grow weary of doing good. . . . let us do good to everyone" (Galatians 6:9–10). But St. Paul says nothing about social action until he has been at Calvary. "I have been crucified with Christ" (Galatians 2:20). There and there alone is the dynamic of love kindled that drives a man out into the world to help and serve his fellow men. No whipping or prodding by the demands of the Law will drive a man to this kind of Christian living for others. On the contrary, Luther says,

> direct your attention to the point at issue here, namely, that Jesus Christ, the Son of God, dies on the cross and bears my sin, the Law, death, the devil, and hell in His body. . . . Afterwards, when Christ has thus been grasped by faith and I am dead to the Law, justified from sin, and delivered from death, the devil, and hell through Christ—then I do good works, love God, give thanks, and practice love toward my neighbor.[41]

It is the Holy Spirit who through the Cross fans the spark of faith into a flame of love and good works toward the neighbor. "For the believer has the Holy Spirit; and where He is, He does not permit a man to be idle but drives him to all the exercises of devotion, to the love of God, to patience in affliction, to prayer, to thanksgiving, and to the practice of love toward all men."[42] This is the meaning of St. Paul's "faith working through love" (Galatians 5:6). "That is, as Erasmus shows from the Greek, a faith which is powerfully active, not one that snores once it has been 'acquired' or one that is strong through miracles but one that is powerfully active through love."[43]

Luther never tired of preaching this "faith working through love." It is never faith only, never love only, but faith and love together, the touchstone of the Christian life. Sunday after Sunday, year after year, his followers at worship heard him pour forth this Gospel of the cross—this theology to live by. And his appeal for Christian living in faith and love was never more forcefully put than in the First Wittenberg Sermon of March 9, 1522. Let Luther preach to us as he did to them.

> [W]e must also have love and through love we must do to one another as God has done to us through faith. For without love faith is nothing, as St. Paul says (I Cor. 2 [13:1]). . . . And here, dear friends, have you not grievously failed? I see no signs of love among you, and I observe very well that you have not been grateful to God for his rich gifts and treasures.
>
> Here let us beware lest Wittenberg become Capernaum [cf. Matt. 11:23]. I notice that you have a great deal to say of the doctrine of faith and love which is preached to you, and this is no wonder; an ass can almost intone the lessons, and why should you not be able to repeat the doctrines and formulas? Dear friends, the kingdom of God,—and we are that kingdom—does not consist in talk or words [I Cor. 4:20], but in activity, in deeds, in works and exercises. God does not want hearers and

repeaters of words [Jas. 1:22], but followers and doers, and this occurs in faith through love. For a faith without love is not enough—rather it is not faith at all, but a counterfeit of faith, just as a face seen in a mirror is not a real face, but merely the reflection of a face [I Cor. 13:12].[44]

This lifts the plane of Christian life to glorious heights. No philosophy of life has ever touched it. There is no doubt that here lies one of the secrets of Luther's power and influence. In his heart were two great loves: the love of truth and the love of men; and behind them both a burning love for his Lord. He reveled in his Christian freedom. Refusing to be hemmed in by laws and commandments, he lived a free and triumphant Christian life that proclaimed to the world, "I can do all things through Him who strengthens me" (Philippians 4:13). "Who then can comprehend the riches and the glory of the Christian life? It can do all things and has all things and lacks nothing. It is lord over sin, death, and hell, and yet at the same time it serves, ministers to, and benefits all men."[45]

That First Wittenberg Sermon is as relevant today as it was way back there. This theology of the cross is a theology to live by for every generation. True love originates in the heart of God. Its great manifestation is the cross, where Christ dies, not for the righteous but for sinners. He prayed for those who crucified Him, even as He said, "I came not to call the righteous, but sinners" (Matthew 9:13). And this, says Luther, "is the love of the cross, born of the cross, which turns in the direction where it does not find good which it may enjoy, but where it may confer good upon the bad and needy person."[46] Anders Nygren has summed it up in two neat sentences, "Only at the Cross do we find God, but there we really find Him. '*Theologia crucis*' is the only true theology."[47]

CHAPTER NINE

THE LIFE WE RECEIVE— THE MEANS OF GRACE

To accomplish His purpose of bringing us to faith and into His kingdom, God uses visible means and signs. This element in Luther's theology was fully developed in his struggle with the "enthusiasts," people he today might have called the radical left—men like Zwingli, Karlstadt, and Muenzer.

"Enthusiasts" (*Schwaermer*) is a loose term that Luther could apply to all who in any way separate the activity of the Holy Spirit from the Word and the Sacraments. He uses the term also of those who fail to distinguish the two realms or kingdoms of God's activity, between His preserving and His redeeming work, between Law and Gospel. Thus he can apply the name to his opponents all the way from Calvin and Zwingli to Karlstadt, Muenzer and the Zwickau prophets, Anabaptists, and many others. Ernst Troeltsch sees this humanist theology, this sectarian Anabaptism, and this individualist-subjectivist spiritualism as the

forerunner of modern, liberal, individualistic Protestantism.[1] Karl
Holl holds that Anabaptism, mysticism, and spiritualism all
belong to the same family.[2] George Williams speaks of "the
Lutheran and Zwinglian movement and its analogues across the
Channel and elsewhere as the Magisterial Reformation or, when
one has in mind more its doctrine than its manner of establish-
ment, as classical Protestantism." On the one side stand the
Lutherans and the Reformed (the Zwinglians and the Calvinists).
On the other side are the exponents of the radical Reformation:
Anabaptists, spiritualists, and rationalists, who oppose "the
Lutheran-Zwinglian-Calvinist forensic formulation of justifica-
tion" and their doctrine of original sin and predestination.[3]

These *Schwaermer*, as Luther called them, held that the Holy
Spirit works His miracles of grace directly in a person and not necessarily through the means of grace: Word and Sacrament. In his
treatise *Against the Heavenly Prophets in the Matter of Images and
Sacraments* Luther exposes their error in some of his picturesque
language. He explains that God deals with us in a twofold manner,
first outwardly, then inwardly. "Outwardly he deals with us
through the oral word of the gospel and through material signs,
that is, baptism and the sacrament of the altar. Inwardly he deals
with us through the Holy Spirit, faith, and other gifts. . . . The
inward experience follows and is effected by the outward."[4] And
here Luther lays down one of the most significant principles in his
theology. "For he wants to give no one the Spirit or faith outside of
the outward Word and sign instituted by him, as he says in Luke 16
[:29], 'Let them hear Moses and the prophets.' Accordingly Paul can
call baptism a 'washing of regeneration' wherein God 'richly pours
out the Holy Spirit' [Titus 3:5]. And the oral gospel 'is the power of
God for salvation to every one who has faith' (Rom. 1:[16])."[5]

This is where Luther finds the enthusiast in error. For he
"seeks to subordinate God's outward order to an inner spiritual
one." He does not look to the Gospel for the reception of the
Spirit,

but to some imaginary realm, saying: Remain in "self abstraction" where I now am and you will have the same experience. A heavenly voice will come, and God himself will speak to you. . . . With all his mouthing of the words, "Spirit, Spirit, Spirit," he tears down the bridge, the path, the way, the ladder, and all the means by which the Spirit might come to you.[6]

How does God save the sinner? The answer of Scripture, says Luther, is that He does it through the means of grace, the Word and the Sacraments, and in no other way. We meet the same language in *The Smalcald Articles*. "[W]e must firmly hold that God grants His Spirit or grace to no one, except through or with the preceding outward Word, in order that we may [thus] be protected against the enthusiasts, *i.e.*, spirits who boast that they have the Spirit without and before the Word. . . . "[7] Luther does not limit this power to the spoken Word, as we shall see in the discussion of the Word of God. Whether spoken or written, heard or read, the Word of God is a means of grace. So are Baptism and the Lord's Supper, which will require our special attention. For it is the same Gospel that meets us in the Word and in the Sacraments. It is the same Christ who comes to us in all of them. It is the same Holy Spirit who works His miracles of grace through all of them, bringing sinners to repentance and faith, uniting them with Christ, and ushering them into the kingdom of God and into the life eternal. All this, says Luther, happens in the Church through the administration of the Keys of the Kingdom.

1. The Word of God

Luther believes that God speaks to us in four different ways. The term "Word of God" may refer to

1. Jesus Christ, the Word of God Incarnate, the Logos of John 1:1–14;

2. The written Word of God, Holy Scripture, the Bible;

3. The spoken Word of God;

4. The sacramental Word of God in Baptism and the Sacrament of the Altar.

In all of these God speaks to us, addresses us. In all of them we are confronted by Jesus Christ. He is the Word of God in the most profound and basic sense. He is the "Word of Life" that, St. John says, "we have heard, which we have seen with our eyes, which we have looked upon and touched with our hands" (1 John 1:1). Luther comments on this verse: "[T]he Word, who is God's only-begotten Son, rested in the bosom of the Father and revealed Him to us. . . . To say that He, in His divine essence, is the Word of the eternal Father is a sublime way of introducing the discussion of the divine nature and majesty of our dear Lord and Savior Jesus Christ."[8]

Luther uses the term "Word of God" as Scripture does, sometimes with specific emphasis on the personal Word, Jesus Christ, or on the written Word of Scripture, or on the preached Word, or on the sacramental Word, sometimes embracing any or all of these meanings. But whether he is referring more particularly to the written Word or the spoken Word or the sacramental Word, he is also always speaking of the Word made flesh. For the written, spoken, or sacramental Word is the Word of God only for two reasons: first, because God is speaking through it, and second, because its content and message is Jesus Christ, the Word made flesh. It is nevertheless perfectly clear that Luther sometimes is speaking specifically of Holy Scripture in using the term "Word of God." Or he may be referring to the Word or words that Jesus speaks or that any preacher or Christian speaks. As to distinguishing between Christ and the Word spoken by Christ or by a minister, Luther says,

> The first is the Word Incarnate, which was true God from the beginning. This Word has been revealed. This Word is substantially God. But that Word (spoken) is effectively God; it is the power and the virtue of God, but

> not substantially God. For it is characteristic of man, whether of Christ or of the minister. Nevertheless it accomplishes what it says. For through this instrument God deals with us and does everything and offers us all his treasures.[9]

In all three instances it is the Word of God, God's address to man, Christ's confrontation of man, a means of grace. The same is true of the written Word or of the sacramental Word.

In Luther's thinking, therefore, it is futile to try to measure the relative power of the Word in these four forms, or to suggest that one is the living Word, the other is not. The Word of God to Luther is a living Word in whichever of these forms it comes to us. To say that the spoken Word is the living Word, the written Word a dead Word, has no foundation in Luther's theology. When Luther insists that ministers preach the Word of God, he means that they are to preach what God says in the Holy Scriptures. In this way the written Word of Scripture holds a certain priority over the preached Word. For the authority of the sermon lies where Jesus and St. Paul put it with that word that closed every argument: *gegraptai*, it is written. The prophet said, "Thus saith the Lord." St. Paul said, "It is written." The preacher today according to Luther must be able to say, "Thus saith the Lord." But no one should believe him unless he can also say, "It is written." Luther says this in a thousand different ways. The Church is our holy mother and our teacher. The voice of the minister is the voice of the Church. His life can be sinful and untrue. Indeed life is "very untrue—but doctrine must be straight as a plumb line, sure, and without sin. Therefore nothing must be preached in church except the sure, pure, and one word of God." This is the Word the preacher finds in Scripture. "[T]he church must teach God's word alone, and must be sure of it. . . . But whatever else is taught or whatever is not with certainty God's word, cannot be the doctrine of the church, but must be the doctrine, falsehood, and idolatry of the devil."[10]

The written Word of Scripture is thus the *Urkunde*, the source, the well of living water from which the preacher draws in order that his word may be the *living* Word of God. Scripture is the Word of God in a basic sense, because there God says what He wants to say exactly the way He wants it said. He says it through men, but through men who are His chosen and uniquely "inspired" men, who say in their own way what God wants them to say. Luther accepts without question the age-old doctrine of the Church of an *inspired* and *infallible* (or *inerrant*) Scripture. Some contemporary scholars who reject this doctrine themselves attempt to prove that Luther rejected it. As evidence they invariably cite his reference to the Epistle of St. James as a "straw epistle." This only indicates that he had questions about the canon. But whatever that canon was, he had no doubts about its divine inspiration and inerrancy. And this he applied to the entire Bible, Old Testament as well as New. For the Bible is one Book, and God is the Author. "Scripture is His own witness concerning Himself."[11] It is written by men, yet it is not *Menschenlehre*, human teaching, for both the writers and what they wrote were inspired by God. "[M]en spoke from God as they were carried along by the Holy Spirit" (2 Peter 1:21), and what they wrote, too, is "breathed out by God" (2 Timothy 3:16).[12] Luther comments on this passage that the Holy Scripture is "inspired and taught by God Himself." And to have this faith in Scripture as God's own Word is to Luther part of our Christian faith. "Oh, if we could only believe that God Himself is speaking to us in the Scripture!"[13]

In all of this Luther shows how completely he rejects the popular contemporary idea that the Bible is merely a human book. It is a human book, but much more, since the men whom God chose to write it were under the guidance of the Holy Spirit and were "moved" by Him as they wrote. Hence it is also a divine Book, "the *verbum Dei infallible*," as Luther calls it.[14] Since it is God's Word and since God is speaking through it, Luther can come to no other conclusion than that it is infallible, without error. In fact, he makes no problem of this. He takes it for granted, taking Scripture's own testimony at face value. With this article of faith, together with the fact that Scripture is "the manger in which Christ lies," we can understand Luther's utter dependence upon Scripture as the absolute truth, the final and absolute authority.

This did not mean that to Luther the Bible was a static sort of encyclopedia, a musty sourcebook where he could find the answer to all questions. No, the written Word, like the preached Word, is the dynamic and powerful Word of God, which is "living and active, sharper than any two-edged sword" (Hebrews 4:12). It is the power of God whether it is written or spoken, read or heard. Luther condemns those who call the written Word a dead thing. He rails against the spirits "swarming everywhere . . . who regard Scripture as a dead letter, extolling nothing but the spirit and yet keeping neither the Word nor the spirit. But there you hear how St. Paul uses Scripture as his strongest witness and shows that there is nothing solid to support our doctrine and faith except the material or written Word, put down in letters and preached verbally by him and others; for there it is clearly stated: 'Scripture, Scripture.'"[15]

Throughout his writings we find Luther speaking indiscriminately of the written and spoken Word as the living Word of God through which the Holy Spirit works His miracles of grace. He sees himself in the company of St. John fighting the enthusiasts who want to separate the Spirit from the Word. And that means the Word of God, whether written or spoken. For he quotes John 17:20 ("I do not pray for these only, but also for those who believe in Me through their Word") and adds, "Certainly through the spoken or written Word, not through the internal Word." Therefore, he says, it is necessary to "listen to and read the Word, which is the vehicle of the Holy Spirit. When the Word is read, the Holy Spirit is present; and thus it is impossible either to listen to or to read Scripture without profit."[16]

St. John is a prime witness to Luther of the power of the written Word as a means of grace. St. John says, "I write these things to you who believe in the name of the Son of God that you may know that you have eternal life" (1 John 5:13). Luther turns this against the "fanatics." "To them the letter is something dead on paper. But John says: 'I am writing to you'; for Scripture must serve the purpose of bringing it about that his epistle is a means and a vehicle by which one comes to faith and eternal life." Luther then quotes John 20:31 ("These are written that you may believe") and explains: "Accordingly, we should know that God's testimony does not come to us except through the spoken Word or through Scripture."[17] The apostle, too, bears witness to the Scripture as the "living Word": "Until I come, devote yourself to the public reading of Scripture, to exhortation, to teaching" (1 Timothy 4:13). "Why," says Luther, "do they themselves produce and write books if the letter avails and profits nothing?"

Because the written Word of Scripture is the *living* Word of God, Luther's logical conclusion is that we must constantly be occupied with the Word, reading it, hearing it, remembering it, meditating upon it.

> [I]t is an exceedingly effectual help against the devil, the world, and the flesh and all evil thoughts to be occupied with the Word of God, and to speak of it, and meditate upon it. . . . Undoubtedly, you will not start a stronger incense or other fumigation against the devil than by being engaged upon God's commandments and words. . . . For this is indeed the true holy water and holy sign from which he flees, and by which he may be driven away.[18]

For this reason alone, we ought to "read, speak, think and treat of these things." In other words, there is nothing more important for the Christian for the sanctification of life than to meditate upon the Word of God in Scripture. God Himself enjoins us (in Deut. 6:6 ff.) "that we should always meditate upon His precepts, sitting,

walking, standing, lying down, and rising, and have them before
our eyes and in our hands as a constant mark and sign."[19] This is
the way the Holy Spirit accomplishes our sanctification. "At whatever
hour, then, God's Word is taught, preached, heard, read or
meditated upon, there the person, day, and work are sanctified
... because of the Word."[20] Meditation on the Word is sure to bear
fruit, because "such is the efficacy of the Word, whenever it is seriously
contemplated, heard, and used, that it is bound never to be
without fruit, but always awakens new understanding, pleasure,
and devoutness, and produces a pure heart and pure thoughts. For
these words are not inoperative or dead, but creative, living
words."[21] Here again is a theology to live by.

Since it is the Gospel that is "the power of God unto salvation,"
it is the Gospel particularly that is the object and content of
our meditation. And this is the Gospel that shines through the
entire Scripture, Old Testament as well as New. For there is only
one Gospel, and its content is Christ. Luther never ceases to exalt
the Old Testament and to condemn those who downgrade it.[22] To
meditate on the Word of God is to contemplate the Gospel wherever
it is found in Scripture, whether in Genesis or in the Prophets
or in the New Testament. Scripture is one, and it proclaims one
Gospel, one Christ. The New Testament is based on the Old, and
the evangelists and apostles build on the Old. "Everything that the
apostles taught and wrote they drew out of the Old Testament; for
there is proclaimed everything which Christ should do and preach
in the future." Luther learns this from St. Paul, who says to the
Romans that God proclaimed the Gospel of His Son beforehand
through the prophets in the Holy Scriptures. "Therefore they base
all their preaching on the Old Testament, and there is no word in
the New Testament that does not refer back to the Old Testament
in which it was previously proclaimed."[23]

It is Christ who binds the two Testaments together into the
one unified revelation of God, proclaiming one Gospel, one way
of salvation, one faith accomplished by the one Holy Spirit.

Luther's interpretation of the Old Testament is consistently Christocentric. Moses, the prophets, the psalms, and the historical
books all point to Christ. Luther does not lose himself in allegory.
He interprets the Old Testament stories first literally in their historical setting and as part of holy history, then spiritually in their
relation to Christ. It is the Lord Himself who teaches us the right
way of interpreting Moses and the prophets. "He teaches us that
Moses points and refers to Christ in all his stories and illustra-
tions." Yes, Luther goes so far as to say that "all the stories of Holy
Writ, if viewed aright, point to Christ."[24] All the prophets are concerned about the same thing: "to see the future Christ or his future
kingdom. All of their prophecies are centered in this. . . . "[25]

The Psalms likewise proclaim the Gospel of Christ, the resurrection and life eternal.

> At this point we should learn the rule that whenever in
> the Psalter and Holy Scripture the saints deal with God
> concerning comfort and help in their need, eternal life
> and the resurrection of the dead are involved. All such
> texts belong to the doctrine of the resurrection and eter-
> nal life, in fact, to the whole Third Article of the Creed
> with the doctrines of the Holy Spirit, the Holy Christian
> Church, the forgiveness of sins, the resurrection, and
> everlasting life.[26]

It has become proverbial to call the Psalter "the prayer book
of the church." No one has understood that better than Luther.
And no one will understand it unless he sees what Luther saw, that
the heart and marrow and message of the Psalter is Christ.
Luther's simple faith radiates beautifully from his exposition of
Psalm 8, with his charming introduction: "We want to talk a little
about our dear Lord and Savior Jesus Christ. . . . To give us an
occasion to talk about Him, we shall take up the Eighth Psalm of
David, which was written about our Lord Jesus Christ, and follow
the example of this prophet as he prophesies to us."[27] Then comes

one of those rich Christocentric interpretations so characteristic of Luther's commentary on the Psalter.

> This Psalm is one of the beautiful psalms and a glorious prophecy about Christ, where David describes Christ's person and kingdom and teaches who Christ is; what kind of kingdom He has and how it is formed; where this King rules, namely, in all lands and yet in heaven; and the means by which His kingdom is founded and regulated, namely, only through the Word and faith, without sword and armor.[28]

Luther sees a profound kinship between New Testament Christians and the Old Testament people of God. For we share a common faith, theirs in the Christ who is to come, ours in the One who has come. From St. Paul (Romans 4) he learns that Abraham is indeed "the father of us all" (Romans 4:16), and we "share the faith of Abraham." The whole doctrine of justification the apostle bases on God's dealing with Abraham who "believed God, and it was counted to him as righteousness. . . . But the words, 'it was counted to him,' were not written for his sake alone, but for ours also. It will be counted to us who believe in Him who raised from the dead Jesus our Lord, who was delivered up for our trespasses and raised for our justification" (Romans 4:3, 23–25). The faith of Abraham and all the Old Testament saints was the faith in Christ that justifies the sinner. The blessing promised to Abraham "is simply that grace and salvation in Christ proclaimed to the whole world through the Gospel." All the prophets, says Luther, "wrote about the coming of Christ, His grace and Gospel."[29] Abraham "had the same faith which we have. There is one faith, one Spirit, one Christ, one fellowship of all saints; only they preceded Christ, we come after Him."[30]

From all this we can understand why Luther was so enamored of the Old Testament and why he insisted that it be not neglected in our contemplation of Christ in Scripture. For our meditation must get to the heart of the Gospel, which is the cross.

And Luther finds the Passion and crucifixion of our Lord nowhere more vividly described than in Isaiah 53.

The secret of effective meditation lies in the believer's confidence that through the Word he is reading or recalling what God is speaking to him. Luther had a double-barreled formula: *Deus dixit* and *Deus loquens*, God has spoken, and God is still speaking through His Word. And this is a dynamic, Spirit-filled speaking. For when God speaks to us, He comes to us in the very Word He is speaking. When we believe the Word He speaks, we believe Him. When we put our faith in what He says, we are putting our trust in Him. There can be no talk of faith in God apart from faith in what He says. *Gegraptai* means "it stands written." Everything Jesus said and did was "according to the Scriptures." Everything the apostles preached, they preached "according to the Scriptures." Everything the Church believes, it believes "according to the Scriptures." In the Nicene Creed we confess that we believe "in one Lord Jesus Christ. . . . And the third day He rose again according to the Scriptures. . . . And I believe in the Holy Ghost . . . who spake by the Prophets." Who will give less authority to the Scriptures than Christ and the apostles and the Church give them?

We have seen that in Luther the written Word of God in Scripture is a living Word, where God is speaking to us as we read, confronting us, addressing us. This existential aspect of the Word of God is also true of the spoken or preached Word. Luther is of course aware that in the history of the Church there is good evidence that many more people have been brought to faith by hearing the Word preached than by reading it in Scripture. The command of the Lord is unequivocal. The Word of God must be preached. "Faith comes by hearing." The Bible is no mere talisman that can lie closed on a shelf and radiate its magic power, transforming a home. Its message must be heard or read.

Luther must have sensed the urgency of the Lord's command to go and preach the Gospel. For all his life he was busy preaching the Word of God, whether from his pulpit in Wittenberg or from pulpits and platforms and supper tables around the country. Preaching the Word to Luther meant preaching the Gospel of Jesus Christ. But it meant preaching the "whole counsel of God," Law and Gospel. For the aim of preaching and the goal of every sermon was to bring people to repentance and faith, and then to Christian living for the benefit of the neighbor and to the glory of God.

With this goal of preaching always before him, Luther knew that he must stick to preaching the Word of God from Scripture and not the word of men or human opinions about human affairs. For immortal souls were at stake. This was serious business to Luther. "These two facts are entirely logical: that those who preach the Word of God must necessarily be sent by God; and, conversely, that those who are sent by God cannot proclaim anything but the Word of God." But what man is capable of this? "It is impossible to derive the Word of God from reason; it must be given from above."[31] Luther was convinced that he was sent by God to preach and that the message he preached was given him by God. As long as he faithfully preached the Word from Scripture he could maintain a cool confidence that through his preaching God would accomplish His purpose in the hearers. Preach the Word, he told himself and other preachers, and leave the results to God. The abandon with which Luther applied this principle is illustrated in his Second Wittenberg Sermon. "I simply taught, preached, and wrote God's Word; otherwise I did nothing. And while I slept [cf. Mark 4:26–29], or drank Wittenberg beer with my friends Philip and Amsdorf, the Word so greatly weakened the papacy that no prince or emperor ever inflicted such losses upon it. I did nothing; the Word did everything."[32]

We begin to understand this confidence in the power of his preaching when we read Luther's sermons. For they are invariably concerned with the central facts of our faith and life and revolve around Christ and the loving plan of God for our salvation. He has no patience with any preaching that does not move within this frame. "[N]othing but God's Word alone should be preached in Christendom. The reason for this is no other, as we have said, than this, that a Word must be proclaimed that remains eternally—a Word through which souls may be saved and may live forever."[33]

Luther chastises not only the preachers who presume to solve all the problems of society from their pulpits, but he chides also the people for their itching ears, by which they drive their pastors to this kind of preaching. He pictures a peasant coming to him and saying: "You proclaim God's Word, you preach about God the Creator and about Christ the Redeemer. But this is not enough for me. I want you to supplement your sermon with a pronouncement that ten groschen should be the price of a bushel of grain." Luther would answer the peasant: "Go and consult the market about that."[34] No, says Luther, this is not what he was sent to preach. "Here on this pulpit it is our duty to preach the Word which has not been invented by man but has been sent from heaven. Then a Christian can say that he derived his faith and message, not from the philosophers of Persia, Greece, or Rome but from the Word of God, which came from heaven."[35]

We meet Luther here as a great teacher of preachers. He gives them confidence in the effectiveness of their message and inspires them to stick to their knitting and, like St. Paul, to preach the Word in season and out of season. But while he is encouraging the faithful preacher to trust the power of the Word he is preaching, he wants no negotiation with the milk-toast preacher who is uncertain both of his message and of its power. "A preacher should neither pray the Lord's Prayer nor ask for forgiveness of sins when he has preached (if he is a true preacher), but should say and boast with Jeremiah, 'Lord thou knowest that which came out of my lips is true and pleasing to thee' [Jer. 17:16]." He should say like the apostles: "*Haec dixit Dominus*, 'God Himself has said this.' " He should dare to say, "In this sermon I have been an apostle and a prophet of Jesus Christ [I Thess. 4:15]." Don't ask for forgiveness as if you had not taught the truth, "for it is God's Word and not my word, and God ought not and cannot forgive it, but only con-firm, praise, and crown it, saying, 'You have taught truly, for I have spoken through you and the word is mine.' Whoever cannot boast like that about his preaching, let him give up preaching, for he truly lies and slanders God."[36]

A preacher who has this confidence that he is preaching the Word of God, and therefore the truth, will inspire confidence in his hearers. It will be easier for them to get the idea that God is confronting them and addressing them. And His address is a call to faith and action. Where this response occurs, there is salvation. Where the response is unbelief and inaction, there is judgment. For this Word of the Gospel is a "living Word" in and through which the Spirit is active, calling, convicting, converting to faith, sanctifying, and saving those who hear. It is a living Word because its content is the risen and living Christ, and it is the "power of God unto salvation" today just as it was when Jesus walked on the earth as the living Word calling men to life in Him. Our preaching of the Gospel is the living Word because it proclaims the event of Calvary and the resurrection as our redemption and applies it to sinners everywhere and at all times.

And this "event of Calvary" is not something that first hap-pens in the consciousness of the hearer of the Gospel. It happened 1,900 years ago, and that happening is the Good News the Church proclaims. The cross to Luther, like the resurrection, is history. It is not only an "eschatological event." The existential element was heavy in Luther's preaching, but he never allowed God's act in his-tory to be overshadowed by it. Schniewind put his finger on the danger of an overemphasis on the existential factor when he said, "Everything Bultmann says about the cross is located not at Cal-vary but in our human experience. His talk about 'the legend of the empty tomb' makes Easter Day not the resurrection itself but the beginning of the disciples' faith in the resurrection."[37] Luther showed a remarkable balance in his preaching between the histor-ical and the existential elements. He did not lose the "then" in an overemphasis on the "now." He allowed no one to forget the *Deus dixit* in his enthusiasm for the *Deus loquens*. The redemption has been accomplished, and it is bestowed as a gift on every sinner when he comes to faith through the Word. And at this point the written Word, the spoken Word, and the sacramental Word merge in the one Word, the Gospel.

Every true preacher strives, like Luther, to make his preaching contemporaneous, to bring Christ's incarnation, crucifixion, and resurrection into the present. He lives in the written Word. He preaches the Gospel that he finds there. He contemplates the old story of our redemption. Then like St. Paul he "placards" Christ before the eyes of his hearers (Galatians 3:1). He takes us back to the first Christmas: "For unto you is born this day in the city of David a Savior, who is Christ the Lord" (Luke 2:11). Then he brings this Christmas into the present: "Behold, now is the favorable time; behold, now is the day of salvation" (2 Corinthians 6:2). Paul Althaus, no mean Luther scholar, brings this out forcibly in a discussion of history and proclamation.

> Although the history of Jesus Christ is once-for-all, finished, by-gone history, it has nevertheless contemporaneity for us, for in the proclamation of the church it confronts us with a contemporary address. In this it differs from all other history. To other history we gain a relationship by studying its sources and presentation. It becomes for us an experience in culture. But it is otherwise with this history. True, it is borne witness to in the Holy Scriptures and has been transmitted in many books since the origin of Scripture. But Holy Scripture may not be placed alongside other historical sources and presentations. It is from beginning to end only a unique form of Christian witness. What John says at the end of his Gospel is true of all Biblical writings which present the history of Jesus: "written that ye might believe that Jesus is the Christ, the Son of God, and that, believing, ye might have life in His name" (John 20, 31). It belongs in

the category of Christian preaching which calls people to faith. . . . The Bible is not a sourcebook of ancient history which merely tells a bygone story. Rather, Scripture proclamation confronts and courts and claims me. And so past history confronts me in the present moment. . . . Therefore the history of Jesus ceases to be merely an historical fact of the past which one can recollect. . . . But rather the day of the proclamation is "the day of salvation."[38]

In the proclamation of the Gospel, therefore, the crucified and risen Lord confronts us, speaks to us, calls us. And the Word preached is a means of grace that God uses to make us what He wants us to be. The heart of the Word is the Gospel of the Lord Jesus Christ. It is God's Word of forgiveness. It is absolution. All this we have in the Church. "We further believe that in this Christian Church we have forgiveness of sin, which is wrought through the holy Sacraments and Absolution, moreover, through all manner of consolatory promises of the entire Gospel."[39]

2. THE SACRAMENTS

A. The Necessity of the Sacraments

"[W]e have yet to speak of our two Sacraments instituted by Christ, of which also every Christian ought to have at least an ordinary, brief instruction, because without them there can be no Christian."[40] This summary statement separates Luther from all Protestants, sectarians, and later Lutherans who de-emphasize the Sacraments. It again plants him squarely in the historic Catholic tradition. When he deals with the necessity of the sacraments in the Christian life, he is always positive. He has no interest in quibbling about exceptions or about the possibility that God might save someone without the Sacraments. The Word of God commands the Church to use them for our salvation. That is enough. Jesus says to go and to baptize: "Unless one is born of water and

the Spirit, he cannot enter the kingdom of God" (John 3:5). Then
He institutes the blessed sacrament of His body and blood and
says, "Do this in remembrance of Me" (Luke 22:19). So the
Church baptizes people into the life in Christ and feeds them with
the bread of life in the blessed Sacrament.

This position never causes Luther to minimize the supreme
importance of the Word of God. Without the Word there is no
Sacrament, there is only water, only bread and wine. But add the
Word of God and you have the Sacraments: Baptism and the
Sacrament of the Altar. And each of these is a means of grace, just
as the Word alone is a means of grace. Through them God works
His miracles of grace, creating the new life of faith and sustaining
it "till faith in vision end." "[B]y this means, and in no other way,
namely, through His holy Word, when men hear it preached or
read it, and the holy Sacraments when they are used according to
His Word, God desires to call men to eternal salvation, draw them
to Himself, and convert, regenerate, and sanctify them."[41]

The relation between Word and Sacrament and the relative
importance of the two have caused much debate. In the history of
the Church the pendulum has swung back and forth in giving
preeminence to one or the other. Various churches of Christendom reflect differing attitudes toward the problem. In the Roman
Catholic Church the Mass exalts the Sacrament. Until Vatican II
the preaching of the Word from the pulpit seems to have held a
relatively unimportant position. Many Protestant churches have
no altar, while the pulpit looms large. Preaching dominates the
service, while the Sacrament is relegated to a place of minor
importance.

Within Lutheranism there has been a wide range of emphasis. From Reformation to orthodoxy, from pietism to enlightenment, from neoorthodoxy to the liturgical revival, the pendulum
has swung to and fro. One can almost trace the change of emphasis in the interior architecture of the churches. Usually the altar
has the central focus according to historical tradition. Occasion-

ally the baptismal font dominates. In some churches the pulpit towers over the altar, a silent but powerful testimony to the relative importance of the two means of grace in the thinking of the time. In a prominent church in southern Germany the pews are ranged almost in a circle around the pulpit. The altar is in the distant background and not used except for an occasional celebration of the Eucharist. The worshipers enter the church and stand at their pews facing the pulpit for silent prayer, some turning their backs on the altar. In the old log church built at Muskego, Wisconsin, in 1845 by Norwegian Lutheran pioneers the pulpit is placed directly over the altar, reflecting the pietism out of which they came. The Sacrament must not be allowed to challenge the supremacy of the Word.

Luther felt that the balance between the Sacrament and the preached Word, which was characteristic of the Early Church, had been seriously upset in the Medieval Church. In the service, he says, "God's Word has been silenced, and only reading and singing remain in the churches."[42] The balance must be restored. Let the Sacrament remain as the climax of the service, but preaching of the Word must be revived. In his treatise *Concerning the Order of Public Worship* Luther even went so far as to say that "a Christian congregation should never gather together without the preaching of God's Word and prayer."[43]

When Luther in his teaching and practice reduced the number of sacraments from seven to two, the rationale is to be found in his definition of a sacrament. Not every ceremony or symbolic act of the Church is a sacrament. A sacrament must be instituted by God and must contain a visible "sign" and a Word of promise. The sign alone cannot make a sacrament, be it water or bread or wine. But let the Word of promise be added to the sign or element according to the command of the Lord, and you have a sacrament. "We have said that in every sacrament there is a word of divine promise, to be believed by whoever receives the sign, and that the sign alone cannot be a sacrament."[44]

With this definition, Luther could not give the name "sacrament" to marriage or confirmation or the other symbolic acts that the Roman Church called sacraments. "There is not even a divinely instituted sign in marriage, nor do we read anywhere that marriage was instituted by God to be a sign of anything."[45] Only Baptism and the Sacrament of the Altar could qualify as sacraments under this definition. "*Hence there are, strictly speaking, but two sacraments in the church of God—baptism and the bread.* For only in these two do we find both the divinely instituted sign and the promise of forgiveness of sins."[46]

It is true that the early Luther occasionally spoke of three sacraments: Baptism, the Lord's Supper, and penance. He uses this language in a letter to George Spalatin of December 18, 1519. Likewise in the treatise *The Babylonian Captivity of the Church* of 1520 he says, "*I must deny that there are seven sacraments, and for the present maintain that there are but three: baptism, penance, and the bread.*"[47] But before the treatise is finished he concludes, "The sacrament of penance, which I added to these two, lacks the divinely instituted visible sign, and is, as I have said, nothing but a way and a return to baptism."[48]

In the divine institution of the sacraments Luther sees further evidence of the goodness of God. Recognizing the fragility of our faith, He gives us a visible sign to make it easier for us to believe His Word of forgiveness. "True enough, he [the Lord] says, all this is external, but it is necessary and helpful to you, in order that you may have a definite image by which you can take hold of me, for you will never reach me in naked majesty; therefore I must present myself to you in these external images, in order that you may grasp me."[49] It is like the Incarnation, where the hidden God has revealed Himself in the incarnate Christ to make it easier for men to know God. "This has always been the custom of our Lord God, to put signs or ceremonies beside His Word. . . . That has always been the way of our Lord God, that not only should the ears hear, but the eyes should see."[50]

Luther makes it plain in all this that faith is "a necessary part of the sacrament."[51] Not that faith is constitutive of the Sacrament or determines its validity. The Sacrament is valid though faith be missing. But the blessing is lost, for faith receives the Sacrament and its blessing. Only presumptuous and stupid minds will conclude that "[w]here there is not the true faith, there also can be no true Baptism." Baptism remains valid "and retains its full essence, even though a single person should be baptized, and he, in addition, should not believe truly. For God's ordinance and Word cannot be made variable or be altered by men."[52] Nevertheless, Luther is careful to reject what he sees as the Roman idea that the Sacrament works *ex opere operato*, by the outward act, even if there be no faith.

The relation of faith and Sacrament has always been a major problem in Lutheran theology, and Luther himself realized that here we are involved in the mystery of faith. But one thing he is sure of: the answer must lie within the framework of grace alone. So in the Sacrament of the Altar he takes the words of institution and declares, "These words require and also convey faith, and also exercise it in all those who desire this sacrament, and do not act against it; just as Baptism also brings and gives faith, if it be desired."[53] This statement from the Schwabach Articles of Luther is reflected in Article 13 of the Augsburg Confession, which states that the sacraments were "instituted to awaken and confirm faith in those who use them."[54] This faith is no vague and general faith in God, but must also relate to the Sacrament and particularly to the promise in the Sacrament. "For to constitute a sacrament there must be above all things else a word of divine promise, by which faith may be exercised."[55]

Luther here leaves no room for the person who says, "I am a Christian and a member of the church. So I'll take Baptism and the Lord's Supper with the others, even though I don't believe this business about regeneration and about the real body and blood of Christ." For here is demanded what Melanchthon in the Apology

calls "special faith." Luther defines it in the Small Catechism when
he says, "[H]e that believes these words ['Given and shed for you
for the remission of sins'] has what they say and express, namely,
the forgiveness of sins. . . . he is truly worthy and well prepared
who has faith in these words: *Given, and shed for you, for the remission of sins*."[56] This means that those who gather at the Supper
must share the faith, not only a general faith in God, but faith in
the Sacrament itself and the promise connected with it. We reserve
discussion of this problem for a later chapter on the Sacrament of
the Altar.

Word or Sacrament, Luther knows he is dealing with the
Gospel. It is the Gospel that is "the power of God for salvation." It
is the Gospel that brings man into union with Christ and the life
with God. And this He accomplishes in the Church through the
means of grace, Word and Sacrament. "Gospel," then, appears as
the overarching concept. It must be so, for its content is Christ.
The broadness of the concept in Luther's thinking is expressed in
the Smalcald Articles, Part III, Article IV, which declares that the
Gospel

> offers counsel and help against sin in more than one way,
> for God is surpassingly rich in his grace: First, through
> the spoken word, by which the forgiveness of sin (the
> peculiar function of the Gospel) is preached to the whole
> world; second, through Baptism; third, through the holy
> Sacrament of the Altar; fourth, through the power of the
> keys; and finally, through the mutual conversation and
> consolation of brethren.[57]

The Gospel of God's grace and love in Christ looms ever
larger as Luther unfolds his doctrine of the sacraments. God wants
all men "to be saved and to come to the knowledge of the truth"
(1 Timothy 2:4). Maybe He could have accomplished this by giving us only His Word and by having the Gospel proclaimed to all
the world. But "by His superabundant grace our merciful Father
always placed some outward and visible sign of His grace along-

side the Word, so that men, reminded by the outward sign and
work or Sacrament, would believe with greater assurance that God
is kind and merciful."[58] Men in all ages weighed down by the bur-
den of guilt have cried out for forgiveness. And so "Baptism and
the Eucharist have been given as the visible signs of grace, so that
we might firmly believe that our sins have been forgiven through
Christ's suffering and that we have been redeemed by His death."[59]
Thus not only the naked Word of promise, but the sacraments
with their accompanying and constituting Word become the
object of faith. The believer "clings" to the Word, to his Baptism,
to the Eucharist, and to the promises contained therein. And
through each of them God kindles and strengthens faith. Luther
calls them "lightbearers today, toward which we look as depend-
able tokens of the sun of grace." For we can be perfectly sure that
"where the Eucharist, Baptism, and the Word are, there are Christ,
forgiveness of sins, and eternal life."[60] Luther most commonly uses
the term "signs of grace" (*Gnadenzeichen*). But these signs are also
"means of grace." For God has given men "signs by means of
which they might comfort themselves."[61] When we come to consider what Luther has to say about Baptism and the Eucharist,
there is no question that they are means through which God con-
veys His grace, forgiveness, life, and strength. Hence Luther could
call the Sacraments "effective signs" of grace.[62]

B. The Sacrament of Baptism

If Luther had given up the Church's historic doctrine of Baptism,
he would no longer have furnished us with a theology to live by.
For the theology of the cross is not complete without Baptism. A
theology to live by must have within it the wellsprings of life eternal. And in Luther's theology we are ushered into the life with
God through Holy Baptism. Luther took Jesus at His word. To
enter the kingdom and the life with God, one must be "born
again." More specifically, one must be born of "water and Spirit."
There was no question in Luther's mind that this referred to the
Church's Sacrament of Holy Baptism.

From the testimony of Scripture, of the Church's tradition, and of experience, Luther was compelled to speak of the *necessity* of Baptism for salvation. For it is *an institution of God*, confronting us with both His *command* and His *promise*. As instituted by God, Baptism has three parts. The first is water, "just natural water." The second is God's Word "beside and with the water." And this is the Word of Christ in Matthew 28:19, "Go therefore and make disciples of all nations, baptizing them in the name of the Father and of the Son and of the Holy Spirit." When these words are added to the water, it is no longer just natural water, "but a holy, divine, blessed water." Water and Word, like water and Spirit in John 3:5, belong together. "[T]he Word with and beside the water constitutes the substance of baptism." The third part necessary to make it a sacrament is the "institution or the Word which institutes and ordains baptism." Here Luther speaks of "two kinds of Word. . . . One which is spoken with the water or baptizing, the second that which orders and commands us to baptize in this way, that is, to immerse in water and to speak these words."[63] In the Smalcald Articles, Part III, Article V, he says simply, "Baptism is nothing else than the Word of God in the water, commanded by His institution, or, as Paul says, *a washing in the Word*."[64] The most concise definition of Baptism is probably the one in the Small Catechism, "Baptism is not simple water only, but it is the water comprehended in God's command and connected with God's Word."[65] And this is the Word of Christ in Matthew 28:19.

Because of this divine institution and command, together with other testimony of Scripture and of the Lord Himself, the Church has said that Baptism is necessary for salvation. Luther and his fellow reformers never repudiated this doctrine, but proclaimed it with great emphasis and wrote it into every one of the Lutheran Confessions. Luther never ceased to extol Baptism, and all through his life we hear him reveling in the fact that he was baptized. For in his baptism he knew that God entirely by His grace had given him a new birth, ushered him into His kingdom, forgiven his sin, delivered him from death and the devil, and granted him eternal salvation. For he had been baptized into Christ and into His death. This was a vital part of Luther's faith and the source of his greatest comfort. He was talking from experience when he professed in his treatise on *The Holy and Blessed Sacrament of Baptism* of 1519, "Therefore there is no greater comfort on earth than baptism. For it is through baptism that we come under the judgment of grace and mercy, which does not condemn our sins but drives them out by many trials."[66]

Luther now unfolds his great new emphasis, which is not new at all but which he feels has been buried in the Medieval Church. There is no disagreement on the initial blessing in Baptism as the washing of regeneration and initiation into the Church of Christ. But the blessing and power of Baptism do not cease here. Where a man has fallen away from his baptism Rome directs him to the sacrament of penance, as though his baptism had now lost its effectiveness or importance. Luther, on the other hand, calls this man to repentance and says: Return to your baptism. Rome calls the sacrament of penance "the second plank after shipwreck,"[67] as if the power of Baptism were broken. Luther counters that if anyone abandons the faith and leaps into the sea, the ship is not broken but remains intact. The sinner must be brought back to the ship by God's grace, and it is "in the solid ship itself that he is borne to life."[68] He need only return by faith to the "abiding and enduring promise of God"[69] in the covenant of his baptism. So Baptism, to Luther, is "something permanent," a continuing power for sanctification in the Christian life. You may wander away into sin, but the way back is to "return to the power of your baptism."[70]

Luther will not let the Christian forget his or her baptism and the important part it plays in daily Christian living. "It signifies that the old Adam in us should, by daily contrition and repentance, be drowned and die with all sins and evil lusts, and, again, a new man daily come forth and arise, who shall live before God in righteousness and purity forever."[71] This observation in the

Small Catechism receives its full meaning in the Large Catechism. There Luther makes it plain that Baptism not only "signifies" such a new life but also creates it and nourishes it. "For therein are given grace, the Spirit, and power to suppress the old man, so that the new man may come forth and become strong."[72] Repentance is "an earnest attack upon the old man and an entering upon a new life[.] Therefore, if you live in repentance, you walk in Baptism, which not only signifies such a new life, but also produces, begins, and exercises it."[73] Luther's conclusion in his article on Baptism in the Large Catechism is one of his finest statements. "For this reason let every one esteem his Baptism as a daily dress in which he is to walk constantly, that he may ever be found in the faith and its fruits, that he suppress the old man and grow up in the new."[74]

Luther found it necessary to make another correction in the medieval doctrine of Baptism. It must agree with the central doctrine of justification. As Paul Althaus says, "His doctrine of baptism is basically nothing else than his doctrine of justification in concrete form."[75] Since justification is through faith, Baptism, too, must be accompanied by faith. For Baptism carries with it a promise of life and salvation, and where "there is a divine promise, there faith is required. . . . Hence, to seek the efficacy of the sacrament apart from the promise and apart from the faith is to labor in vain and to find condemnation."[76]

Luther does not mean to say that the validity of Baptism depends on a man's faith. Baptism is "God's work," not man's, and faith does not make the sacrament.

> God's works, however, are saving and necessary for salvation, and do not exclude, but demand, faith. . . . it becomes beneficial to you if you have yourself baptized with the thought that this is according to God's command and ordinance, and besides in God's name, in order that you may receive in the water the promised salvation. Now, this the fist cannot do, nor the body; but the heart must believe it.[77]

This faith Luther sometimes speaks of as "special faith," especially when he is discussing the Sacrament of the Altar. But the same holds good in Baptism. Here he is not speaking simply of a general faith in God. The faith must embrace Baptism and its promises.

> [F]aith must have something which it believes, that is, of which it takes hold, and upon which it stands and rests. Thus faith clings to the water, and believes that it is Baptism, in which there is pure salvation and life; not through the water . . . but through the fact that it is embodied in the Word and institution of God, and the name of God inheres in it. Now, if I believe this, what else is it than believing in God as in Him who has given and planted His Word into this ordinance, and proposes to us this external thing wherein we may apprehend such a treasure?[78]

There is a fine dialectic involved here. While Luther insists on faith in Baptism, he does not want one to depend on faith for salvation, but on the institution and promise of God. "[W]e are not so much concerned to know whether the person baptized believes or not; for on that account Baptism does not become invalid; but everything depends on the Word and command of God. . . . Baptism is valid, even though faith be wanting. For my faith does not make Baptism, but receives it."[79]

This emphasis is particularly important when we are talking about infant Baptism. The sectarians attacked Luther at this point. Infants cannot believe, hence infant Baptism is wrong. Luther refuses to be tied up in a psychological argument over whether children can believe or, if they can, what the nature of that faith is. God has commanded us to baptize, and in obedience to that command we baptize infants because the Word of God does not exclude them. "We bring the child in the conviction and hope that it believes, and we pray that God may grant it faith; but we do not baptize it upon that, but solely upon the command of God."[80]

Luther believes that God supplies the faith in and through Baptism to the infant. Hence he can say, "even though infants did not believe, which, however, is not the case, yet their baptism as now shown would be valid, and no one should rebaptize them."[81]

It is Luther the pastor who is speaking much of the time when he discusses Baptism. He believes God meant it to be a source of comfort to the Christian. He should therefore not begin to worry about whether he had faith when he was baptized. "[I]f you did not believe, then believe now and say thus. . . . I myself also, and all who are baptized, must speak thus before God: I come hither in my faith and in that of others, yet I cannot rest in this, that I believe, and that many people pray for me; but in this I rest, that it is Thy Word and command."[82] As a pastor Luther directed his parishioners to their Baptism. When Dr. Weller was in anguish of soul, Luther simply asked him, "Are you baptized?" In this way Luther, true to a theology to live by, pointed his people to the grace and promise of God. The Christian lives in the tension of Romans between the Spirit and the flesh. He is never through with sin any more than St. Paul was. But he is a forgiven sinner who clings to the promises of God and therefore also to his baptismal covenant. "We must humbly admit, 'I know full well that I cannot do a single thing that is pure. But I am baptized, and through my baptism God, who cannot lie, has bound himself in a covenant with me. He will not count my sin against me, but will slay it and blot it out.' "[83]

Luther's doctrine of Baptism is like a brilliant gem planted in a double setting. On the one side is the theology of the cross. On the other the theology of justification by grace through faith. Luther took his cue from St. Paul. "Do you not know that all of us who have been baptized into Christ Jesus were baptized into His death? We were buried therefore with Him by baptism into death, in order that, just as Christ was raised from the dead by the glory of the Father, we too might walk in newness of life" (Romans 6:3–4). Luther says St. Paul is speaking here of "the power of baptism, which derives its efficacy from the death of Christ. . . . So we, also, through his death have obtained forgiveness of sins; that sin may not condemn us, we die unto sin through that power which Christ—because we are baptized into him—imparts to and works in us." Christ died unto sin, destroyed and buried it, "and he acquired life and victory over sin and death by his resurrection, and bestows them upon us by baptism."[84]

How closely Baptism is tied in with Luther's doctrine of justification becomes evident in his treatment of Galatians 3:27: "For as many of you as were baptized into Christ have put on Christ." Luther comments, "But to put on Christ according to the Gospel is a matter, not of imitation but of a new birth and a new creation, namely, that I put on Christ Himself, that is, His innocence, righteousness, wisdom, power, salvation, life, and Spirit. . . . This does not happen by a change of clothing or by any laws or works; it happens by the rebirth and renewal that takes place in Baptism."[85] The idea of justification as imputation or as covering the sinner with the righteousness of Christ Luther found in the Psalms as well as in St. Paul. "Therefore Paul teaches that Baptism is not a sign but the garment of Christ, in fact, that Christ Himself is our garment. Hence Baptism is a very powerful and effective thing. For when we have put on Christ, the garment of our righteousness and salvation, then we also put on Christ, the garment of imitation."[86] "Therefore I admonish you, if a heretic comes, if he makes anything else greater than Baptism, then let him be suspect to you."[87]

C. The Sacrament of the Altar

It would be a mistake to regard Luther's tangle with Rome on the Sacrament of the Altar as an effort to minimize the importance of it. He did indeed accuse the Romans of de-emphasizing the Word. And his concern was to restore the Word to its proper place beside the sacraments of Baptism and Eucharist. Holding as he did that it is the Word that makes the water Baptism, and the consecrated bread and wine the means that convey the true body and blood of

Christ, Luther does appear to give a certain preeminence to the Word. "A Christian should know that nothing on earth is more sacred than God's Word; for even the Sacrament itself is made, blessed, and sanctified by God's Word. . . . "[88] "Therefore though there are many great gifts of God in the world, given for the benefit of man, yet the one gift which includes and sustains all the others is the Word, which proclaims that God is merciful and promises forgiveness of sins and life everlasting."[89]

At the same time it must be said that Luther maintained the Church's reverence for the Sacrament. And what is more, he gave it back to the people. He rejected as unbiblical the idea that the priest could celebrate Mass for the people while they sat in their pews praying with their rosaries instead of partaking of the body and blood of the Lord. And both in his preaching and writing he impressed on the people the necessity of frequent Communion for the sustaining and strengthening of their Christian life. Let those who would be Christians "make ready to receive this venerable Sacrament often." For "such people as deprive themselves of, and withdraw from, the Sacrament so long a time are not to be considered Christians. For Christ has not instituted it to be treated as a show, but has commanded His Christians to eat and drink it, and thereby remember Him."[90]

The balance between Word and Sacrament must be maintained. While the Romans tipped the balance to the Sacrament at the expense of the Word, Luther saw the Swiss reformers and the enthusiasts as reversing this and de-emphasizing the sacraments to the point of neglect. Most serious of all to him was their rejection of the real presence of the body and blood in the Sacrament. This was taking the very heart out of the Supper and was a blatant denial of the clear words of Christ. It even raised the question in his mind whether they had the Sacrament at all. It was shortly before his death that he wrote: "*I rate as one concoction, namely, as Sacramentarians and fanatics, which they also are, all who will not believe that the Lord's bread in the Supper is His true natural body,*

which the godless or Judas received with the mouth, as well as did St.
Peter and all [other] saints; he who will not believe this (I say) should
let me alone, and hope for no fellowship with me; this is not going to
be altered."[91]

It is this thinking that causes Luther more and more to shift
his attack from the papists to the enthusiasts. The former, in spite
of their errors, do have the Sacrament of the body and blood,
while the latter "have only bread and wine."[92] The catholicity of
Luther's theology stands out when he declares, "For instance we
confess that in the papal church there are the true holy Scriptures,
true baptism, the true sacrament of the altar, the true keys to the
forgiveness of sins, the true office of the ministry. . . . "[93] He regards
as sectarians and schismatics those who want to throw out everything that smacks of Rome.

> We do not rave as do the rebellious spirits, so as to reject
> everything that is found in the papal church. For then we
> would cast out even Christendom from the temple of
> God, and all that it contained of Christ. . . . the Antichrist
> sits in the temple of God through the action of the devil,
> while the temple still is and remains the temple of God
> through the power of Christ.[94]

This theology of Luther is echoed in the Apology of the
Augsburg Confession. "And we have ascertained that not only
the Roman Church affirms the bodily presence of Christ, but
the Greek Church also both now believes, and formerly believed,
the same."[95]

It becomes evident that in Luther's thinking we are dealing
here with a fundamental doctrine. Historic Lutheranism has followed the Reformer up to the twentieth century, holding that until
there is unity in this doctrine, there can be no unity in the Church.
Whether it will maintain its position against the mounting ecumenical pressures remains to be seen.[96]

As in all his theology, Luther draws his doctrine of the Supper from Holy Scripture and bases it particularly on the institu-

tion of Christ. In all his debates, whether with papists or enthusiasts, Zwingli or Karlstadt, his appeal is always to Scripture. When his opponents appeal to the fathers and tradition, Luther drives them back to Scripture. Nevertheless, having stated his case from Scripture, he does not hesitate to appeal to the fathers in support of his position. "The amazing thing, meanwhile, is that of all the fathers . . . not one has spoken about the sacrament as these fanatics do. . . . actually, they simply proceed to speak as if no one doubted that Christ's body and blood are present. . . . They all stand uniformly and consistently on the affirmative side."[97] Tertullian, Irenaeus, Cyprian, Hilary, Augustine, name whom you will, Luther claims them on his side.[98]

Luther's doctrine of the Lord's Supper has three watchwords: sacramental union, or real presence (*unio sacramentalis*), oral eating (*manducatio oralis*), and Communion of the unworthy (*cornmunio indignorum*).[99] It was on this threefold front that he waged his lifelong battle with the "left wing."

Unio Sacramentalis

The sacramental union of bread and body, wine and blood, is another way of speaking of the real presence of the body and blood of Christ "in, with, and under" the bread and wine in the celebration of the Sacrament. This is the frontline of Luther's struggle to preserve the historic doctrine of the Church on the Lord's Supper. If this teaching is confessed, Luther recognizes the presence of the Sacrament. If it is denied, he questions the very presence of the Sacrament. Here we begin to understand "why Luther recognized the sacrament in the Roman Church but denied that the Swiss had it."[100]

We can sense here how Luther is torn between the mother Church on the right and the "radical reformers" on the left. On the one hand, he thunders against the Antichrist in Rome and the errors that are perverting the Gospel and destroying the faith of the Church. But at the same time he pleads with Rome to reform herself and correct the errors so that the unity of the Church may not be broken. On the other hand, he recognizes that those on the left are fighting some of the same errors that trouble him. To that extent they are allies in the cause of reformation. But in their revulsion against the corruption and errors of Rome they have lost their sense of the Church and become schismatics. With a new sectarian individualism they reject basic doctrines that the Church has held for 15 centuries. Luther sees a certain insidious rationalism destroying the Sacrament and even threatening the very doctrine of the person of Christ. The divorce is inevitable, and the Marburg Colloquy collapses with Luther's fateful words to Zwingli: "You are of another spirit."[101]

Throughout the long two-fronted struggle around the Sacrament it becomes apparent that here lay the prime cause of Luther's and Lutheranism's separation from Reformed Protestantism. And at the same time it was this doctrine that caused Luther and his followers to this day to claim continuity with the "one holy catholic and apostolic church." Neither orthodoxy nor pietism, enlightenment nor modernism, existentialism nor spiritualism has been able to destroy the sense of kinship with the Roman Catholic Church. History refuses to let the Lutheran Church forget those fateful words of her patron saint: "I contend that in the papacy there is true Christianity, even the right kind of Christianity and many great and devoted saints."[102]

Luther must have anticipated the endless struggle that has been going on since his own day regarding the presence of Christ in the Sacrament. He heard the same confusing voices then as we hear now. "We all believe in the presence of Christ in the Sacrament, so why bicker and let the details of that presence separate us?" Luther recognized a blind spot in these crusaders for peace. Can't they see from the words of our Lord and the apostle that the issue is not whether Christ is present in the celebration? They all believe that He is present there as He is wherever two or three are gathered in His name. The issue is whether the body and blood of our Lord is present in the bread and wine in the celebration.

"There is quite a difference between speaking of Christ and of the body and blood of Christ."[103] And to spike this confusing argument, which is beside the point, Luther states the doctrine in a dozen different ways. In the Small Catechism he says that the Sacrament of the Altar "is the true body and blood of our Lord Jesus Christ, under the bread and wine, for us Christians to eat and to drink, instituted by Christ Himself."[104] Some object that the preposition "under" is a Germanism and doesn't make sense in English. The same objection is made to Luther's talk of "in, with, and under" the bread and wine.

Zwingli's error is basically Christological, holding that Christ in His human nature is localized at the right hand of God, and therefore He cannot be bodily present in the Sacrament. So the believer must by faith ascend to heaven and partake spiritually of Christ. Calvin found Christ's presence not in the elements but in the celebration.

To make his difference with Zwingli and the others clear, Luther made the unequivocal declaration in the Smalcald Articles: "Of the Sacrament of the Altar we hold that bread and wine in the Supper are the true body and blood of Christ, and are given and received not only by the godly, but also by wicked Christians."[105]

It is evident that at this time, around 1536, Luther is stating the doctrine of the Eucharist in a way that is quite acceptable to the Roman Catholics, but anathema to Zwingli and the enthusiasts. For the statement clearly condemns those who deny the real presence of the body and blood and say that the Lord is not giving the same gift to the wicked as to the godly. This does not mean that he has become reconciled to the Roman doctrine. The idea of the "sacrifice" of the Mass and making it a good work is still anathema to him. But, as we have noted, the fact that they believe in the real presence of the body and the blood makes their doctrine less deadly than that of those who deny this presence. Transubstantiation Luther rejects as a "sophistical subtlety," trying to give a rational explanation to the miracle of the real presence.[106]

Luther refused to be drawn into a philosophical argument over the manner of Christ's presence. Zwingli's talk about a spiritual presence or a spiritual body he found wholly inadequate. "Here the words are plain and clear, that it is not the spiritual body of Christ which is present, but his natural body."[107] Christ is present "substantially and naturally."[108] When Christ says, "This is my body," the words must be taken at face value. And when Zwingli says Christ means, "This signifies my body," Luther says, "they have not adhered to the words."[109] "They have taught nothing more than that the bread signifies the body and the wine signifies the blood of Christ. . . . One must not do such violence to the words of God as to give any word a meaning other than its natural one, unless there is clear and definite Scripture to do that."[110]

Luther is flush with his adjectives when he speaks of the presence of the body and blood in the bread and wine. "Truly present," "really present," "bodily present," "physically present" are some of the terms he uses. Still clearer is his declaration, "Christ is truly present in the sacrament with his flesh and blood as it was born of Mary and hung on the holy cross."[111] To make it so clear that a child can understand it and no theologian can confuse his meaning, he says, "everyone knows what 'this is my body' means, . . . namely, that which was born of Mary, suffered, died, and rose again."[112] The body we receive in the Sacrament is "the same body which was given for us, not in the same form or mode but in the same essence and nature."[113]

The presence of Christ in the Sacrament is a *unique* presence. "In dungeon, torture, and death" Christ is with me. "He is present there through the Word, although not in the same way as here in the sacrament, where through the Word he binds his body and blood so that they are also received corporeally in the bread and wine. . . . He has put himself into the Word, and through the Word he puts himself into the bread also."[114] There is no doubt: This kind of language has caused the church to speak of the Consecration.

"Take, eat, this is my body, given for you, this do in remembrance of me." When we say these words over the bread, then he is truly present, and yet it is a mere word and voice that one hears. . . . For as soon as Christ says: "This is my body," his body is present through the Word and the power of the Holy Spirit. If the Word is not there, it is mere bread; but as soon as the words are added they bring with them that of which they speak.[115]

The Large Catechism is even more explicit. In the Sacrament we have not mere bread and wine, "but bread and wine comprehended in, and connected with, the Word of God. It is the Word . . . which makes and distinguished this Sacrament, so that it is not mere bread and wine, but is, and is called, the body and blood of Christ."[116] As St. Augustine says, "If the Word be joined to the element, it becomes a Sacrament."

It is evident that Luther has a *dynamic* conception of the Sacrament. Christ puts Himself into the Sacrament. In giving His body and blood to the communicant, He is bringing the cross to the altar. For the sacrifice of Christ on the cross for the forgiveness of sins is here brought to the individual. Here indeed the communicant enters into the "power of His resurrection, and may share His sufferings" (Philippians 3:10). "The passion of Christ occurred but once on the cross. But whom would it benefit if it were not distributed, applied, and put to use? And how could it be put to use and distributed except through Word and sacrament?"[117] The dynamic element will appear again when we consider the gift of the Sacrament, the blessing bestowed through it. For it is clear to Luther that something happens in the celebration, that power and grace are transmitted. The Sacrament is a means of grace.

Manducatio Oralis

The oral eating of the body and blood of Christ in and with the bread and wine was another angle of the historic doctrine that Luther maintained and the Swiss reformers and the enthusiasts rejected. Here again he stood with Mother Church and with the Church fathers from the beginning. Again he was bound by the words of Christ and the inspired record of the institution of the Sacrament as told by the evangelists and St. Paul. Luther found particular assurance in the apostle's account in 1 Corinthians 10:16: "The cup of blessing that we bless, is it not a participation in the blood of Christ? The bread that we break, is it not a participation in the body of Christ?" This verse, says Luther, "is a thunderbolt on the head of Dr. Karlstadt and his whole party. This verse has been also the life-giving medicine of my heart in my trials concerning this sacrament. Even if we had no other passage than this we could sufficiently strengthen all consciences and sufficiently overcome all adversaries."[118] When he asks wherein this participation consists, he comments, "It cannot be anything else than that as each takes a part of the broken bread he takes therewith the body of Christ. . . . they all in common and as one receive the one body of Christ and become partakers of it bodily."[119]

This leaves no room, Luther believes, for the spiritual interpretation of Zwingli and others, either of the Presence or of the eating. "Paul does not here speak of the spiritual participation, which only the saints have, of which Dr. Karlstadt dreams. But he speaks of a bodily participation, both by the holy and the unholy, just as both break bread."[120] Since they hold that the bread and wine are only symbols of the body and blood, there can be no talk of bodily eating and drinking. Furthermore, Christ in His human nature is localized at the right hand of God in heaven. He cannot therefore be bodily present in the Sacrament. Hence there can be no bodily eating. The only eating one can speak of is the participation by faith. The soul of the communicant is lifted to heaven, and there in faith through the Spirit he receives the body and blood of Christ, that is, the fruit of His life, sufferings, death, and resurrection. This describes the difference between Luther and all the others, be it Zwingli or Calvin or the many sects that follow them.[121]

Luther, of course, does not deny the "spiritual" eating that the Swiss reformers speak of. For unless there is faith, the communicant does not receive the blessing of the Sacrament. This confronts us with the third issue that separated Luther from the Swiss and the enthusiasts in the doctrine of the Sacrament.

Communio Indignorum

St. Paul says in 1 Corinthians 11:27–29, "Whoever, therefore, eats the bread or drinks the cup of the Lord in an unworthy manner will be guilty of profaning the body and blood of the Lord. Let a person examine himself, then, and so eat of the bread and drink of the cup. For anyone who eats and drinks without discerning the body eats and drinks judgment on himself."

From this passage Luther gathers that the "unworthy" communicant also receives the body and blood of the Lord. But for the unworthy it brings not blessing, but judgment or condemnation, as some versions translate the Greek word *krima*. And who is worthy or unworthy? In the Small Catechism Luther answers, "[H]e is truly worthy and well prepared who has faith in these words, *Given, and shed for you, for the remission of sins*. But he that does not believe these words, or doubts, is unworthy and unfit; for the words, *For you* require altogether believing hearts."[122]

Whatever interpretation is given to the presence of the body and blood, the Swiss and the enthusiasts held that this was received only by the believer. The unbeliever or the unworthy received only bread and wine. To Luther the apostle's words were convincing proof of the real presence of the body and blood. For if these were not present and only bread and wine were received, unworthiness could not be such a serious matter. But St. Paul makes it deadly serious. And the sin lies in "not discerning the body." The context in which the apostle spoke these words is clear. "[T]he Corinthians ate the bread with the misconception and misunderstanding that it was ordinary bread, and discerned no difference between this bread and other bread. This certainly is what is meant by 'unworthily eating the body of Christ'. This is why Paul admonishes them to examine themselves and perceive who they are and how they regard this bread. If they do not regard it as the body of Christ, or treat it as if it were not the body of Christ, then they do not discern the body of Christ; and this offense will not go unpunished."[123] So there must be two kinds of eating or partaking, says Luther, namely, the physical, oral eating and the spiritual eating by faith. The unworthy cannot partake spiritually, lacking faith; so his eating is only physical. "Therefore the true, real body of Christ must of necessity be physically present in the bread which we break, and the unworthy may partake of it physically, because they cannot partake of it spiritually."[124] "How can you sin in eating the body of the Lord, if he is not present in the eating or the bread?"[125]

Here is a very important point in a theology to live by. For it has serious practical implications for our sacramental life. In the present moment of the Church's history there is a swing back to more frequent use of the Sacrament. In some congregations it can almost be called a mass movement. Encouraging as this appears to be, it carries with it a serious threat, which Luther sensed as he urged people to come frequently to the Lord's Table. It can become a routine, a habit, a mass movement that sweeps us along to the Supper without the individual personal preparation which the apostle calls for.

Luther insists on *preparation* for Communion on the basis of St. Paul's words, "Let a person examine himself, then, and so eat of the bread and drink of the cup" (1 Corinthians 11:28). The traditional preparation meant fasting and prayer and private confession to the priest. Luther approved of this, but held that it must be a matter of liberty and not of law. "Fasting and bodily preparation is, indeed, a fine outward training; but he is truly worthy and well prepared who has faith in these words: *Given, and shed for you, for the remission of sins.*"[126] The best preparation, says Luther, is "a soul troubled by sins, death, and temptation and hungering and thirsting for healing and strength."[127]

The priest or minister is responsible to see to it that this kind of discipline is maintained in connection with Communion. On the one hand he is to watch over the sanctity of the Lord's Table. Pearls must not be thrown to the swine (cf. Matthew 7:6). On the other hand, he must try to protect people from eating and drinking judgment to themselves. There are two ways in which the minister can do this. He should know the communicant's name and manner of life.

> And let him not admit the applicants unless they can give a reason for their faith and can answer questions about what the Lord's Supper is, what its benefits are, and what they expect to derive from it. In other words, they should be able to repeat the Words of Institution from memory and to explain that they are coming because they are troubled by the consciousness of their sin, the fear of death, or some other evil, such as temptation of the flesh, the world, or the devil, and now hunger and thirst to receive the word and sign of grace and salvation from the Lord himself through the ministry of the bishop, so that they may be consoled and comforted.[128]

This kind of examination might be conducted once a year, in some cases once in a lifetime, or not at all.

The normal way of preparation, of course, was private confession, which Luther insisted on retaining, not as a matter of law but as a privilege. To him it was one of the great treasures of the Church.

> Indeed, I rejoice that it exists in the church of Christ, for it is a cure without equal for distressed consciences. For when we have laid bare our conscience to our brother and privately made known to him the evil that lurked within, we receive from our brother's lips the word of comfort spoken by God himself. And, if we accept this in faith, we find peace in the mercy of God speaking to us through our brother.[129]

This is not the place for a full-dress discussion of private confession. What concerns us here is its importance as a preparation for Holy Communion and as a way of guarding the sanctity of the Lord's Table.

> I do advise that you make confession gladly before you go to the sacrament, or at least that you do not despise confession. For although the absolution is present in the words of the mass, which is primary, nevertheless you should not for that reason despise the other absolution in the confession. God has given us his absolution richly and in various ways, and no one of them is to be despised for the sake of the others.[130]

Communion

In Holy Communion we are united with Christ. This means that the gift of the Sacrament is nothing less than Christ Himself. For when we receive His body and blood we receive Him, and with Him we receive all that He has done for us. In Holy Communion Christ unites Himself with us, yes, identifies Himself with us. At that moment comes true for me the experience of St. Paul: "I have been crucified with Christ. It is no longer I who live, but Christ who lives in me" (Galatians 2:20).

This union with Christ is a living, pulsating, dynamic experience where Christ applies all His redemptive work to me personally. His incarnation brings God to me. His cross redeems me. His resurrection gives me victory; His ascension declares His lordship over me. All this becomes mine in Holy Communion, for it is communion with Christ.

Luther puts the cross at the center of the Sacrament. For there we meet the *Agnus Dei*, the Lamb of God, who takes away the sin of the world. So to Luther the primary and overarching gift of the Sacrament is the forgiveness of sin. "For where there is forgiveness of sins, there is also life and salvation."[131] This must account for the stress he puts on preparation and self-examination before Communion. He finds this emphasis in the Lord's own words of institution: "[T]his is My blood of the covenant, which is poured out for many for the forgiveness of sins" (Matthew 26:28). "It is as if Christ were saying, 'See here, man, in these words I promise and bequeath to you forgiveness of all your sins and the life eternal. In order that you may be certain and know that such a promise remains irrevocably yours, I will die for it, and will give my body and blood for it, and will leave them both to you as a sign and seal, that by them you may remember me."[132] Starting with forgiveness, the blessings pour forth upon the communicant from the Sacrament as from the cross itself: faith, assurance, strength, comfort, life eternal. In ecstasy he exults:

> Here my Lord has given me his body and blood in the bread and wine, in order that I should eat and drink. And they are to be my very own, so that I may be certain that my sins are forgiven, that I am to be free of death and hell, have eternal life, and be a child of God, and an heir of heaven. Therefore I go to the sacrament to seek these things. I am a poor sinner with death before me, I must go through it; and the devil threatens me with all kinds of trouble and danger. Because I am in sin, a captive of death and the devil, because I feel that I am weak in faith, cold in love, wayward, impatient, envious, with sin clinging to me before and behind, therefore I come hither where I find and hear Christ's word that I shall receive the gift of the forgiveness of sins.[133]

One cannot read this outpouring of Luther's heart without seeing here the profound piety of the man, his frightful sense of sin, his hunger for the forgiving fellowship of Christ. It reminds us of the apostle in the seventh chapter of Romans, "Wretched man that I am! Who will deliver me from this body of death?" (Romans 7:24). It gives us a glimpse of what Luther calls his *Anfechtung*, his spiritual agony under the attacks of the Tempter.[134] This man is really spiritually involved in his theology. It is a life-and-death theology, a theology to live by and a theology to die by. It is a theol-

THE LIFE WE RECEIVE

ogy of the cross on which hangs the forgiving Christ. And
nowhere does this Christ embrace us more lovingly than in the
Supper. Here is to Luther a kind of "holy of holies" where he experiences the ultimate in communion both with Christ and with
other Christians. Here is the ultimate *koinonia* of the early Christians in Acts 2:42, "And they devoted themselves to the apostles'
teaching and fellowship, to the breaking of bread and the prayers."

Here, above all places, Luther discovers the glory of being a
member of the Church, the communion of saints, the body of
Christ. He longs for this communion like St. Ignatius, who on the
way to Rome and a martyr's death wrote to his faithful: "I care no
longer for corruptible food, nor for the pleasures of this life: I
desire only the bread of God, the bread of heaven, which is the
flesh of Jesus Christ, the Son of God, born of the race of David and
Abraham; I desire the drink of God, His blood, which is love
incorruptible and life without end."[135]

While Luther shared this longing for communion with
Christ in the Sacrament, his longing embraced also the joy of
communion with other Christians. For communion with Christ
only became more poignant with the awareness of his communion with the body of Christ, the Church. The glory of this communion with Christ and the saints has probably never been
expressed more beautifully or preached more powerfully than in
Luther's sermon "The Blessed Sacrament of the Holy and True
Body of Christ, and the Brotherhoods," delivered in 1519.[136]
"Christ and all saints are one spiritual body." And to receive the
Sacrament is "to receive a sure sign of this fellowship and incor-
poration with Christ and all the saints." With this fellowship
comes a share in "all the spiritual possessions of Christ and his
saints," but also in their sufferings and sins. "[T]hus love engenders love in return and [mutual love] unites."[137]

This fellowship involves us in both privilege and responsibility. The evil spirit attacks us with sin and affliction. A guilty
conscience assails us, and there is the fear of death and the pains

of hell. "All of these afflictions make us weary and weak, unless we seek strength in this fellowship, where strength is to be found."[138] Our refuge is in the Sacrament of Christ's body and blood.

> Whoever is in despair, distressed by a sin-stricken conscience or terrified by death or carrying some other burden upon his heart, if he would be rid of them all, let him go joyfully to the sacrament of the altar and lay down his woe in the midst of the community [of saints] and seek help from the entire company of the spiritual body. . . . The immeasurable grace and mercy of God are given us in this sacrament to the end that we might put from us all misery and tribulation [anfechtung] and lay it upon the community [of saints], and especially on Christ. Then we may with joy find strength and comfort, and say, "Though I am a sinner and have fallen, though this or that fortune has befallen me, nevertheless I will go to the sacrament to receive a sign from God that I have on my side Christ's righteousness, life, and sufferings, with all holy angels and the blessed in heaven and all pious men on earth. If I die, I am not alone in death; if I suffer, they suffer with me. [I know that] all my misfortune is shared with Christ and the saints, because I have a sure sign of their love toward me." See, this is the benefit to be derived from this sacrament; this is the use we should make of it. Then the heart cannot but rejoice and be strengthened.[139]

But as Luther says, love engenders love and carries with it a responsibility. Therefore "you must in turn share the misfortunes of the fellowship. . . . Here your heart must go out in love and learn that this is a sacrament of love."[140] St. Paul calls us to share one another's burdens (Galatians 6:2). As the Christian communicant receives love and support in the fellowship, so he must in turn "render love and support to Christ in his needy ones."[141] Luther becomes impatient with those who will enjoy the privileges of the sacramental fellowship but will not carry the responsibilities.

"There are those, indeed, who would gladly share in the profits but not in the costs." For this treasure is not to be hoarded, but shared. And here Luther's social consciousness waxes eloquent.

> They will not help the poor, put up with sinners, care for the sorrowing, suffer with the suffering, intercede for others, defend the truth, and at the risk of [their own] life, property, and honor seek the betterment of the church and of all Christians. . . . They do not want to have to suffer disfavor, harm, shame, or death, although it is God's will that they be thus driven—for the sake of the truth and of their neighbors—to desire the great grace and strength of this sacrament.[142]

There is no limit to this obligation to love and sacrifice for others. We "must make the evil of others our own, if we desire Christ and his saints to make our evil their own. Then will the fellowship be complete, and justice be done to the sacrament. For the sacrament has no blessing and significance unless love grows daily and so changes a person that he is made one with all others."[143]

This accent on love and social concern appears again in Luther's Seventh Wittenberg Sermon of 1522, where he says that the fruit of this sacrament is love. And he utters a sharp rebuke, as we have seen earlier, to those who fail at this point. "It is true, you have the true gospel and the pure Word of God, but no one as yet has given his goods to the poor, no one has yet been burned, and even these things would be nothing without love. You are willing to take all God's goods in the sacrament, but you are not willing to pour them out again in love."[144]

With this exalted view of the Sacrament it is not surprising that Luther urges faithful and frequent use of it, even as he rebukes those who neglect it. Because it is the sacrament in which there is forgiveness, "it is not to be despised." A man should come with his family, "if they want to be Christians."[145] No man should be compelled to go to the Sacrament. "You have four doors here—go on out!" God offers you His body and blood given for you. "If you want to despise God and neglect the forgiveness of sins, then stay away. So I do not compel you, but Christ pleads with you lovingly."[146] Our attendance at Communion is our witness that we belong to Christ. "For this is how we know which are Christians and which are not." Before closing his sermon Luther reaches out to the young people. "If you will not go, then let the young people come; for us so much depends upon them. . . . For even if you adults want to go to the devil, we shall nevertheless seek after your children."[147]

Luther's sense of the holiness of the Sacrament compelled him to surround the celebration with safeguards. What we call "open Communion," where anybody comes who wants to, was unthinkable to him. We have already seen how he glorifies this *fellowship of love*. But it is also a *fellowship of faith*, a *fellowship in the truth*. Jesus has defined the fellowship. St. Paul has told us who is worthy to come into it at the Lord's Table. Because it is a fellowship of faith, Luther insists that there can be no sharing of the fellowship except with those who share the faith. For these alone are the "worthy" ones according to the apostle. But to Luther this faith includes particularly faith in the Sacrament of the Lord's Body and Blood, faith in our Lord's words of institution. "[H]e is truly worthy and well prepared who has faith in these words: *Given, and shed for you, for the remission of sins*."[148] A man must believe the Lord is giving him His body and blood in the Sacrament. The man who does not believe this, does not "discern" the body of the Lord in the bread, but regards this like any other bread. It was on this basis that Luther felt he had to refuse fellowship with Zwingli at Marburg and warn his followers not to commune with the followers of Zwingli and the enthusiasts. Rather than communing with them at the Lord's Table, "suffer patiently your tribulation and comfort yourselves meanwhile with reading and teaching the Holy Word and with longing and praying . . . desiring the Sacrament with sighing. . . . The Enthusiasts have no Baptism or Sacrament."[149]

Luther felt so strongly about guarding the truth at this point that he pulled no punches in his condemnation of those who denied the real presence and who therefore should not be admitted to the Lord's Table. "If we are to practice Christian unity with them and extend Christian love to them, we must also love and be satisfied with, or at least tolerate, their doctrine and behavior. Let anyone do that if he wishes. Not I. For Christian unity consists in the Spirit, when we are of one faith, one mind, one heart."[150] He will gladly consort with them in civil matters. "But in spiritual matters, as long as we have breath, we intend to shun, condemn, and censure them, as idolators, corrupters of God's Word, blasphemers, and liars." He will continue to pray for them and admonish them. "But to acquiesce in, keep silence over, or approve their blaspheming, this we shall not and cannot do."[151]

In his "Great Confession" of 1528 we can see that the controversy over the real presence had reached white heat. His attack on the papists over their doctrine of the sacrifice of the Mass and the like seems almost to fade into the background as he is confronted by what he saw as a monstrous denial of the real presence. This seems much more serious than anything he faced from the papist side. Hence in the great treatises on the Sacrament of 1527 and 1528 he unleashes all his theological forces against the "fanatics" and the Swiss: Karlstadt and Zwingli and all their sympathizers. He lumps them all together "in one pot" and refuses all fellowship with them in the celebration of the Sacrament. And when they object that he should be turning his guns against the papists with their transubstantiation, he answers: "I do not argue whether the wine remains wine or not. It is enough for me that Christ's blood is present; let it be with the wine as God wills. Sooner than have mere wine with the fanatics, I would agree with the pope that there is only blood."[152]

It is tempting to speculate about this affinity that Luther felt toward Rome through their common doctrine of the real presence of the body and blood in the Sacrament, an affinity he never found with the Swiss and the others. Is this one big reason why Lutherans, who for decades have been striving almost exclusively toward fellowship with the Reformed churches, now rather suddenly have moved into serious conversations with Rome? It is a fact that even after muddling through orthodoxy and pietism, enlightenment and modernism, the Lutheran Church has never wholly lost Luther's deep conviction that the doctrine of the sacraments is a fundamental doctrine and is deadly serious business. This seriousness he saw in the Roman Church to a far greater degree than he did in the Swiss and the enthusiasts.

The concern for doctrinal truth that characterized Luther and his followers has often brought the charge of "bigotry" and "intolerance." He is damned for his "personal invective" in debate. But "when doctrine is concerned, no man is too great for my criticism; I consider him a mere bubble or even less."[153] One had to be thick-skinned to take part in sixteenth-century controversy, and he warned his followers: "If you want to testify to the truth, then be prepared to have as enemies the devil with his angels, the world with its wisdom and its greatest intellect, nay, to have as enemies your parents, your father and mother, and your best friends. There is no other way."[154]

Hardly less than his concern for truth was his desire for unity in the Church. His deep sense of the communion of saints and the body of Christ compelled him to strive for unity, but always unity in the truth. Schism was abhorrent, a wound in the body of Christ. His ecumenical approach was indeed tough and his language in debate often violent. But this was the order of the day. Our ecumenical scene today would never tolerate the language used by the reformers on both sides in debate. But with all their violence, one thing is their glory. They knew what they believed, and they fought for the truth with the passion of martyrs. Nothing mattered but the truth. Compromise was a foreign word to Luther where truth was at stake.

The ecumenical scene has changed. Not truth but love is the password. To Luther, too, love was the driving force in his lifelong battle for truth. But the love of truth transcended the love of men, or rather it inspired it. When pushed for compromise for the sake of unity, he sputtered, "A curse on a love that is observed at the expense of the doctrine of faith, to which everything must yield— love, an apostle, an angel from heaven, etc!"[155]

Our ecumenical conversations today do indeed show more kindliness and self-control in debate. But one is sometimes constrained to ask whether the loss of the reformers' realistic language has brought with it some loss of conviction and concern for truth. Joseph Lortz, the eminent Roman Luther scholar, has seen the problem as he faces Lutherans and others across the ecumenical table.[156] And he has laid down some pretty good ground rules for interchurch conversations, rules that breathe the spirit of the reformers with their bold conviction and concern for truth:

> Decisions presuppose unreserved, uncompromising truthfulness. . . . Every form of relativism must be rejected as leading to the death of truth. . . . This is especially important in the realm of revealed truth. The core of the Christian truth is dogma, a truth that can be known and set down in human words. . . . Dogma is protection for the truth of salvation. . . . we cannot expect tolerance but rather intolerance in matters pertaining to dogma. Tolerance in matters of dogma would be nothing less than sacrificing truth.

> Just as I speak, as a Catholic Christian and priest, from the conviction that the Christian truth is fully expressed only by our Catholic faith, so the Evangelical partner of this dialogue will have to be filled with the same conviction that his faith presents the Christian fullness in its purity. Only men so convinced for the truth they possess can be willing to stand with their very lives for what they believe. Only then is the question of truth posed in its sublime inexorability.[157]

That is the kind of language Luther understood and spoke. It echoes beautifully his belief that controversy and debate can be healthy for the Church when there is honesty and openness and a passionate concern for the truth. "My eyes are directed to nothing but the cause of the truth as such. This I heartily love. In case I am, or at times were to be, too free and forceful in the interest of this cause, I desire everybody kindly to forgive me the offense. I do not know what I can do beyond this. God's will be done on earth as it is in heaven. Amen."[158] This is Luther's way of saying that a theology to live by must be a theology of truth, a theology of certainty, and above all a theology of the cross.[159]

CHAPTER
TEN

IMMORTALITY
AND RESURRECTION

What a strange world we live in! He who made heaven and earth and created man in His image continues to let the sun shine and the rain fall and the earth provide food and clothing enough for all His creatures. He offers life and love, peace and plenty to all men. But men choose death rather than life, darkness rather than light. And there is the smell of death all around us. It is like the world at the end of the Thirty Years' War. The very air they breathed reeked with the stench of disease, bloodshed, and death. Now we find ourselves in a generation whose moral sense has been dulled, whose hope for a world of peace and justice has been snuffed out, whose reverence for life has been killed. Here is a generation brought up on two world wars and an endless ongoing slaughter in various parts of the world, a generation breathing an air so polluted that the password has become "survival," a generation so dehumanized by technocracy that man has become a slave to his own inventiveness. The language of the media of communication is the language of violence, tragedy, revolution, death. Universities offer seminars on death.

The Church, too, seems to be catching the plague. During the Passion season we follow the Lord indifferently to Jerusalem. We scoff at the disciples who "forsook Him and fled." But we ourselves seem to get bogged down on Holy Saturday. We never seem to reach the empty tomb to hear the angel say, "He is risen." We creak out of Jerusalem with the two weary disciples on the road to Emmaus. But we appear to have left them before the Stranger joined them. And so our hearts never burn like theirs. We look around in the Church for signs of life, enthusiasm, resurrection joy. Here and there come signs of awakening and life. *Jesus Christ Superstar* explodes on Broadway and Jesus People tell us, "This is it. Christ is breaking down the barriers." But the curtain goes down and He is still in the grave. A leading church periodical puts out an Easter issue, and the lead article by a theological professor proclaims that the biggest obstacle to new life in the church is the naive idea of Christians that Jesus actually rose from the grave in the flesh. Death, not life, is the theme song that is dinned into our ears by the world and too often by the churches.

But now come signs of hope. Suddenly plastered on the front page of the press, both secular and religious, is a new theme: Resurrection and Immortality! The secular press, carrying the ball for a new school of theologians, announces that the idea of resurrection has replaced the Greek idea of immortality.

Without analyzing the multitude of different interpretations of the resurrection, it is evident that many articles in both the religious and the secular press have left readers in a state of confusion. The humble Christian, who with his father and grandfather and saints back to St. Paul has been comforted by the promise that when he dies, he will be alive with the Lord, is suddenly given to understand that when he dies, he is dead all over, out like a light, annihilated body and soul. His little brain finds it hard to grasp the idea that there can be a resurrection of someone or something that does not exist. And these Christians are the people whom pastors and counselors are called upon to comfort and give hope to when death is approaching.

We complicate the question by thinking that we have to choose between immortality and resurrection, or between Althaus and Thielicke, Cullmann and Weatherhead, Stendahl and Father Shannon. One wonders how many pastors before visiting the dying have asked or answered for themselves two questions: What happens when I die? Am I with the Lord or not? Until he has answered those two questions is he really in a position to bring comfort and hope to the Christian who knows what he believes and is dying in the blessed hope that with St. Paul and the dying thief and untold millions of Christians he will be with Christ— alive—when he dies?

Where can I find the right word for this dying man? I read a dozen front-page theologians and find as many different answers. Philosophers and columnists offer their solutions, each different. I am constantly tempted to speculate about these mysteries of the Kingdom that are only grasped by faith and only revealed to those who believe. Certainly all generations, all great philosophers, all great religions have speculated about the problem of life and death. And some of them, like Plato and Socrates, have come up with some remarkable theories. But then I am reminded of what Luther once said: "We know no more about eternal life than children in the womb of their mother know about the world they are about to enter."[1]

So I turn to Mother Church. First I ask the contemporary theologians. Most of them agree that there will be a resurrection of all the dead on Judgment Day. Resurrection of what? Not of "the body," as the Church confesses, or of "the flesh," as the earliest Christian creeds said it. But of what, then? Here they differ. Most of them will say it is the resurrection of the whole man—

body, soul, person, spirit—everything that constitutes man. But between death and Judgment Day what happens? Some say the deceased is totally annihilated. But somehow God will create him on the Last Day. Here there can clearly be no talk of a resurrection of someone who does not exist. Most of the contemporary theologians will reject the word "annihilation." They use the same language up to a point. The whole person dies—body and soul. No dualism is permitted between body and soul in death. The whole person is dead. And yet they say he will be resurrected on the Last Day. Where is he meanwhile, between his death and his resurrection on the Last Day?

Here we need beware lest we invent a nice, comforting deathbed theology with which to drug our dying parishioner to sleep, all the while thinking that science and contemporary theologians have made it quite clear, as Stendahl says, that "the whole long and glorious tradition of speaking about the immortality of the soul is coming to an end."[2] It is significant for our study to note that Luther represents this "whole long and glorious tradition of speaking about the immortality of the soul." He finds it a solid, unbroken tradition right out of the early church and sees nothing in Scripture to persuade him to depart from it. It is safe to say that the average humble Christian still lives in this tradition and in this hope. In their uncomplicated faith the great majority of Christians, like Luther, still live in the blessed hope that when they die they are with the Lord, and their bodies will be raised on the Last Day according to the Scriptures and the historic creeds of the Church.

Immortality and resurrection! Luther finds both concepts clearly appearing in Scripture, both Old Testament and New, as do the terms "body," "soul," and "spirit." Luther and the church fathers see both concepts in both Testaments and sense no contradiction. Luther says on Genesis 2:13, "the Prophets have carefully searched those passages in which Moses intimates the resurrection of the flesh and the life immortal."[3] He finds the heart of the Gospel in Genesis 3:15:

> Therefore this statement includes the redemption from the Law, from sin, and from death; and it points out the clear hope of a certain resurrection and of renewal in the other life after this life. If the serpent's head is to be crushed, death certainly must be done away with. . . . He frees those who are overwhelmed by death, and transports them into eternal life. This he does, as Moses teaches here, by crushing the head of the serpent.[4]

Hebrews 11 speaks of the faith of the patriarchs and the Old Testament saints, looking for the life to come. Luther takes Abel as an example. God uses his death to point out "somewhat obscurely that the soul is immortal and that there is eternal life." Though Abel is dead he still speaks, "so that he who, when he was alive, could not teach his one brother through his faith and example, now that he is dead, that is, lives far more vigorously, teaches the whole world."[5] As the Old Testament says, the dead "go to their fathers." They are "gathered to their people." Life is never snuffed out. It continues through the grave.

It is worth pausing here to note that in Luther all the talk of immortality and resurrection of the dead begins with the resurrection of Jesus. He is "the firstfruits of them that sleep." And my resurrection and life eternal have their source and guarantee in His resurrection. "[B]eing redeemed, by the resurrection, from death and sin, we shall live eternally."[6]

Luther finds emphatic testimony in the New Testament that life continues when we die. He preaches on Jesus' words to Martha and Mary ("I am the Resurrection and the Life. Whoever believes in Me, though he die, yet shall he live, and everyone who lives and believes in Me shall never die," John 11:25–26). "The natural death" is nothing else than that "the soul separates itself from the body." To the believer there is no fear, and "where there is no fear there death is no death, but a sleep."[7]

Eternal life—the Church has always believed that eternal life begins here. If it does, then the question arises: How can I cease to live when I die? "And this is life eternal, that they know You. . . . " (John 17:3). To Luther this means to know Him in this life. "Yes," says Luther, "natural life is a part of eternal life, its beginning, but on account of death it has an end, because it does not honor . . . him from whom it comes. . . . On the other hand, those who believe in him . . . shall never die; but this natural life of theirs will be extended into eternal life, so that they will never taste death, as John says, 8,51."[8] Paul says he desires to "depart and be with Christ" (Philippians 1:23). He must be saying that he believes he will continue to live with Christ when he dies.

Luther preaches on the pericope text for the Fifth Sunday in Lent, which has the significant word of Jesus: "Truly, truly, I say to you, if anyone keeps My Word, he will never see death" (John 8:51). Here Luther finds the assurance that there is continuity between the life here and the life hereafter. The Christian "enters death calmly and quietly, as though falling asleep, and yet he does not die." But in the same sermon Luther recognizes the mystery of death. He sees no problem for speculation when the Bible speaks on the one hand of immortality and on the other of resurrection. They belong together. Both are true, and he leaves the mystery in the hands of a gracious God. So it does not surprise us when he in the same breath with the above statement declares, "For just as he who falls asleep does not know how it happens, and he greets the morning when he awakes; so shall we suddenly arise on the last day, and never know how we entered and passed through death."[9]

This is the theology of hope with which people of God have lived and died through all generations. And a part of that hope is the promise that our bodies will not forever molder in the grave, but will be raised on the Last Day. Then we shall enter, body and soul, into the full glory of heaven. Luther rests securely in the Church's faith in an intermediate state between death and the final resurrection. That means to him uninterrupted continuity of life at death. The sticky question is: What is it that continues to live? The answer of the Church has quite consistently been the soul. Many contemporary theologians, with the help of science and anthropology and philosophy, now maintain that this "Greek dualism" must be rejected. Man is a whole. Body and soul can never be separated in life or in death. Some even seem to hold that there is no such thing as a soul. Some speculate as to whether the soul has substance or is a substance. In this confusion some will translate psyche as "life" instead of as "soul," as the old translations have it. But they have difficulty avoiding the term "soul" in Matthew 10:28, "And do not fear those who kill the body but cannot kill the soul. Rather fear Him who can destroy both soul and body in hell." (Cf. New English Bible, Jerusalem Bible, Good News for Modern Man, and other versions.)

Luther has numerous references to "immortality of the soul." He knows very well that the Greeks used the term, but that does not bother him. This was common language with Luther, as with Augustine and the other fathers right up to his day. He can speak of immortality of the soul and resurrection of the dead in one breath, indicating that he sees no conflict between them. Thus he can write in his Genesis Commentary,

> There is extant a delightful account by Augustine concerning a certain physician who regarded the doctrine of the resurrection of the dead and the immortality of the soul as uncertain. While he is sleeping, a very handsome young man appears to him, addresses him familiarly and asks whether he knows him. When the sleeping physician says no and yet admits that he sees and hears him, the young man says: "How is it that you see me when your eyes are closed in sleep? How is it that you hear me when your ears are not open but you are asleep?"
>
> Therefore, learn and believe that there are other spiritual eyes with which those who believe in Christ see when the eyes of the body have been closed by death or have rather been entirely destroyed.[10]

It is easy to see how Luther's theology of death and life eternal is rooted in the Church fathers. "We see Augustine gladly extolling this endowment of our nature and proving the immortality of our souls from it, since man alone counts time and has an understanding of it."[11]

Luther's understanding of the soul appears in his exegesis of 1 Corinthians 15:45 ("Thus it is written, 'The first man Adam became a living being'; the last Adam became a life-giving spirit,'"). It comes in again in 1 Thessalonians 5:23 ("Now may the God of peace Himself sanctify you completely, and may your whole spirit [*pneuma*] and soul [*psyche*] and body [*soma*] be kept blameless at the coming of the Lord Jesus Christ,"). Luther finds both trichotomy and dichotomy in Scripture's description of man, but sees no conflict there. The soul is the seat of life. In fact, he says, "In the Scriptures it is frequently put for the life; for the soul may live without the body, but the body has no life apart from the soul. Even in sleep the soul lives and works without ceasing."[12] Hence Luther has no problem in speaking of the soul's sleep with God after death.

In exegeting the Genesis account of creation Luther frequently slips into the language of the immortality of the soul. Discussing the fourth day of creation, he says: "But here the immortality of the soul begins to unfold and reveal itself."[13] And the "difference between the origin of man and that of cattle also points to the immortality of the soul."[14] This soul departs from the body at death. In the story of Rachel, Luther comments, " . . . *as her soul was departing (for she died), she called his name Benoni.*" "Rachel herself commended her soul to God and found rest in the consolations offered by Jacob. . . . She was taken to heaven into the bosom of Abraham, her father."[15]

The last words of Jesus from the cross were a great comfort to Luther: "Into Thy hands I commend My spirit." This tells him, says Luther, that "He Himself will provide a place where my soul may continue to exist."[16] This continued existence is a kind of sleep, says Luther. But it is different from our sleep here on earth.

> For in this life a man, fatigued by the day's work, enters his bedroom at night in order to sleep in peace and enjoy rest during the night. Nor is he conscious of any evil that is happening. . . . But the departed soul does not sleep in this manner; it is, more properly speaking, awake and has visions and conversations with the angels and God. Therefore the sleep of the future life is deeper than that of this life, and yet the soul lives before God. . . . He thinks that he has slept scarcely an hour or two, and yet he observes that the soul sleeps in such a way that it is awake at the same time. Thus the soul enters its chamber and peace after death and is at rest, though it is not conscious of its sleep, and God keeps the soul awake in it.[17]

This is more than Luther usually likes to say about the condition of the one who dies. He prefers to say that

> this question is too ambitious and difficult for us to answer. For God did not want us to understand the mooted matter in this life. We should, therefore, be satisfied to know that souls do not leave their bodies only to be threatened by the torments and punishments of hell, but that a chamber has been prepared for them in which they rest in peace.

"It is true, souls hear, think, see after death, but how they do it we do not understand[.]"[18] "If we knew how the souls are kept, faith would be unnecessary."[19]

Luther reverses the old hymn verse, "In the midst of life we are in death." "This is the song of the Law only; for the Gospel and faith reverse it and sing thus: 'In the midst of death we are in life; we praise Thee, Lord God, our Redeemer. . . . So we sing because the Gospel teaches that in death itself there is life."[20]

In his preaching Luther will not let us forget that our life after death and our resurrection are wholly the result of Christ's death and resurrection. Commenting on 1 Thessalonians 4:14 ("Jesus died and rose again, even so, through Jesus, God will bring with Him those who have fallen asleep."), Luther says, "God intends to bring with him you and all others who have been baptized and have fallen asleep in Christ, because he has wrapped them in Christ's death and included them in his resurrection."[21] So be comforted! "After all, it is only a man that dies, and not even the whole man, but only a part, the body."[22]

You can hear the pastor preaching when Luther says in his sermon at the funeral of the Elector, Duke John of Saxony, that life here is

> nothing compared to a man's leaving this life and dying to sin and the world; for then God opens both his eyes and all the angels must be there to wait upon him, below and above and round about him, if it be so that he is clothed with the baptism of Christ and faith and God's Word that he may be counted among those who are called God's saints.[23]

While many contemporary theologians will reject this view of Luther and the language of immortality of the soul, of separation of body and soul at death, it is interesting to hear Karl Barth say, "Death as separation of the immortal soul from the mortal body confirms the fact that we *still* exist in a state of ambiguity as children of Adam and as children of God. . . . "[24] That makes Luther sound quite contemporary when he says, "Natural death, which is the separation of the soul from the body, is simple death."[25] But through it and beyond it flows the unbroken stream of life, life with Christ and all the saints. Death is only "the narrow gate and the small way to life which every man must joyfully ponder. For while it is narrow, it is not long." Just as a child is born into the great world from his little dwelling in his mother, "so a dying man must courageously face anxiety with the knowledge that there will be great space and much joy afterwards."[26]

omes to Luther the crowning ele-
to bring our eyes, our hearts and
. heaven and in a lively hope await

tians, the ultimate objects of our
ying, selling. . . . But our ultimate
er and higher: the blessed inheri-
ιss away."[27]

NOTES

Chapter One

1. Dorothy Sayers, *Christian Letters to a Post-Christian World* (Grand Rapids: Eerdmans, 1969), 31, 32.

2. Sayers, *Christian Letters*, 31–32.

3. LW 51:71.

4. LW 31:371.

5. As Peter Meinhold points out, Luther's great purpose in the Reformation was to bring the proclamation and the life of the Church under the authority of Scripture and to bring theology and life into harmony. See *Luther heute* (Berlin and Hamburg: Lutherisches Verlagshaus, 1967), 138–41.

6. Wilhelm Loehe, *Three Books Concerning the Church*, trans. Edward Horn (Reading, Pa.: Pilger Publishing House, 1908), 11.

7. Adolf Herte, *Das katholische Lutherbild im Bann der Lutherkommentare des Cochläus* (Münster: Aschendorff Verlagsbuchhandlung, 1943), IXff. Thomas Mann in his "Washingtoner Rede," June 1945, quoted by Kurt Ihlenfeld, *Angst vor Luther* (Eckart-Verlag, Witten and Berlin, 1967), p. 257: "Martin Luther. Ich liebe ihn nicht. . . . Und das spezifisch Lutherische, das cholerisch Grobianische, das Schimpfen, Speien und Wueten, das fuerchterlich Robuste, verbunden mit zarter Gemuetstiefe und dem massivsten Aberglauben an Daemonen, Incubi und Kielkroepfe, erregt meine instinktive Abneigung. Ich haette nicht Luthers Tischgast sein moegen."

8. Joseph Lortz is a leading Roman Catholic Luther scholar, always objective and sympathetic to Luther's efforts to reform the Church. Cf. his *How the Reformation Came*, trans. Otto M. Knab (New York: Herder and Herder, 1964).

9. WA 51:487.

10. WA 7:219; Phila. 2:373.

11. Martin Luther, *Evangelium Auslegung*, Part 5 (Göttingen: Vandenhoeck & Ruprecht, 1950), 201–202.

12. Lenker 12:76.

13. Gerhard Ebeling, *Luther: An Introduction to His Thought*, trans. R. A. Wilson (Philadelphia: Fortress, 1970), 228–29. WATr 4:490, 24–26, no. 4777 (1530ff.); WA 49:257–58.

14. J. I. Packer and O. R. Johnston, trans., *The Bondage of the Will* (Westwood, N. J.: Fleming H. Revell, 1957), 66–67.

15. Packer and Johnston, *Bondage of the Will*, 67–70.

16. Lenker 12:76.

17. WA 54:32.

18. WA 36:186f.

Chapter 2

1. For our study, Luther's theological milieu is more important than the political, social, or economic. For the latter, see Charles S. Anderson, *The Reformation Then and Now* (Minneapolis: Augsburg, 1966).

2. LW 35:247.

3. WA 2:288.

4. WA 24:19.

5. WA 24:19.

6. LW 22:151f.

7. LW 22:152.

8. LW 22:153.

9. LW 22:153–54.

10. LW 22:154.

11. Martin Luther, *Luthers Episteln-Auslegung* (on Acts 15), ed. Chr. G. Eberle (Stuttgart: Verlag der Evangelischen Bücherstiftung, 1866), 54. Cf. Ruediger Lorenz, *Die vollendete Befreiung vom Nominalismus* (Guetersloh: Guetersloher Verlagshaus, Gerd Mohn, 1973).

12. Roland H. Bainton, *Here I Stand* (New York: Abingdon-Cokesbury Press, 1950), 185.

13. Bainton, *Here I Stand*, 185.

14. WABr 1:90; LW 48:40.

15. Heinrich Bornkamm, "Faith and Reason in the Thought of Erasmus and Luther," in *Religion and Culture: Essays in Honor of Paul Tillich*, ed. Walter Leibrecht (New York: Harper & Row, 1959), 134.

16. Bornkamm, "Faith and Reason," 133.

17. E. Gordon Rupp, *The Righteousness of God* (London: Hodder and Stoughton, 1953), 271.

18. LW 48:36.

19. Heiko A. Oberman, *The Harvest of Medieval Theology* (Cambridge: Harvard University Press, 1963), 360.

20. Karl Holl, *Gesammelte Aufsaetze zur Kirchengeschichte* (Tübingen: Mohr, 1948), 1:11.

21. WA 1:557.

22. Franz Lau, *Luther*, trans. R. H. Fischer (Philadelphia: Westminster Press, 1963), 61.

23. LW 31:9–11.

24. LW 31:40.

25. Heiko A. Oberman, "*Facientibus quod in se est Deus non denegat gratiam.* Robert Holcot and the Beginnings of Luther's Theology," *Harvard Theological Review* 55 (October 1962): 317–42.

26. WATr 1:146. For further discussion of the tune of the "Turmerleb-nis," cf. Ernst Bizer, *Fides ex Auditu* (Neukirchener Verlag des Erziehungsvereins Neukirchen-Vluyn, 1966); Erich Vogelsang, *Die Anfaenge von Luthers Christologie* (Berlin und Leipzig: deGruyter, 1929); Rupp, *Righteousness of God*; Heinrich Bornkamm, *Luthers Bericht ueber seine Entdeckung der iustitia Dei*, ARG, 1940.

27. LW 34:336–37.

28. Bernhard Lohse says that when the question of truth is involved, there can only be an answer that is radical and even one-sided, "but which in its one-sidedness nevertheless expresses the whole of the Christian faith. In this sense we can still say that Luther redis-covered Paul." *Lutherdeutung Heute* (Göttingen: Vandenhoeck & Ruprecht, 1968), 32.

Chapter 3

1. *The Lutheran Hymnal* (St. Louis: Concordia, 1941), no. 376, v. 3.

2. Otto Ritschl, *Dogmengeschichte des Protestantismus* (Leipzig: J. C. Hinrichs'sche Buchhandlung, 1912), 2:43.

3. Walther von Loewenich, *Luthers Theologia Crucis*, 2nd ed. (München: Chr. Kaiser Verlag, 1933).

4. WA 9:18/9.

5. LW 35:247.

6. LW 35:247–48.

7. WA 3:646/20.

8. LW 13:319.

9. LW 35:254.

10. LW 31:53.

11. LW 31:53.

12. LW 31:52–53.

13. Paul Althaus, "Die Bedeutung des Kreuzes im Denken Luthers," in *Luther*, Vierteljahrschrift der Luthergesellschaft (München: Chr. Kaiser Verlag, 1926), 100.

14. Althaus, "Die Bedeutung des Kreuzes im Denken Luthers," 101.

15. LW 1:11–13.

16. LW 1:14.

17. LW 42:74.

18. *The Lutheran Hymnal*, 6.

19. Lenker 9:236–37.

20. Lenker 9:224.

21. Lenker 10:96.

22. Lenker 14:185.

23. Lenker 14:186–87.

24. Lenker 14:187–88.

25. When Luther speaks of the conflict between spirit and flesh in his Romans and Galatians commentaries, he hardly seems to distinguish between spirit and Spirit (Holy Spirit). He uses lower case in both instances. On Galatians 5:17 he writes, *Caro vetus homo enim concupiscit: spiritus novus homo autem adversus carnem.* . . . On Galatians 5:18, *Quod si spiritu novo homine ducimini* . . . (WA 57:41). But on Romans 8:3 he writes, *Ideo dicit, quod Deus damnavit et destruxit in carne peccatum et nos destruere facit per spiritum suurn per fidem Christi diffusum in cordibus nostris* (J. Picker, *Luthers Vorlesung ueber den Roemerbrief, 1515–1516* [Leipzig: Dietrich'sche Verlagsbuchhandlung, 1930], 188). This indicates that in the conflict "flesh" (*sarx, caro*), "the old man," the old sinful nature, is in conflict with "spirit" (*pneuma, spiritus*), "the new man," man's spirit, or man as spirit under the control of the Holy Spirit.

26. Pauck, 204.

27. Pauck, 208.

28. *Anfechtung* has no adequate English synonym. It can be defined as testing, trial, agony of conscience under temptation.

29. LW 35:322.

30. LW 35:260.

31. LW 35:260.

32. LW 26:63.

33. LW 26:63–64.

34. LW 26:65.

35. LW 26:65–66.

36. LW 35:264.

37. LW 34:285.

38. LW 34:285–86.

39. LW 34:286.

40. LW 34:287.

41. LW 34:287–88.

42. Pauck, 261–63.

43. Pauck, 263.

44. Matthew Fox, *Religion USA* (Dubuque, Iowa: Listening Press, 1971), 376.

Part II: Introductory Comments

1. *The Lutheran Hymnal* (St. Louis: Concordia, 1941), 6.

2. See Herschel Baker, *The Image of Man* (New York: Harper & Row, 1946), 51.

3. LW 34:137.

4. LW 34:137.

5. LW 34:138.

6. LW 34:137.

7. LW 34:142.

8. LW 32:258.

9. H. J. McSorley, *Luthers Lehre vom unfreien Willen* (München: Hueber, 1967), 137.

10. LW 32:258.

11. LW 32:92.

12. LW 31:39.

13. LW 31:75. Luther is speaking of *A German Theology*, by an unknown mystic. Cf. Susanna Winkworth, trans. *Theologia Germanica*, rev. ed. (New York: Belgrave Press, Inc., 1949).

14. LW 31:322. Leif Grane throws out a warning against tying Luther too closely to Augustine's theology: "Luther derimod er bunden til den historiske åbenbaring, og derfor er hans opfattelse af den kristnes gudsforhold en ganske anden end Augustins." *Protest og Konsekvens* (Denmark: Gyldendal, 1968), 59.

15. WA 50:526. The translation is from Phila. 5:149.

16. LW 35:150.

17. LW 35:150.

18. LW 34:337.

19. Cf. Bonaventura, "Of the Stages in the Ascent to God," in *The Mind's Road to God*, trans. George Boas (New York: Liberal Arts Press, 1953).

Chapter 4

1. WA 24:18.

2. WA 24:21–22.

3. WA 18:636.

4. David Loefgren, *Die Theologie der Schoepfung bei Luther* (Göttingen: Vandenhoeck & Ruprecht, 1960), 22.

5. LW 1:47.

6. WATr 4:197, no. 4201.

7. Rudolf Hermann, *Gesammelte Studien zur Theologie Luthers und der Reformation* (Göttingen: Vandenhoeck & Ruprecht, 1960), 158. WATr 4:197, no. 4201, to which he refers, does not have the quotation.

8. LW 1:67.

9. Otto Piper, *God in History* (New York: Macmillan, 1939), 52.

10. *Triglotta*, 543.

11. LW 1:85.

12. LW 1:86.

13. WA 24:67.

14. WA 24:68.

15. LW 21:303.

16 LW 21:303.

17. Johann Gerhard, Locus 26 in *Loci Theologici* (Berlin: Gust. Schlawits, 1869), 8:52.

18. Notice how Luther here uses interchangeably spirit (*Geist*) and

soul (*Seele*). WA 7:550–51; LW 21:303.

19. LW 21:303.

20. LW 21:303.

21. Pauck, 237.

22. LW 21:303–04.

23. LW 21:304.

24. LW 21:304.

25. LW 24:106.

26. LW 21:307.

27. WA 40:2/609.

28. LW 1:65. Werner Elert, *The Christian Ethos*, trans. Carl J. Schindler (Philadelphia: Muhlenberg Press, 1957), 23: "The idea of the image of God is of fundamental importance in the New Testament. Only on this basis could Christ present God as 'the Father.' The New Testament term 'Father' denotes more than logical or mechanical 'cause.' . . . God is both Creator and eternal pattern. The image of God remains a valid concept even in the face of divine judgment."

29. LW 1:62.

30. LW 1:62.

31. LW 1:62–63.

32. LW 1:63. This resembles the language of Aquinas, who according to Maritain holds that "the deepest layer of the human person's dignity consists in its property of resembling God—not in a general way after the manner of all creatures, but in a *proper* way. It is the *image of God*. For God is spirit and the human person proceeds from Him in having as principle of life a spiritual soul capable of knowing, loving and of being uplifted by grace to participation in the very life of God so that, in the end, it might know and love Him as He knows and loves Himself." Jacques Maritain, *The Person and the Common Good*, trans. John J. Fitzgerald (New York: C. Scribner's Sons, 1947), 32.

33. *Triglotta*, 108.

34. LW 1:168.

35. WA 24:50.

36. Maritain, *Person and the Common Good*, 32.

Chapter 5

1. D. R. Davies, *Down, Peacock's Feathers* (New York: Macmillan, 1944), 9.

2. LW 1:144.

3. LW 1:145.

4. LW 1:179.

5. LW 1:179.

6. Davies, *Down, Peacock's Feathers*, 46.

7. Lewis Mumford, *The Condition of Man* (New York: Harcourt, Brace & Co., 1944), 293.

8. LW 1:96.

9. LW 1:162.

10. LW 1:146.

11. LW 1:147.

12. Julius Köstlin, *The Theology of Luther*, 2 vols., trans. C. E. Hay (Philadelphia: Lutheran Publication Society, 1897), 2:345.

13. *Triglotta*, 477.

14. WA 10/1:508. See also Wilhelm Maurer, *Kirche und Geschichte* (Göttingen: Vandenhoeck & Ruprecht, 1970), 1:177: "Weil es sich bei dem Problem der Schuld nicht um eine theoretische, sondern um eine praktisch-seelsorgerliche Frage handelt, tun wir gut, von Luthers beiden *Katechismen* auszugehen."

15. Pauck, 170.

16. LW 1:67.

17. LW 1:67.

18. Martin Luther, *The Bondage of the Will*, trans. Henry Cole (London: Sovereign Grace Union, 1939), 79.

19. LW 1:90.

20. WA 24:51.

21. WA 42:86.

22. Rudolf Hermann, *Gesammelte Studien zur Theologie Luthers und der Reformation* (Göttingen: Vandenhoeck & Ruprecht, 1960), 400. Hermann takes the quote from Aurifaber, but does not give the source otherwise.

23. Walch 11:1,277.

24. WA 42:86; Lenker 1:186.

25. LW 1:143.

26. George Long, trans., *The Meditations of the Emperor Marcus Aurelius Antoninus*, (New York: A. L. Burt), 6:16, 195.

27. LW 1:142.

28. LW 1:143.

29. Philip S. Watson, *Let God Be God* (London: The Epworth Press [Edgar C. Barton], 1947), 86. "Reason, then, is not the appropriate organ of knowledge in the Spiritual Kingdom. The only source of spiritual knowledge is the Word." B. A. Gerrish, *Grace and Reason* (Oxford, Clarendon Press, 1962), 20. Luther's harsh language against reason and the philosophers is a favorite grist for the mill of his critics. Jacques Maritain's sharpest criticism comes at this point. Cf., for instance, his *Three Reformers*, where he calls Luther "that enemy of philosophy" (New York: Charles Scribner's Sons), 4.

30. Reinhold Niebuhr, *An Interpretation of Christian Ethics* (New York: Harper & Brothers, 1935), 91. The most violent attacks against Luther and his concept of sin now seem to come from psychiatrists and psychologists. Thus from the French neuropsychiatrist A. Lamache comes the outburst: " . . . je la conclurais . . . que Luther était complètement irresponsable dans le domaine religieux. Je ne conteste acunement que dans la vie de tous les jours il ait pu se comporter en homme normal. Mais dès qu'il abordait le thème du péché, il était saisi par un sentiment morbide de culpabilité d'une violence telle que l'exercice de son libre arbitre était suspendu." His Preface to *L'Angoisse de Luther*, by Roland Dalbiez (Paris: Téqui, 1974), 9.

31. Emil Brunner, *Man in Revolt*, trans. Olive Wyon (London: Lutterworth Press, 1947), 128–29.

32. Paul Tillich, *Systematic Theology* (London: James Nisbet & Co. Ltd.), 2:46.

33. Tillich, *Systematic Theology*, 2:50.

34. Tillich, *Systematic Theology*, 2:64.

35. Rudolf Bultmann, *Theology of the New Testament*, trans. Kendrick Grobel (New York: Charles Scribner's Sons), 1:251.

36. Bultmann, *Theology of the New Testament*, 1:252.

37. Tillich, *Systematic Theology*, 2:42.

38. Tillich, *Systematic Theology*, 2:44.

39. LW 1:115.

40. LW 1:44.

41. LW 1:46.

42. LW 1:56.

43. LW 1:114–15.

44. LW 1:104.

45. LW 1:57.

46. LW 34:137.

47. LW 34:138–39.

48. LW 29:126–28.

49. *Triglotta*, 557.

50. WA 31:2/547.

51. Pauck, 86.

52. LW 29:130.

53. LW 26:345.

54. Adolf Harnack declares that "Luther was also able to describe the whole of Christianity under the scheme of law and gospel." See his *History of Dogma*, trans. W. M'Gilchrist (London: Williams and Norgate, 1899), 7:204.

55. LW 26:117.

56. LW 51:18.

57. LW 51:19.

58. LW 26:117.

59. LW 51:22.

60. LW 54:128.

61. Pauck, 252.

62. LW 32:94.

63. LW 31:48–49.

64. *De Libero Arbitrio Diatribe sive Collatio*, ed. Johannes von Walter (Leipzig: A. Deickert'sche Verlagsbuchhandlung, 1910). In the Weimar Edition, the title of Luther's response to Erasmus is, in contrast, *De Servo Arbitrio*. WA 18:551.

65. This Erasmus saw in Luther's treatise Assertio Omnium Articulorum M. Lutheri per Bullam Leonis X Novissimam Damnatorum (Wittenberg, 1520, WA 7:91 ff.).

66. We use the translation of Ernst F. Winter in his edition entitled *Erasmus—Luther: Discourse on Free Will* (New York: Frederick Ungar Publishing Co., Inc., 1961), 20.

67. Winter, *Erasmus—Luther*, 5–6.

68. Winter, *Erasmus—Luther*, 6.

69. "In spite of its animosity the debate was conducted on a high level. One can feel Luther's pleasure in crossing swords for once with an opponent of the highest caliber, instead of the petty, yapping critics

for whom he needed only a rough cudgel, and who now bored him
so much that as a rule he no longer answered them." Richard
Friedenthal, *Luther: His Life and Times*, trans. J. Nowell (New York:
Harcourt, Brace Jovanovich, Inc., 1970), 454. Hence we can hardly
apply to Luther's treatment of Erasmus H. G. Koenigsberger's reference to Luther's "self-righteousness and his moral callousness
toward those whom he judged as the enemies of God's Word."
Luther: A Profile (New York: Hill and Wang, 1973), xvi.

70. WABr 8:99.

71. Daniel Callahan, ed., *The Secular City Debate* (New York: Macmillan, 1966), 207.

72. "Luther always insisted that *The Bondage of the Will* was among the
best and most important of his writings. It was on this issue, he
said, that the basic differences between his theology and that both
of his scholastic predecessors and contemporary humanists were
most evident. If we want to understand Luther we must make
some effort to hear what he has to say at this point. At stake are the
basic questions of man's thinking about God and the nature of his
relationship to God." Gerhard O. Forde, *Where God Meets Man*
(Minneapolis: Augsburg, 1972), 19.

73. Carl Stange, ed., "De Servo Arbitrio als Ausdruck Lutherischen
Christentums," *Zeitschrift für Systematische Theologie* 14, no. 2
(Berlin: Alfred Toepelmann, 1937): 307.

74. Joseph Lortz, *How the Reformation Came*, trans. Otto M. Knab
(New York: Herder and Herder, 1964), 85–86.

75. Lortz, *How the Reformation Came*, 88.

76. "Faith and Reason in the Thought of Erasmus and Luther," in *Religion and Culture*, ed. Walter Leibrecht (New York: Harper and
Brothers, 1959), 137.

77. Harnack, *History of Dogma*, 7:203.

78. Franz Lau, *Luther*, trans. R. H. Fischer (Philadelphia: Westminster
Press, 1963), 108.

79. Martin Luther, *The Bondage of the Will*, trans. Henry Cole (Grand
Rapids: Eerdmans, 1931), 38.

80. Luther, *Bondage of the Will*, 64.

81. Luther, *Bondage of the Will*, 69.

82. Luther, *Bondage of the Will*, 70–71.

83. Luther, *Bondage of the Will*, 72.

84. Luther, *Bondage of the Will*, 79.

85. LW 1:165.

86. LW 1:142.

87. D. R. Davies, *Thirty Minutes to Raise the Dead* (New York: Macmillan Co., 1950), 100.

88. Luther, *Bondage of the Will*, 295.

89. LW 27:355.

90. WA 27:152. "I have sinned; then comes the evil conscience, because the Law pricks him in his heart."

91. Lenker 14:148.

92. Lenker 14:148.

93. Lenker 14:149, 148.

94. Luther, *Bondage of the Will*, 374.

95. Martin Luther, *Luthers Episteln-Auslegung* (on Acts 15), ed. Chr. G. Eberle (Stuttgart: Verlag der Evangelischen Bücherstiftung, 1866), 54.

96. Heinrich Bornkamm, *Luther's World of Thought*, trans. M. H. Bertram (St. Louis: Concordia, 1958), 82–84.

97. LW 13:93.

98. Werner Elert, *The Structure of Lutheranism*, trans. Walter A. Hansen (St. Louis: Concordia, 1962), 1:20.

99. Lenker 14:150.

100. "Luther kender ingen menneskelig mulighed for at *vælge* Gud, som om han var en genstand blandt andre genstande (omend en særlig ophoeiet)." Leif Grane, *Protest og Konsekvens* (Denmark: Gyldendal, 1968), 101.

101. Luther, *Bondage of the Will*, 79.

102. Luther, *Bondage of the Will*, 363.

103. Lenker 14:150–51.

104. LW 33:110.

105. LW 33:124–25.

106. LW 33:127.

107. LW 33:135.

108. LW 33:135.

109. LW 33:136.

110. LW 33:137.

111. LW 33:138–39.

112. LW 33:140.

113. Lenker 14:29–30.

114. Lenker 14:29–30.

115. Lenker 14:31.

116. Luther, *Bondage of the Will*, 73.

117. *Triglotta*, 545.

118. *Triglotta*, 45.

119. Walch 9:2,331.

120. Walch 9:1,981.

Chapter 6

1. Lenker 8:306.

2. LW 32:235.

3. WA 18:750/8; Cf. E. Gordon Rupp, *The Righteousness of God* (London: Hodder and Stoughton, 1953), 277.

4. WA 18:632/30. Trans. Rupp, *Righteousness of God*, 278.

5. "The Babylonian Captivity of the Church," in *Works of Martin Luther* (Phila.: Muhlenberg Press, 1943), 2:224.

6. *Triglotta*, 689.

7. LW 26:130.

8. See *Proceedings of the Fourth Assembly of the Lutheran World Federation*, Helsinki, July 30–August 11, 1963 (Berlin and Hamburg: Lutherisches Verlagshaus, 1965).

9. LW 26:372.

10. Martin Luther, *Luthers Episteln-Auslegung* (on Acts 15), ed. Chr. G. Eberle (Stuttgart: Verlag der Evangelischen Buecherstiftung, 1866), 697.

11. LW 31:353.

12. LW 26:130.

13. LW 26:132.

14. LW 31:351.

15. LW 26:227.

16. *Triglotta*, 543, *emphasis added*.

17. LW 32:235–36.

18. LW 26:177.

19. LW 26:177.

20. LW 26:179.

21. Pauck, 104.

22. Pauck, 102.

23. Pauck, 81.

24. Pauck, 76.

25. Pauck, 18.

26. LW 26:129–30, *emphasis added.*

27. Phila. 2:368.

Chapter 7

1. Lenker 14:218–19.

2. *The Lutheran Hymnal* (St. Louis: Concordia, 1941), 6, *emphasis added.*

3. Inter-Lutheran Commission on Worship, *Contemporary Worship Services: The Holy Communion* (Minneapolis, Philadelphia, Concordia; Augsburg, Board of Publication Lutheran Church in America, Concordia, 1970), 9, *emphasis added.*

4. G. Cope, J. G. Davies, and D. A. Tytler, *An Experimental Liturgy*, No. 3 (Richmond, Va.: John Knox Press, 1958), 32.

5. *Services for Trial Use* (The Church Hymnal Corporation, New York, 1971).

6. LW 1:114.

7. Erl. 15:49–50.

8. Erl. 15:50.

9. LW 27:363.

10. LW 27:364.

11. Pauck, 204.

12. LW 1:197.

13. WA 2:415, 6ff.

14. Karl Holl, *Gesammelte Aufsätze zur Kirchengeschichte* (Tübingen: Verlag von Mohr, 1927), 62.

15. Pauck, 204–05.

16. Pauck, 206.

17. Pauck, 201.

18. Pauck, 201–02.

19. Pauck, 207.

20. Pauck, 208.

21. Pauck, 208.
22. Pauck, 125.
23. Pauck, 135.
24. LW 32:173.
25. LW 32:175.
26. LW 32:181.
27. LW 32:190.
28. LW 32:209.
29. LW 32:213.
30. LW 32:230.
31. LW 32:239.

Chapter 8

1. LW 32:220.
2. LW 35:33–34.
3. LW 35:34.
4. LW 27:68.
5. LW 27:74.
6. WA 7:50, 23. Here the translation in the Philadelphia edition is more accurate than the Concordia-Fortress edition of *Luther's Works*.
7. LW 31:348.
8. LW 31:348–49, 353.
9. LW 31:349.
10. LW 35:370–71.
11. Pauck, 183.
12. LW 27:347.
13. Erdmann Schiott, *Fleisch und Geist nach Luthers Lehre* (Leipzig: Deichertsche Verlag, 1928), 55. This book contains one of the most penetrating discussions of Luther's concept of the *totus homo*.
14. LW 31:344.
15. LW 31:371. "Love, the fruit of faith, is both love for God, our Creator, and love for man, our fellow creature." Regin Prenter, "The Lutheran Tradition," in *Man's Concern with Holiness*, ed. Marina Chavchavadze (London: Hodder and Stoughton, 1970), 142. Cf. George Forell, *Faith Active in Love* (Minneapolis: Augsburg, 1954); Adolf Köberle, *The Quest for Holiness* (Minneapolis: Augsburg, 1936).

16. LW 31:367.

17. LW 31:367.

18. LW 31:367.

19. LW 31:367–68.

20. LW 51:96.

21. Lenker 8:71.

22. Lenker 8:69.

23. Lenker 8:68.

24. Lenker 8:67.

25. LW 44:26.

26. LW 44:27.

27. LW 44:27–28.

28. LW 32:159.

29. LW 44:37.

30. LW 32:186–87.

31. LW 32:172.

32. LW 44:26.

33. LW 44:38.

34. *Triglotta*, 687.

35. *Triglotta*, 693.

36. LW 41:145–46.

37. LW 41:146.

38. Lenker 8:67.

39. Lenker 8:67–68.

40. LW 26:133.

41. LW 26:160–61.

42. LW 26:155.

43. LW 27:336.

44. LW 51:71.

45. LW 31:368.

46. LW 31:57.

47. Anders Nygren, *Agape and Eros*, trans. Philip S. Watson (London: S. P. C. K., 1953), 740.

Chapter 9

1. Ernst Troeltsch, *Die Bedeutung des Protestantismus fuer die Entstehung der Modernen Welt* (Aalen: Otto Zeller Verlagsbuchhandlung, 1963), 26.

2. Karl Holl, *Gesammelte Aufsätze zur Kirchengeschichte* (Tübingen: Mohr, 1927), 1:424 (Luther).

3. George Hunston Williams, *The Radical Reformation* (Philadelphia: Westminster Press, 1962), xxv.

4. LW 40:146.

5. LW 40:146.

6. LW 40:147.

7. *Triglotta*, 495.

8. LW 22:8 and 14.

9. WATr 4, no. 5177.

10. LW 41:217.

11. WA 50:282. Cf. WA 48:31, "Scripture is written by the Holy Ghost."

12. Paul Althaus takes Luther at face value and says without hesitation that "although Luther criticized the Bible in specific details, he nonetheless followed the tradition of his time and basically accepted it as an essentially infallible book, inspired in its entire content by the Holy Spirit. It is therefore the 'Word of God,' not only when it speaks to us in law and gospel . . . but also—and this is a matter of principle—in everything else that it says. Seen as a totality, its historical accounts, its world-view, and all the miracle stories are 'God's Word' given by the Holy Spirit; they are therefore all unquestionable truth, to be 'believed' precisely because they are contained in the book." *The Theology of Martin Luther*, trans. Robert C. Schultz (Philadelphia: Fortress Press, 1966), 50–51.

13. Martin Luther, *Luthers Episteln-Auslegung* (on Acts 15), ed. Chr. G. Eberle (Stuttgart: Verlag der Evangelischen Buecherstiftung, 1866), 796, 795.

14. WA 2:288, "the infallible Word of God."

15. WA 36:500.

16. LW 30:321.

17. LW 30:321.

18. *Triglotta*, 569–571.

19. *Triglotta*, 571.

20. *Triglotta*, 607.

21. *Triglotta*, 609. Note the summary statement of Jaroslav Pelikan: "Ultimately, then, there was only one 'Word of God,' which came in various forms. In its written form it was the Bible." *Luther the Expositor*, LW Companion Volume, 70. In the light of all the evidence cited in these pages, one may question this author's statement that " . . . the written word of the New Testament became a means of grace by being transposed into preaching." Jaroslav Pelikan, *Spirit Versus Structure* (New York: Harper and Row, 1968), 119.

22. "Few people would challenge the assertion that the Reformation meant a kind of rediscovery of the Old Testament in the Western church." James Samuel Preus, *From Shadow to Promise* (Cambridge, Mass.: Harvard University Press, 1969), 5.

23. WA 10/1/1.181.

24. LW 22:339.

25. WA 13:88.

26. LW 14:87.

27. LW 12:97.

28. LW 12:98.

29. WA 10/1/1.4–5.

30. WA 10/1/1.6.

31. LW 22:477.

32. LW 51:77.

33. LW 30:167.

34. LW 22:480–81.

35. LW 22:478.

36. LW 41:216.

37. *Kerygma and Myth*, ed. H. W. Bartsch, trans. R. H. Fuller (London: S. P. C. K., 1957), 66, 69.

38. Paul Althaus, *Die Christliche Wahrheit* (Guetersloh: Bertelsmann, 1949), 1:132ff.

39. *Triglotta*, 693.

40. *Triglotta*, 733.

41. *Triglotta*, 901.

42. LW 53:11.

43. LW 53:11.

44. LW 36:92.

45. LW 36:92.
46. LW 36:124.
47. LW 36:18.
48. LW 36:124.
49. LW 51:327.
50. WA 49:74f.
51. LW 36:67.
52. *Triglotta*, 747.
53. J. M. Reu, "Schwabach Articles," in *The Augsburg Confession: A Collection of Sources* (Chicago: Wartburg Publishing House, 1930), Article 10, p. 43.
54. *Triglotta*, 49.
55. LW 36:92.
56. *Triglotta*, 557.
57. Tappert, 310.
58. LW 1:248.
59. LW 1:248.
60. LW 1:249.
61. LW 1:250.
62. LW 36:64.
63. LW 51:320–21.
64. *Triglotta*, 491.
65. *Triglotta*, 551.
66. LW 35:34.
67. LW 36:61.
68. LW 36:61.
69. LW 36:61.
70. LW 36:69.
71. *Triglotta*, 551.
72. *Triglotta*, 751.
73. *Triglotta*, 751.
74. *Triglotta*, 753.
75. Althaus, *Die Christliche Wahrheit*, 356.
76. LW 36:67.
77. *Triglotta*, 741.

78. *Triglotta*, 739.

79. *Triglotta*, 745.

80. *Triglotta*, 747.

81. *Triglotta*, 745.

82. *Triglotta*, 747.

83. LW 35:36.

84. Sermon on the Sixth Sunday after Trinity on Romans 6:3–11. Lenker 9:144.

85. LW 26:352.

86. LW 26:353.

87. WA 36:111.

88. WA 10/2.19f.

89. WA 40/3.76ff.

90. *Triglotta*, 761, 763.

91. WA 54:155; quoted in the Formula of Concord, *Triglotta*, 983.

92. LW 37:367. Cf. WABr 6:244: "The *Schwaermer* have no Baptism or Sacrament."

93. LW 40:231.

94. LW 40:232–33.

95. *Triglotta*, 247.

96. Paul C. Empire and James I. McCord, ed., *Marburg Revisited: A Reexamination of Lutheran and Reformed Traditions* (Minneapolis: Augsburg, 1966), a report of meetings between Lutherans and Reformed, concludes: "As a result of our studies . . . we see no insuperable obstacles to pulpit and altar fellowship and, therefore, we recommend to our parent bodies that they encourage their constituent churches to enter into discussions looking forward to intercommunion and the fuller recognition of one another's ministries." (P. 191)

97. LW 37:54.

98. LW 37:106f.

99. These Latin terms are used because the sacramental debates, which have been going on in the church since before the Reformation, have revolved around them. They are much used by Luther and the Lutheran Confessions.

100. Elert, *Structure of Lutheranism*, 309.

101. Some scholars question the accuracy of this quotation. If they are not the exact words, they reflect Luther's position. Walther Koehler

quotes him at one stage of the debate: "I am not your lord, nor your judge, nor your teacher; for it is quite apparent that we do not have the same spirit." From "Das Marburger Religionsgespraech, 1529," *Schriften des Vereins fuer Reformationsgeschichte* (Leipzig, 1929), 48:1, 38.

102. LW 40:232.

103. LW 40:220.

104. *Triglotta*, 555.

105. *Triglotta*, 493.

106. *Triglotta*, 493.

107. LW 36:284.

108. LW 36:275.

109. LW 36:337.

110. LW 36:279.

111. LW 36:275.

112. LW 36:338.

113. LW 37:195.

114. LW 36:343.

115. LW 36:341. Cf. Hermann Sasse, *This Is My Body* (Minneapolis: Augsburg, 1959), 171–72: "It seems that Luther would share the Roman view about the 'moment of consecration'. . . . Actually, however, he never established a theory about this. The same is true of the question as to the precise moment when the body and blood of Christ cease to be present. It is not lack of clarity that causes him to refrain from answering such questions, but rather the fact that they cannot be answered from the Word of God."

116. *Triglotta*, 755.

117. LW 37:193.

118. LW 40:177.

119. LW 40:178–81.

120. LW 40:180.

121. Cf. *Consensus Tigurinus* of 1549 (*Collectio Confessionum*, in *Ecclesiis Reformatis Publicatarum*, Leipzig, 1840, ed. H. A. Niemeyer), where Calvin consolidates the Geneva and Zurich movements in a common theology of the Lord's Supper. Here Calvin speaks of the Lutheran teaching of the presence of the body and blood "under the elements of the world" as a "false and godless superstition." Cf. p. 196.

122. *Triglotta*, 557.

123. LW 37:347.

124. LW 37:354.

125. LW 40:183.

126. *Triglotta*, 551.

127. LW 53:34.

128. LW 53:32.

129. LW 36:86.

130. LW 36:258.

131. *Triglotta*, 557.

132. LW 35:85.

133. LW 36:350.

134. Cf. Helmut Thielicke, *Theologie der Anfechtung* (Tuebingen: Mohr [Paul Siebeck], 1949).

135. G. de Lai, *The Real Presence of Jesus Christ in the Eucharist* (Dublin: Brown & Nolan, Ltd., 1926), 60.

136. LW 35:49–73.

137. LW 35:51.

138. LW 35:53.

139. LW 35:53–54.

140. LW 35:54.

141. LW 35:54.

142. LW 35:57.

143. LW 35:57–58.

144. LW 51:96.

145. LW 51:190–91.

146. LW 51:191.

147. LW 51:192.

148. *Triglotta*, 557.

149. From Luther's letter to Kaspar Huberinus in 1532, WABr 6:244f.

150. LW 37:27.

151. LW 37:27.

152. LW 37:317.

153. WA 23:28.

154. WA 28:321.

155. LW 27:38.

156. Cf. *Catholic Scholars Dialogue with Luther*, ed. Jared Wicks, S. J. (Chicago: Loyola University Press, 1970).

157. Joseph Lortz, *How the Reformation Came* (New York: Herder and Herder, 1964), 21–23.

158. WA 6:477.

159. A chapter on the church might be expected at this point. The author has already treated this topic in his *Communion of Saints* (Minneapolis: Augsburg, 1948).

Chapter 10

1. WaTr 3, no. 3339.

2. Krister Stendahl, in a lecture at Gustavus Adolphus College, quoted in *The Minneapolis Tribune*, Feb. 13, 1972.

3. LW 1:80.

4. LW 1:196–97.

5. LW 29:233.

6. Lenker 9:146.

7. *Luthers Evangelien-Auslegung*, ed. Chr. G. Eberle (Stuttgart: Verlag der Evangelischen Buecherstiftung, 1877), 288.

8. Lenker 10:188.

9. Lenker 11:179.

10. LW 3:10–11.

11. LW 1:44.

12. Phila. 3:132. I use the Holman Edition, which translates Leben with soul, whereas LW translates it as spirit. Luther is talking about the soul (*Seele*) throughout the paragraph.

13. LW 1:45.

14. LW 1:84.

15. LW 6:272–73.

16. WATr 4, no. 4833.

17. WA 43:360.

18. WATr 5, no. 5534.

19. WA 10/1B.118.

20. WA 43:218f.

21. LW 51:235.

22. LW 51:234.

23. LW 51:247.

24. Karl Barth, *Credo*, trans. J. S. McNab (London: Hodder and
      Stoughton, 1936), 168.

25. LW 4:115.

26. WA 2:685.

27. WA 34/2.111.